Women, Development, and the UN

United Nations Intellectual History Project

Women, Development, and the UN

A Sixty-Year Quest for Equality and Justice

Devaki Jain

Foreword by Amartya Sen

Indiana University Press
Bloomington and Indianapolis

This book is a publication of

Indiana University Press
601 North Morton Street
Bloomington, IN 47404-3797 USA

http://iupress.indiana.edu

Telephone orders   800-842-6796
Fax orders   812-855-7931
Orders by e-mail   iuporder@indiana.edu

The paper used in this publication meets the minimum requirements
of American National Standard for Information Sciences—Permanence
of Paper for Printed Library Materials, ANSI Z39.48-1984.

Manufactured in the United States of America

Library of Congress Cataloging-in-Publication Data

Jain, Devaki, date-
  Women, development, and the UN : a sixty-year quest for equality and justice /
Devaki Jain.
    p. cm. — (United Nations intellectual history project)
Includes bibliographical references and index.
    ISBN 0-253-34697-5 (cloth : alk. paper) — ISBN 0-253-21819-5 (pbk. : alk. paper)
    1. United Nations. 2. Women in development—International cooperation—History.
3. Women's rights—International cooperation—History. I. Title. II. Series.
    HQ1240.J35 2005
    305.42'09172'4—dc22   2005003698

1 2 3 4 5 10 09 08 07 06 05

Dedicated to the United Nations

My notion of democracy is that under it, the weakest should have the same opportunity as the strongest.

—Mahatma Gandhi

Contents

Boxes and Tables

Boxes

Tables

Series Editors' Foreword

It is surprising that there is no comprehensive history of the United Nations family of organizations. True, a few of the UN funds and specialized agencies have or are in the process of writing their institutional histories. But this is a mostly recent endeavor and, indeed, it is no more than should be expected of all public organizations, especially internationally accountable ones, along with enhanced efforts to organize their archives so that independent researchers can also document and analyze dispassionately their efforts and achievements. All this is an essential part of the record of international governance.

Faced with this major omission—which has substantial implications for the academic and policy literatures—we decided to undertake the task of beginning to write an *intellectual* history; that is, a history of the ideas launched or nurtured by the United Nations. Observers should not be put off by what may strike them as puffed-up billing. The working assumption behind this effort is straightforward: ideas and concepts are a main driving force in human progress, and they arguably have been one of the most important contributions of the world organization.

The United Nations Intellectual History Project (UNIHP) was launched in 1999 as an independent research effort based in the Ralph Bunche Institute for International Studies at The Graduate Center of The City University of New York, with a liaison office in Geneva. We are grateful for the enthusiastic backing from the Secretary-General and other staff, as well as from scholars and analysts and governments. We are also extremely appreciative for the generosity of the governments of the Netherlands, the United Kingdom, Sweden, Canada, Norway, Switzerland, and the Republic and Canton of Geneva, as well as of the Ford, Rockefeller, and MacArthur Foundations, the Carnegie Corporation of New York, and the Dag Hammarskjöld and UN Foundations. This support ensures total intellectual and financial independence. Details of this and other aspects of the project can be found on our Web site: www.unhistory.org.

The work of the UN can be divided into two broad categories: economic and social development, on the one hand, and peace and security, on the other. The UNIHP is committed to produce fourteen volumes on major themes in the first arena and a further three volumes if sufficient resources can be mobilized focused on the latter. Áll these volumes are being published in a series by Indiana University Press. In addition, the Project has completed an oral history collection of some seventy-three lengthy interviews of persons who have played major roles in launching and nurturing UN ideas—and sometimes in hindering them! Extracts from these interviews was published in 2005 as *UN Voices: The Struggle for Development and Social Justice.*[1] Authors of the Project's various volumes, including this one, have drawn on these interviews to highlight substantive points made in their texts. Full transcripts of the oral histories will also be disseminated in electronic form at the end of the Project to facilitate work by other researchers and interested persons worldwide.

There is no single way to organize research, and certainly not for such an ambitious project as this one. This UN history has been structured by topics—ranging from trade and finance to human rights, from transnational corporations to development assistance, from regional perspectives to sustainability. We have selected world-class experts for each topic, and the argument in all of the volumes is the responsibility of the authors whose names appear on the cover. Each have been given freedom and responsibility to organize their own digging, analysis, and presentation. Guidance from ourselves as the project directors as well as from peer review groups is provided to ensure accuracy and fairness in depicting where the ideas came from, how they were developed and disseminated within the UN system, and what happened afterward. We trust that future analyses will build upon our series and go beyond. Our intellectual history project is the first, not the last, installment in depicting the history of the UN's contributions to ideas.

Women, Development, and the UN is the seventh volume in the series—and in some respects the most broad-ranging. This is because Devaki Jain, with strong encouragement from us as editors of the UNIHP series, goes far beyond narrow boundaries in exploring the topic of women and gender. As the title makes clear, she traces through the many different ways in which women have enriched the UN: by the strong if tiny presence of the four women present at the UN's founding conference in San Francisco who ensured that equality of the sexes was included as one of the UN's basic principles; by the remarkable leadership of Eleanor Roosevelt as first chairperson of the UN Commission of Human Rights; by the intellectual leadership of others from Bodil Begtrup (who called in 1947 for a global survey of the status and treatment of women and thus established the country survey as a continuing tool in the analysis of women's issues); to the pioneering intellectual leadership of Esther Boserup two decades later. Boserup's pioneering book, *The Role of Women in Development*, documented and analyzed women's activities in developing countries which had been largely neglected until that time. There are many, many others mentioned in Jain's account who at different times and in different countries and regions have led the way in ensuring that matters of concern to women and issues of gender equality came into the spotlight at times when they were otherwise being forgotten or ignored.

But her account contains far more than remarkable and pioneering individuals. *Women, Development, and the UN* is even more an account of women and social movements, regionally and globally. Jain traces how the work of the UN, and especially of the four global women's conferences in Mexico, Copenhagen, Nairobi, and Beijing, fundamentally altered the situation of women in country after country, by raising awareness, building confidence, spreading ideas, and creating alliances which changed the face of the earth. These conferences also changed the UN, providing the mandates which gave the world CEDAW, the Convention for the Elimination of All Forms of Discrimination Against Women, and which established in turn UNIFEM, the UN Development Fund for Women, and INSTRAW, the UN International Research and Training Institute for the Advancement of Women. Equally significant, concerns for women raised awareness of broader and more general human concerns in the whole process of development. In elaborating all this, Jain brings her own strong perspective, a view from the South, an awareness that issues of development are often seen differently from the standpoint of countries in Africa, Asia, and Latin America.

This volume is an account of how the intellectual contributions of women and social movements shaped thinking about development at the UN. Jain's account illustrates four ways women's ideas have had an impact: they have altered how issues are perceived and identified agendas for action; they have prodded countries to rethink and redefine their interests in relation to gender issues; they have created new prospects for forming coalitions of political and institutional forces to achieve change; and they have become embedded in institutions to carry these issues forward. In each of these ways, women, and supporters and promoters of women's issues and concerns, have had an impact on development and on the UN.

Jain brings many talents to her task. She is author and activist, teacher and advisor, organizer and promoter and in all of these roles a committed feminist. These qualities have given her a remarkable range of experiences on which to draw. In her early life she worked with the Gandhian activist Vinoba Bhave and later with Gunnar Myrdal, when he was writing *Asian Drama*. She has lectured in economics in Delhi University, advised the National Commission on Women of the Government of India, been a member of the State Planning Board of

Karnataka and, from 1975 to 1994, directed the Institute of Social Studies in Bangalore. Internationally, Devaki Jain initiated the meeting in Bangalore in 1984 which led to the founding of DAWN, Development Alternatives with Women for a New Era, an influential Third World network of women who were deeply engaged with development issues in their region. DAWN developed an alternative framework for analyzing the situation of poor women in the South and used that analysis to recraft development strategies. From 1987 to 1990, she was a member of Julius Nyerere's South Commission, a think tank of twenty-eight economists that worked to create an agenda for South-South economic cooperation. She has been a member of advisory committees or expert groups of UNIFEM, the UNDP, the WHO, the FAO, the ILO, UNESCO, UNICEF, and the UNFPA. She has written numerous articles and books on women and development and participated in countless international meetings on issues of gender equality and women.

We are persuaded that the UN story deserves to be better documented if it is to be better understood and appreciated. *Women, Development, and the UN* makes a significant contribution in this direction. As Kofi Annan, the UN Secretary-General wrote in the "Foreword" to *Ahead of the Curve? UN Ideas and Global Challenges:* "With the publication of this first volume in the United Nations Intellectual History Project, a significant lacuna in twentieth-century scholarship and international relations begins to be filled."[2] With this seventh volume, a further gap in that record is now closed. We are confident that other analysts will now be in a position to use this critical building block to add to the history of UN contributions to women and gender, as well as to women's contributions to the UN.

We hope that readers will enjoy this account, at once a journey through time, a view from the South, and an energizing story of how women have enriched thinking and action within the UN itself. As always, we welcome comments from our readers.

Louis Emmerij, Richard Jolly,
and Thomas G. Weiss
New York, January 2005

Foreword

It was nearly 150 years ago when Mary Ann Evans penned the redoubtable line: "The happiest women, like the happiest nations, have no history." That view may or may not be correct: Evans was writing under the adopted name of George Eliot in a world in which a woman author had serious hurdles to overcome. But women have reason to seek not just happiness but also knowledge, understanding, and empowerment, and can hardly ignore their own history. The world may have been changing far too slowly, but the history of that change and the role of women in the transformation are both exciting and exhilarating.

An important part of this grand history is the subject matter of Devaki Jain's remarkably well-researched and readable book. Even though the United Nations is often separated out these days for particular chastisement for being ineffective (or worse), the UN and the intellectual and political movements associated with it have contributed greatly to making our world a bit less nasty and more liveable. And even though women had to fight to be heard and to influence the making and working of this grand institution, the constructive impact of women's ideas and leadership can be seen in nearly every field in which the UN has made significant contributions.

Devaki Jain's task has been particularly hard for two distinct reasons. The first—and here I speak as an old friend and admirer—is her own ambition. She did not want to confine her account just to women's participation in the development of the UN nor just to the ways in which the UN has addressed issues of women and gender. Devaki wanted to bring out the process through which the vision, the determination, and the resourcefulness of women leaders associated with the United Nations have deeply enriched this global organization and have made it a source of major creative initiatives in many different fields, going well beyond issues of women and gender. Also, Devaki Jain's diagnosis that the history of what has been going on in the UN has to be placed in the broader context of women's movements and activism in the world at large is important but also highly exacting.

By escalating her assignment, Devaki Jain took on an immensely larger task than a minimalist account of women and the UN would have demanded. It is, therefore, particularly pleasing to see how well she has succeeded in meeting her powerfully ambitious objectives. There is certainly a case for celebration there.

The second difficulty comes from the changing understanding of what are taken to be "women's issues" in the deeply unequal world in which we live. Not long ago, women's movements were primarily concerned with working toward achieving better treatment for women—a more "square" deal. The focus was mainly on women's *well-being,* and since that was a greatly neglected subject, it was indeed a good corrective. However, over the years, the aims and objectives of women's movements have gradually evolved and broadened from this "welfarist" focus to incorporate a fuller understanding of the active role of women's *agency.* No longer treated as the passive recipient of welfare-enhancing assistance, women are increasingly seen—by men as well as women—as active agents of change and as dynamic promoters of social transformation that can alter the lives of *both* women and men.

Devaki Jain's history had to be involved with both the well-being aspect and the agency aspect of women's role in the UN and in the world and had to bring out the ways in which the relative priorities have been shifting over the years. This is an evolving history of which the reader gets a finely inclusive view under Devaki Jain's extensive narrative.

As it happens, the UN itself was a pioneer in facilitating this broadening of aims and objectives. It was the UN Human Rights Commission, chaired by Eleanor Roosevelt, that gave the world the Universal Declaration of Human Rights in 1948—the first such declaration with a totally universalist reach and a global successor to such national pronouncements as the American Declaration of Independence of 1776 (which took it to be "self-evident" that everyone is "endowed" with "certain inalienable rights") and the French declaration of "the rights of man" in 1789 (asserting that "men are born and remain free and equal in rights"). The book provides a fine account of how the debates proceeded in those early days sixty years ago. Even Eleanor Roosevelt's preferred language, which referred to "all men," had to change in response to criticisms from other women members of the commission, particularly from developing countries. Hansa Mehta, the Indian delegate, was insistent: "That would never do," since "all men" could be "interpreted to exclude women." The debate paved the way to the now standard language of "all human beings."

Each of the episodes is discussed in absorbing detail, and the totality of the account gives us a commanding view of the history of arguments and reasoning that accompanied the different initiatives and their articulation and use. The richness of the changing subject matter may have made the book harder to write, but it is also, as a result, more rewarding to read.

When Queen Victoria wrote to Sir Theodore Martin complaining about "this mad, wicked folly of 'Woman's Rights,'" she may have underestimated the power of the "wicked folly." The role and extensive reach of women's agency have been having a profound impact on the world, affecting the lives of all: women, men, and children. It is a critically important part of that record—the global developments directly and indirectly connected with the United Nations—that we get from Devaki Jain's splendidly written history. We have compelling reason to be grateful.

Amartya Sen
Harvard University
March 2005

Acknowledgments

The historical journey this volume has taken us on has been a revelation to us. We have come full circle—from skepticism of, if not downright scoffing at, the UN to a true admiration of its value, and when we dedicate it to this hoary institution, it is now with the sincerity of knowledge. For giving us this learning, this enrichment, we thank the directors of the UNIHP project: Louis Emmerij, Richard Jolly, and Thomas G. Weiss, as well as Nancy Okada, the administrator, and Senior Researcher Tatiana Carayannis.

I use the term "we" in this acknowledgment, as we were a team with Shubha Chacko, who was my research assistant for the first phase, and C. P. Sujaya, who came in as consultant periodically, both of whom made invaluable contributions to the volume, and M. V. Jagadeesh and Perce Bloomer, who provided sustained multiple supports throughout.

Kate Babbitt, my scholar-historian-editor, introduced me to the extraordinary powers of editing—the book certainly went up the scale of quality with her touch. E. S. Reddy, former director of the United Nations Centre against Apartheid, initiated me into the values and hardships of archival research and provided me with the richest of material. To all these partners, who enabled the threads of this history to emerge as a woven fabric, wrapping sixty years of world history into a book, my first debt of gratitude.

We could not have managed this book, known how to contain such a vast canvas within the bounds of one volume, without the lived experience of the feminist movement, local, national, and worldwide. This is what has charged our batteries and given us the knowledge base from which we grew to learn what we hope we have been able to share in this volume.

A host of persons and agencies have provided the material and the advice for this book at different times and in a variety of ways. Some read the early texts, in parts or as a whole. Some gave short interviews which gave both historical glimpses and tips on where to find material. Some gave outlines for chapters on themes and others wrote short essays on a topic. Some of these friends are listed here. They include some who were asked by the project to read the penultimate draft and others who read an even earlier draft as friends: Joan Anstee, Lourdes Arizpe, Rawwida Baksh-Sooden, Rasil Basu, Susan Beresford, Charlotte Bunch, Marty Chen, Gordon Conway, Radhika Coomaraswamy, Shanti Dairian, Viru Dayal, Sissel Ekaas, Diane Elson, Monica Fong, Ruchira Gupta, Caroline Hannan, Noeleen Heyzer, Hameeda Hossain, Kareen Jabre, Renana Jhabvala, Ammu Joseph, Angela King, Sunanda and J. Krishnamurty, Annali Kristiansen, Shiv Kumar, Yianna Lambrou, Lin Lim, Amina Mama, John R. Mathiason, Claire Moses, Achan Mungleng, Madhubala Nath, Sakiko F. Parr, Meera Pillai, Elizabeth Prügl, Kala Ramesh, Shahra Razavi, Amy Richards, Nafis Sadik, Joanne Sandler, Hema Sarathy, Kalyani Menon Sen, Kamlesh Sharma, Andrea Menefee Singh, Claire Slatter, Margaret Snyder, Gloria Steinem, Ann Tickner, Kristen Timothy, Joanne Vanek, Sarita Vellani, Marcel Villarreal, Ann Walker, Jennifer Whittaker. A big thank-you to each of you.

To someone who bore the brunt of this home-based work and played the multiple roles of researcher, reader, hand-holder, and cheerleader, my husband, Lakshmi Jain, my love.

Devaki Jain
Bangalore
December 2004

Abbreviations

AAWORD	Association of African Women for Research and Development
AIDS	acquired immune deficiency syndrome
ATRCW	African Training and Research Centre for Women
AWID	Association for Women's Rights in Development
CEDAW	Convention on the Elimination of All Forms of Discrimination Against Women
CONGO	Conference of Non-Governmental Organizations
CSW	Commission on the Status of Women
DAC	Development Assistance Committee
DAW	Division for the Advancement of Women
DAWN	Development Alternatives with Women for a New Era
DEDAW	Declaration on the Elimination of Discrimination Against Women
ECA	Economic Commission for Africa
ECOSOC	Economic and Social Council
ECWA	Economic Commission for Western Asia
ESCAP	Economic and Social Commission for Asia and the Pacific
FAO	Food and Agriculture Organization
FEMNET	African Women's Development and Communication Network
FGM	female genital mutilation
G-77	Group of 77
GDP	gross domestic product
HDR	Human Development Report
IACW	Inter-American Commission of Women
IACWGE	Inter-Agency Committee on Women and Gender Equality
ICTR	International Criminal Tribunal for Rwanda
ICTY	International Criminal Tribunal for the Former Yugoslavia
IDS	International Development Strategy
ILO	International Labour Organization
IMF	International Monetary Fund

INSTRAW	International Research and Training Institute for the Advancement of Women
NAM	Non-Aligned Movement
NGO	nongovernmental organization
NIEO	New International Economic Order
OAS	Organization of American States
OAU	Organization of African Unity
OECD	Organisation for Economic Co-Operation and Development
SEWA	Self-Employed Women's Association
UDHR	Universal Declaration of Human Rights
UNDP	UN Development Programme
UNESCO	UN Educational, Scientific and Cultural Organization
UNFPA	UN Population Fund (originally the UN Fund for Population Activities)
UNHCR	UN High Commissioner for Refugees
UNICEF	UN Children's Fund
UNIDO	UN Industrial Development Organization
UNIFEM	UN Development Fund for Women
UNIHP	UN Intellectual History Project
UNITAR	UN Institute for Training and Research
UNRISD	UN Research Institute for Social Development
UNSNA	UN System of National Accounts
USAID	U.S. Agency for International Development
VAW	violence against women
WEDO	Women's Environment and Development Organization
WFS	Women's Feature Service
WHO	World Health Organization
WID	women in development
WIEGO	Women in Informal Employment: Globalizing and Organizing

*Women, Development,
and the UN*

Introduction

Women, Development, and Equality:
History as Inconclusive Dialogue

> *The search for the correct viewpoint which is superior to all other*
> *viewpoints is an error in itself.*
> —Akiro Kurosawa, *Rashomon*

> *Most historiographic progress—perhaps most intellectual progress—proceeds*
> *by rearranging relationships within old stories, not by writing new stories.*
> —Linda Gordon[1]

The Quest for Equality

The full story of how and what the women of the world contributed to ideas about rights, equality, and development within the UN remains largely untold—it is usually collapsed with the more common narrative of the UN's historical-institutional achievements in the areas of women's rights and women's emancipation. Over the past six decades, different layers of meaning surrounding an idea of gender equality, a value it endorsed in its Charter, have been uncovered. A new constituency in UN politics called "women" was created, as was the entry of a powerfully endowed idea called "women" in UN thought.

The search for what equality actually means for women has never stopped, both within and outside the UN. Six decades of UN history provides a deeply absorbing narrative of the elusiveness of this aspiration. The women's story is embedded within the larger chronicle of the UN itself, and the twists and turns follow the key political, social, and economic events in the world that shaped the global organization's history: the aftermath of a major war, the post-colonial era, the development decades, the Cold War era, the new economic restructuring of the globe, the new millennium. Yet women's ideation did not ride piggyback on the intellectual development of UN thought; their intellectual work constantly defined and redefined what equality meant for women and for those who are unequally placed. As the composition of the UN changed and as the themes, slogans, and formulae for realizing its goals changed, women worked to ensure that the idea of overcoming inequality was recognized in all its endeavors.

Women's participation with the UN's work in development basically questioned and changed the foundations of its knowledge base, especially in its practice. They brought new ways of looking at the conceptualization of work; they challenged the hierarchies in how economic and social contributions are valued; they insisted that women had a right to development—indeed, they insisted that the degree of access women had to just development was a measure of the stage of development of a nation. They also questioned the models of development that were being promoted; some worked within given models and others insisted that the models needed to be overhauled. Sixty years down the line, it could be said that the gender-specific location of women in all spheres of development has been understood. The sharing of knowledge in the venues provided by the UN enabled the building of a visible political entity.

Finding a Niche

One of the challenges in designing this volume has been to find a niche in the literature. Much has been written about development, much has been written about the worldwide women's movement, and a body of literature is growing about the interactions of women with the United Nations. At the turn of the twenty-first century, the idea of a fifty-year review of the United Nations encouraged several reviews of the history of women and the UN. These assessments provided a strong base for the preparation of this volume. But they also made it challenging to deliver a product that adds value. The niche, then, for this story is political. It narrates the interplay of two political forces, the worldwide women's movement and the United Nations, in their engagement with development.

Another niche this story fits into is the narrative of how women's participation in the politics of development transformed or influenced both the politics of the UN and the understanding of development within that body. Special efforts will be made to use the lenses of the struggle against inequality and the struggle to understand poverty and enable its eradication in unfolding the story. Thus, the engagement of the worldwide women's movement with inequality, development, and the UN will be the core threads that will run throughout the chapters.

The Politics of Place

My location has defined the perspective with which this book is written. I am an academic activist, as my tribe is called, with one foot each in research and activism, an outsider to the UN. I am a feminist with a tendency to view ideas, events, and actors through the lens of a perspective from the South. My work has been located in India. I was a member of Julius Nyerere's South Commission, which was set up to define an economic South. I initiated a Third World women's network, Development Alternatives with Women for a New Era, which gave an identity to the voices of women living in the South and put macroeconomic issues firmly on the agenda of the worldwide women's movement.

Writing history from a South perspective is a rewarding yet challenging task. The knowledge base—the identification of sources, the narrations of history, especially as underpinned by ideas—is visibly Eurocentric. Global breezes, defining moments in history, descriptions of the evolution of thought, intellectual paradigms, critical thinkers are attributed to the world, but that world's boundaries are West derived. Thus, the periodization of history is Eurocentric. For example, World War II and its aftermath—the defining events of the Northern Hemisphere that were, in fact, the impetus for the founding of the United Nations—were not the most important externalities for nations in the South. Slavery, including the use of indentured labor; economic plundering; the effacing of cultural and intellectual identities by the imperial powers were the strong forces that shaped the history of those nations. Mahatma Gandhi was more relevant to Indian recovery from colonization than Keynes. To the black people of South Africa, historical periods are defined in apartheid-regime terms, and Nelson Mandela's twenty-seven years in Robben Island on and off between 1952 to 1990 were the definitions of historical time. The list can go on.

Thus, the history in this volume is disjointed at points. As the North followed the trajectory led by such driving forces as Keynesian economics, the Marshall Plan, and new strands of development thought, the South heard a different rhythm of liberation, socialism, and exciting experiments with government. However, key elements in the South's history of the time period from 1945 to 2005 have not been highlighted and given visibility. My efforts to redress the balance of history, however unsatisfactory and incomplete, have often meant the muting of conventional images of resounding "success" or great personas. The book strives to celebrate the successes of movements, of collective action. Linda Gordon's comment on the writing of history seems relevant here: "Among the particular constraints on the activity of producing history which embodies both truth and myth is the finite, capacious, mottled nature of the evidence."[2]

The *Nethi Nethi* Syndrome

In Hamlet, Shakespeare immortalized the ultimate existential question: "To be or not to be?" This philosophical question that distinguishes the human mind touches on the universal experience of doubt, of questioning. Both of these elements of Hamlet's question resonate in this history. Women faced the dilemma of how to proceed most effectively—would separate space, what Virginia Woolf called a room of one's own, enable them to achieve their goals or would it produce a marginalized ghetto? Conversely, should they enter the mainstream or would that dilute their momentum? To be or not to be? The doubt inherent in this question is also relevant. Women brought into the development discourse the questioning mode, revealing the dilemmas that emerge when trying to land justice with some element of universality and revealing the difficulties of arriving at "complete" solutions. Women's continuous questioning of ideas and practices, even those that were designed to support their quest for dignity and equal citizenship, led almost to definition by negation, what is called in the Upanishads *nethi nethi*. In that sacred text, the quest for "the truth" is a process that removes every suggestion that is made with the response "not this, not this"—*nethi nethi*. This concept can be used to understand many layers of history in this book. For several decades now, as women have worked to understand their identities, the movement has searched for an idea that will bring them together across their valuable and legitimate differences. It has been a period of turmoil and uncertainty as they search for that idea.

Women's almost universal and timeless aspiration for a peaceful humankind is another example of *nethi nethi*. Even before the term "peace dividend" came into common parlance, women were showing the connection between absence of war and its values, financial and otherwise, for development. Just as including women revealed that rights were indivisible, just as women showed that the division between public and private space is artificial or that economic and social security cannot be divided, this organized voice of women showed the links between development and peace. Nairobi had a peace tent to illustrate or symbolize that a conference on development has to consider peace. The peace tent is used in this volume as a symbol of the one issue on which the UN and women have worked from the same standpoint. The tent also symbolizes the politics of a room of one's own—powerhouse or ghetto?

Nethi nethi can also be used to understand the engagement of the women's movement with development thought over the past sixty years. The first strand of that engagement was to perceive women as recipients of welfare—consumers of the national income rather than economic contributors. But it did not go farther than that; it did not include women in the process of planning and making decisions about how development should unfold. The next strand, women in development, sought to include women at a deeper level but was not implemented broadly enough to have the needed impact. And so it went; to each new model—women and development, gender and development, mainstreaming—the women's movement eventually said, "Not this, not this."

Language as Politics

Over the years, language to speak about women has changed several times. This book returns to the term "women," or the women word, as an attempt to envelop the political identity "women." In feminist discourse, each word such as "women," each construct such as "gender," and each identification such as "feminist" is being contested. Each of these terms has different definitions and politics. While every phase of the evolution of language has had its value, there is now, in 2005, an increasingly accepted view that to reclaim political identity, to affirm women's collective political will, the word "women" has returned as preferred currency. Nomenclature, or naming as identity or for analysis, has also suffered due to translation difficulties; no universally acceptable language can be affirmed. On another plane, women's use of language to mark identity—fluid, adapting to the issue at stake, from women to gender to feminism back to women—is strategic. It also suggests the presence of the attitude of *nethi nethi*.

The evolution of nomenclature within the history of ideas about development has been an enabling and clarifying process but also a problematique. Words need to be defined, but the definitions may not be generally or universally accepted. They reflect changing times, changing politics, and can be interpreted through the lens of the place from which they are viewed. The former colonies were called "underdeveloped countries" as they arrived as free countries in the global space. This sounded demeaning, as they had great and old civilizations and resources, so they were renamed the "developing countries." That word was also found not quite dignified and the word "South" was coined because most of these countries belonged to the Southern Hemisphere. But this raised several questions—Australia and New Zealand, countries that belonged to the club of the rich, were in the Southern Hemisphere. Another use of the term emerged to denote the poor and undeveloped, so there was the "global South" and the "global North." These would be regions or peoples who were living in poverty in the rich countries—members of the global South—and the rich living in the poor countries—members of the global North. In this volume we use "South" to represent the developing countries, the countries that came out of colonization, the G-77, the Non-Aligned Movement (NAM) groups.

The Problems of Selection

Engaging with the United Nations and its intellectual history on any account is not an easy task.[3] Its kaleidoscopic character, further complicated by the diversity of its users and the locales in which it lands, its chameleon-like adaptation to the atmosphere and threats from the outside, which change over time, escapes a universally acceptable capture within the bounds of a book. The task gets further complicated, if not thwarted, when the subject of study is the interaction of a section of humanity that is the live and energetic worldwide women's movement with the UN. My topic is a living constituency, tangible stakeholders, agents participating in the making and the writing of their history—a live show, not a recording. The story is moving even as it is being told. Every actor would like to be heard—a challenging and moving phenomenon but one that could not be fully accommodated in this narration.

This book covers the interactions of half the world's population with a large and scattered entity called the UN that is expressed in regions, countries, agencies, and funds—a formidable landscape. It was necessary to be selective in telling the story. Hence only a few of the UN's arms have been drawn into this narrative. The United Nations Educational, Scientific and Cultural Organization (UNESCO) was chosen for its unique role in the early years, stimulating inquiry "beyond the veil" into the components that make up status, undertaking field research in many developing countries, becoming a handmaiden for the early efforts of the UN's Commission on the Status of Women to have informed dialogue with the main spaces. It is also highlighted because in the interim, or middle period, UNESCO's role faded out, to reemerge as culture and identity took center stage in world politics in the new millennium.

The International Labour Organization (ILO) is another agency which has stood by women, especially as the central point of women's advocacy hinged around poverty and work. There is a proposition that all poor women work, as without a livelihood strategy they and their families would starve to death. Since the 1970s, the ILO has explored the world of poor women's work as "both the midwife and the principal international institutional home for the concept of the informal sector."[4]

Conferences and agencies have been selected to reveal the birth of ideas and how those ideas were negotiated within the UN's world space. The institutional architecture for women's advancement at the UN has been continuously changing, and its evolution, its contribution, its dilemmas are traced throughout. Its components include the Commission on the Status of Women, the Division for the Advancement of Women, the Convention on the Elimination of All Forms of Discrimination Against Women, UNIFEM, and INSTRAW. These were the bodies and institutions available to women as they sought to bring their intellectual contributions about women and development into the mainstream of the world body. Over time, women emphasized or de-emphasized various components of this architecture, as needs and circumstances demanded.

Institutional Space

Nethi nethi also describes the evolution of the spaces the United Nations has offered women activists. The UN Charter and the Universal Declaration of Human Rights included women in their texts thanks to the insistence of foremothers at the UN who had worked in the prewar international women's movement. The goals of the Declaration would not become a UN priority for decades, but the presence of the language in that document provided a powerful standard to which women could hold the UN and its member states accountable.

In the late 1960s and early 1970s, women inside and outside the UN realized that a document dedicated to the rights of women was needed. The UN's Commission on the Status of Women (CSW) produced two important documents, the Declaration on the Elimination of Discrimination Against Women (DEDAW, 1967) and the Convention on the Elimination of Discrimination Against Women (1979), that articulated new standards with which to measure progress in how governments and bureaucracies engaged with women and gave them a template to follow. DEDAW's statement that discrimination against women was "fundamentally unjust and an offence against human dignity" was powerful, but translating rhetoric into reality proved more difficult. CEDAW spelled out, for the first time, what discrimination against women meant and outlined the steps with which to remedy that injustice. These three documents—the Declaration of Human Rights, DEDAW, and CEDAW—used the tool of language to jump-start change, and the UN provided the institutional space within which this new language was crafted. They expanded the intellectual space within which women could work, and they expanded the role of the UN as the arbiter of international law.

In the 1970s, women shifted their focus to UN conferences. The four UN conferences on women created new energy for an already emerging second wave of the worldwide women's movement. Many alliances were formed, disagreements were aired, and networks were created. They were a space for women from around the world to recognize similarities and begin to understand differences.

At the women's conferences, women gave language to their desire for change. The documents that emerged from Mexico City, Copenhagen, Nairobi, and Beijing spoke about women and development; what was said traces women's increasing understanding of the complexity of the development landscape. They also revealed the interconnections between the otherwise separated concerns of the UN. They united humanitarian concepts, peace, governance, and culture with the development face of the UN. The Mexico City document acknowledged that "under-development imposes upon women a double burden of exploitation" and stated that any obstacle that stood in women's way of "full integration into national development" must be eliminated.[5] Five years later, the Copenhagen document urged governments to explicitly state their commitment to "equal and full participation of women in economic and social development," including "systematic and sustained linking of efforts to integrate women into national development planning."[6]

The Nairobi Forward-Looking Strategy of 1985 moved from pleas to include women in development programs and planning to the more sophisticated understanding that "the advancement of women is not possible without development, and . . . without the advancement of women, development itself will be difficult to achieve." By the time of the Beijing Declaration of 1995, the rhetoric was becoming more forceful; it spoke of the need to "eradicate the persistent and increasing burden of poverty on women by addressing the structural causes of poverty through changes in economic structures."[7] Clearly women had educated each other and the rest of the world a great deal during these twenty years about how to think and talk about development through UN spaces.

Each of these UN spaces was valuable at the time women engaged with them. It was crucial for women to articulate what discrimination meant in the 1960s and 1970s; that created a standard to which governments can be held. The conferences mobilized women as a worldwide political force. New language and networks are two essential aspects of women's work for change. However, at the turn of the century, a large section of the worldwide women's movement thinks that conferences have gone as far as they can as an enabling space and therefore do not consider another conference on women as being of much value. Women's work for change needs to find another path—*nethi nethi.*

Intellectual Space

The creation and dissemination of knowledge has been a way women and the UN have worked with each other. But as in the case of other areas of work, it is women's questioning of the knowledge base that has been the contribution. Women confronted hard-core theorems of epistemology and classificatory systems and the hierarchies embedded within them with an attitude of not this, not this. In so doing, they brought facts and ideas about women as a political society; the range of interventions has been comprehensive. It was in this quest for replacing the existant that women across conventional divides found unity; they were on the same wavelength in critiquing ideas such as the dichotomies of development and rights, public and private, theory and practice, women's rights and human rights, home and workplace. These dichotomies pervaded development and rights discourses, and women challenged all of them.

Women's studies has been a critical actor in the journey. Learning about women came from two sources: the collective voice of those working in communities and those challenging the academy. Knowledge was created and disseminated through a multiple set of sources. One was research that documented grassroots success stories; another was research that provided a more sophisticated analysis of women's location in the world. Women revisited knowledge theories and rebuilt them with their desire to eradicate inequality at the center. It is in this space that feminists of the world found congruence. They may have been divided along many lines, but they found that they could create alliances under the umbrella of thought as the common space that was challenging the foundations of knowledge. Many fruitful and interesting partnerships were formed.

Chronology

Although this volume is organized chronologically to follow the trajectory of development history at the UN, at times the story steps outside that framework to consolidate women's stories within that institution. Sometimes an issue or event straddles both chapters, moves across time. Hence our time barriers are porous and allow for this flow.

Chapter 1 examines the successful efforts of women in the earliest years of the world body to include their choices of issues and the need for and use of their own spaces; this was the beginning of a place of one's own as well as the peace/women's tent within the UN. Chapter 2 shows the consolidation of UN women's thinking about equality as they crafted DEDAW, their alliances with men to change development thought at the UN, and the emergence of strong voices from the former colonies in both the constituency outside and the actors inside the world body. It also examines how women began to shape their thinking about development at the world conference in Mexico City. Chapter 3 features the successes of transforming DEDAW into a convention and increasing the visibility and the intellectual contributions of women worldwide and within the UN and examines views on women's role in development from two institutions located in the South—the Non-Aligned Movement and the African Training and Research Centre for Women. In chapter 4, the oppositional trajectory for women emerges; as the worldwide women's movement gained momentum in preparation for Beijing, UN reports began delivering the news that more women lived in poverty and that their poverty was worse than it had been in previous decades. It examines South-based responses to this disjuncture. Chapter 5 reveals the beginning of a strong divergence of response by the women's movement and the UN to new economic and political configurations.

Taming Development

In Saint Exupéry's *The Little Prince,* a young boy lives alone on a very small planet. But he is very lonely, and he visits Earth in search of his own kind. He meets a fox, who begs the little prince to tame him, saying, "It is an act too often neglected. . . . It means to establish ties." The prince tames the fox by loving it, and in exchange the fox tells him a secret: "What is essential is invisible to the eye." Since the 1950s, women have tried to reconstruct development—to "tame" it—by showing that the linkages between its social, economic, and political elements have been neglected; by establishing ties with the excluded and discriminated against in order to broaden laws and rights to be inclusive; by building alternative indicators that made the invisible visible. Women have brought lived experience to the work of knowledge creation; they have revealed other typologies of progress; they have insisted that localization, tethering the ground as the source, be the mainspring of action; they have revealed that participation and self-strength and human dignity are minimal conditions for engineering development with justice. In short, they have refused to accept inequality. This book is the story of how that happened.

1

Setting the Stage for Equality, 1945–1965

*The true republic: men, their rights and nothing
more; women, their rights and nothing less.*
—Susan B. Anthony (1820–1906)

- **Setting the Standard at the UN's Birth**
- **Early Notions of Women's Rights**
- **Gathering Knowledge**
- **Working Differently**
- **Responding to Stereotypes of Early Development Thought**
- **The Peace Tent**

The United Nations rose—like the proverbial phoenix—out of the ashes of World War II. Its creation was an attempt to garner international involvement in the preservation of global security. Its acceptance as a global forum with an extraordinarily variegated membership enjoying equal voting power was a celebration of the possible. Although there has been some lament that the simultaneous emergence of strongly adversarial power blocs muted, if not nullified, consensus on global issues, the advantages of a level playing field, internationalism, and a space between two warring giants provided exciting opportunities for nations emerging from forms of alien domination, both economic and political. There was a moral perspective at work in ushering in this international arrangement that opened a space for movements fighting against injustice and domination, movements claiming rights, such as citizenship, into which were woven women's rights.[1]

During these earliest decades of the new world body, the voices of women, confident, already well articulated and internationalized, resounded inside and outside the corridors of power. They exchanged knowledge and strategies from their prewar careers and laid foundations at the UN using a work style that diverged from mainstream ways of operating. Dilemmas and questions about accommodating difference while working toward equality emerged that would persist as the story unfolded in later years. This period set the stage for what followed in the coming decades, and the origins of most questions raised in the coming decades were present in embryonic form during these early years.

Setting the Standard at the UN's Birth

A fact of somewhat extraordinary significance that provides many leads to the rest of this story is that there were just four women among the 160 signatories to the UN's founding document at its Charter conference at San Francisco in 1945. Three of them were from what one would now call developing countries or the Third World: Minerva Bernardino (Dominican Republic), Bertha Lutz (Brazil), and Wu Yi-Fang (China). The fourth was Virginia Gildersleeve (United States). Two other women were present at the conference but were not signatories: Cora T. Casselman (Canada) and Jessie Street (Australia). The minuscule number of women reflected and predicted the slender representation women were fated to have in the UN. Yet women were able to balloon this small presence and influence outcomes through their strategic use of power.

The four women signatories established a sound foundation for the UN by making sure that women's issues were present in the text of the Charter. The simple act of inserting the word "women" in the text made sure that the principle of equality between the sexes was part of the founding ideas of the new organization. The old argument that "men" included "women" was simply not good enough for at least this one, very significant, time. The UN's Division for the Advancement of Women (DAW) noted in 1999 that "[t]he international women's movement from its beginning, influenced the founding principles and goals of the UN with regard to women's rights."[2] The "founding mothers," as Hilkka Pietilä refers to them, "laid the groundwork for the struggle for gender equality that has since gained momentum throughout the world."[3]

Women from the Latin American countries contributed their experience to shape the language of women's rights in the UN's founding documents. Their decades of experience with the Inter-American Commission of Women (IACW) gave them deep experience in dealing with governments; one historian goes so far as to say that they had "some influence over governments."[4] They had pioneered conventions on civil and political rights through the Pan-American Union (later renamed the Organization of American States [OAS]). Its Inter-American Commission of Women was created in 1928 to remove all legal incapacities of women and ensure that they enjoyed full civil and political rights. It was responsible for the Montevideo Convention on the Nationality of Married Women (1933) and two other conventions—the Inter-American Convention on the Granting of Civil Rights to Women (1948) and the Convention on the Political Rights of Women (1952).[5] As Ana Figueroa notes, "At the San Francisco Conference, the delegations of Brazil, Mexico and the Dominican Republic, with the support of the delegation of Chile, presented important amendments in order to include specific mention of the equality of rights for men and women in the Charter."[6] The handful of women participating in this event collaborated with forty-two nongovernmental organizations (NGOs) to ensure that the phrase "respect for human rights and for fundamental freedoms for all, without distinction as to race, sex, language, or religion" was included in Article 1 of the Charter.[7] They also succeeded in changing the language of the Preamble and the Charter from "equal rights among men" to read "equal rights among men and women."

Women at the UN were able to have a significant impact on the founding principles of the world body in its early years because of their decades of experience as activists in freedom struggles, peace movements, political forums, and trade unions.[8] Several of these women had combat or military experience or had worked in resistance movements (see box 1.2). Bodil Begtrup, the chairperson of the Sub-commission on the Status of Women, had worked with the League of Nations and was a member of the Danish resistance in World War II. Minerva Bernardino had held a number of executive positions within her government, from which she fought to include women's rights in the laws of her country. She was also a member of the Inter-American Commission on Women. Sophie Grinberg-Vinaver, the chief of the women's section in the UN Secretariat from 1959 to 1962, had been active in the French resistance and was known to be a passionate advocate of women's rights. Margaret Bruce, chief of the Section on the Status of Women from 1963 to 1973, had served in the British military during World War II. Chafika Selami-Meslem, who was head of the Division for the Advancement of Women in the UN Secretariat for ten years and headed the Algerian delegation to the Mexico world conference on women in 1975, had fought the French during her country's struggle for independence as a teenager. Marie-Helene Lefaucheux, who chaired the Commission on the Status of Women in 1948, was also the head of the Comite Social des Oeuvres de la Resistance and received the Legion d'Honneur for her underground work during the years when France was occupied. Mihir Pektas, a member of the CSW in 1948, was a former member of parliament in Turkey. Each of these women brought a commitment to a style of work that valued coalitions with other excluded and oppressed groups, which gave moral weight to the work they engaged in. Though they came from diverse backgrounds, their shared commitment to women's rights gave the tiny alliance of women great strength as it worked to influence the language of the UN texts.

The UN was not the first international or intergovernmental body to deal with questions that affected the status of women. Indeed, the groundwork for its Charter had already been laid by the Hague Conventions on Private International Law in 1902,[9] the Covenant of the League of Nations in 1924, the Pan-American Union's Lima Declaration of 1938, and the Declaration of Philadelphia of the International Labour Conference in 1944.[10] In terms of language and thought, the Charter was more progressive than these documents and quite categorically declared its belief in the equal rights of men and women. However, only about half of the UN's member countries gave women unrestricted rights to vote and hold public office, and very few countries found it necessary to include women in their delegations.

The women who were present at the Charter conference were aware that previous attempts by women to obtain international recognition of women's right to equality in the UN's predecessor, the League of Nations, had brought mixed results.[11] They saw the birth of another forum as a new opportunity to take their past campaigns forward. They succeeded this time. Women inscribed their identity as holders of rights in the founding documents of the UN—the UN Charter (1945) and the Universal Declaration of Human Rights (1948). Minerva Bernardino, Bertha Lutz, Wu Yi-Fan, and Virginia Gildersleeve used their influence to create a separate human rights body for advancing women's rights in the UN almost immediately thereafter; what would become the Commission on the Status of Women was established as a subcommission of the UN's Economic and Social Council (ECOSOC) in 1946.[12] Its mandate was to prepare reports and make recommendations to ECOSOC about women's equality as it related to political, social, economic, civil, and educational rights. From its inception, the CSW embedded its goals and thinking in the ideology of human rights that permeated the UN's founding documents. This was a significant accomplishment at a time when most public agencies across the world viewed women either as mothers or as recipients of welfare services, not as citizens with individual rights.

Several women who had participated in the League of Nations as delegates or as members of committees later served in the Commission on the Status of Women.[13] The experience Latin American women brought was particularly valuable to the early work of women in the UN. In the League of Nations, women from Latin American countries had asked that body to draft an equal rights treaty and place it on the agenda of the assembly of the League. Latin American women had also asked the League to take the initiative in conducting an investigation of the legal status of women worldwide. The IACW was responsible for collecting data to enable the Conference of American States to look at the question of women's civil and political equality; this was the first intergovernmental

> **Box 1.1. The Inter-American Commission of Women**
>
> The IACW was the first intergovernmental body devoted to women's issues. It was established in 1928 at the Sixth International Conference of American States in Havana, Cuba, as the result of extensive lobbying by a well-organized Pan-American women's movement. Members of the IACW gained valuable experience in drafting an international convention in the 1930s, when they worked on the Lima Declaration in Favor of Women's Rights. The declaration listed women's rights to equal political rights with men, civil equality, protective labor laws and the opportunity to work, and protective laws for mothers. The work of drafting the declaration, which was approved in 1938 at the Eighth International Conference of American States, prepared members of the IACW for the role they would play in the drafting of the UN's Universal Declaration of Human Rights in 1948.
>
> *Sources:* Bartkowski, "Comparative Study of Women's Activities in the Inter-War Intergovernmental Organizations"; Miller, "'Geneva—the Key to Equality'"; "Eighth International Conference of American States, Inter-American Commission on Women, The Lima Declaration in Favour of Women's Rights, 1938," *Women Go Global.*

body of women to collect such data. During the 1930s, Latin American women consistently pressured the League to examine women's status in member states and to collect information from governments and women's NGOs.[14] The experience of this group in drafting documents that granted political and civil rights to women helped the CSW prioritize its work by focusing on women's political rights from the very beginning. The 1938 Lima Declaration prepared by the IACW inspired the CSW to take up a similar exercise at the UN. Latin American women were thus able to ensure that the CSW stole a march over the rest of the UN in preparing a convention on women's political rights.[15]

A Space of One's Own: The CSW

In her famous essay "A Room of One's Own," Virginia Woolf speaks of the longing of women in the early decades of the twentieth century to have the freedom and courage to write exactly what they thought, finally concluding that this could not happen unless many women had enough money to live on and rooms of their own in which to think and write. Although a room of one's own can be a productive place, it is also a lonely place, for one must remove oneself from the

Box 1.2. The First Commission on the Status of Women

Jessie Mary Grey Street (Australia): Campaigned for equality of women, equal pay, the status of Aborigines, and world peace; Secretary of the National Council for Women in 1920.

Evdokia Uralova (Byelorussian Soviet Socialist Republic): A history teacher and a senior executive in the Ministry of Education.

Way Sung New (People's Republic of China)

Graciela Morales F. de Echeverria (Costa Rica): An executive in Costa Rica's Social Security Office.

Bodil Begtrup (Denmark): Chief film censor for Denmark.

Marie Helene Lefaucheux (France): Vice President of the Assemblee de l'Union Française; led the French Resistance to the occupation of Paris in the 1940s.

Sara Basterrechea Ramirez (Guatemala): An organic chemist and sole woman member of the faculty of the University of San Carlos.

Shareefah Hamid Ali (India): Organized the All India Women's Conference in the 1920s and represented Indian women in many international gatherings.

Amalia C. de Castillo Ledon (Mexico): A playwright and active participant in women's and social work.

Alice Kandalft Cosma (Syria): An educator and writer who organized the Arab Women's National League in Syria.

Mihri Pektas (Turkey): University professor and former member of parliament.

Elizavieta Alekseevna Popova (Union of Soviet Socialist Republics): Lawyer and trade unionist.

Mary Sutherland (United Kingdom): Leader in trade union activity and chief woman officer of the Labour Party.

Dorothy Kenyon (United States): Former judge of the New York Municipal Court; active as a lawyer in civic and women's organizations.

Isabel de Urdaneta (Venezuela): Teacher and diplomat active in the work of the Pan-American Union.

Source: Women Go Global.

mainstream of society in that room. The notion of "special space" or a "place of one's own" in the UN, as in any other organization, is fraught with problems. The notion of equality as sameness suggests that there is no need for special space for women in an organization such as the UN, which states in its seminal documents that it makes no distinction on the basis of sex. Yet one must ask why women would have wanted their own space within the UN if they were comfortable in the mainstream. These issues of whether to remain separate or integrate with the mainstream—"the common life which is the real life and not of the little separate lives which we live as individuals," as Woolf put it—continue to haunt efforts to land UN values on the ground. Excluded groups in particular face this dilemma and find their own spaces enabling as places from which to strategize before going into broader arenas.

In the early debates there was hesitation among member states to internationalize the issue of women's equality. Many states considered this to be an intrusion into the sovereignty of nations: they felt that the status of women was tied to national and cultural traditions and that setting an international standard would encroach upon national sovereignty.[16] This view had been in place for decades in the international community; when the League of Nations asked for information on the status of women in 1935, the United Kingdom replied with the following statement: "The extent to which effect should be given in any State to the principle of the equality of the sexes is a matter for that State to determine under its domestic law according to its own circumstances and requirements."[17] This question of sovereignty of states and the universalist quality of various international covenants continues to challenge the United Nations in its attempt to set standards. While its articulation that women and their freedoms should be subjected to the discretion of nation-states is one of the more contested examples, there are many other issues, such as culture or governance, where the sovereignty of states continues to challenge multilateral agreements or the rule of international law.

At the UN, the cause of equality for women found its home under the rubric of human rights, which gave it the platform from which to enter political and legal discourse. At the same time, the Commission on the Status of Women claimed autonomy from the Commission on Human Rights. This move was controversial among the small group of women in the UN. Eleanor Roosevelt, chair of the Commission on Human Rights, felt that that body would have more clout than a small commission devoted to women's issues and worried that a separate commission would marginalize women and their issues at the UN.[18] Her U.S. colleague Virginia Gildersleeve agreed. She spoke of how special mechanisms such as a separate commission for women contradicted the ideal of equality between the sexes. "Women should be regarded as human beings. . . . If they should be segregated in this special feminine Commission, then it might well happen that the men would keep them out of other commissions or groups, saying that they had plenty of scope in their own organization. This would be contrary to what we were working for—no discrimination because of sex."[19]

But Bodil Begtrup's arguments prevailed. She told ECOSOC that

> in view of the importance of this world-wide social scheme which covers, in fact, the condition of half the population of the world, the work ought to have the best possible working conditions and not be dependent upon another Commission, and that it would give this work more weight in the social field if it was done by a full Commission.

She was blunt; the view that women's problems should not be separated from those of men was "purely unrealistic and academic." She pointed out that for the first time, women's problems could be studied on an international level and that it would be a tragedy to spoil the historic opportunity by "confusing the wish with the fact."[20] In the normal course, a body that focused on women's issues would have been located in agencies that dealt with social issues and human rights issues; the independence of an autonomous commission devoted to women served women well. John P. Humphrey, the first director of the UN Secretariat Division of Human Rights, recalled in his memoirs that "there was no more independent body in the UN. Many governments . . . appointed . . . as their representatives women who were militants in their own countries."[21]

Within a month of Begtrup's speech, ECOSOC raised the status of the sub-commission to a full commission. The reasons for this speedy decision are not on public record. Speculation on the possible reasons ranges from the likelihood that women were able to convince ECOSOC that the male-dominated human rights "mainstream" was too turbulent and politicized to be useful to women to the argument that women's issues were not considered important and therefore there was no objection (from the men) to dealing with them separately.[22]

In less than a year, the United Nations office for women's affairs that Begtrup had asked for materialized as the Section on the Status of Women within the Division of Human Rights. But again, there were nonbelievers within the UN who held the view that it was not necessary to have a separate women's secretariat and that human rights were gender neutral. Political pressure to maintain a distinct and identifiable women's rights unit protected the section over the next forty-five years, although the financial resources allocated to it were meager.[23]

The justification for "special space" went in tandem with another belief held by women in the UN: that women's issues concern everyone and that accountability must be built into all parts of the system. Begtrup's speech of May 1946 to

ECOSOC reflects this: "work is to be done by different specialized agencies of the United Nations *and not just this Commission,*" and again, "we have to work closely together and many of the things will have to be carried on between these various specialized agencies, such as UNESCO, the ILO, and other sub-commissions."[24]

From its inception, the CSW was conscious of the close functional and ideological links it needed to build and preserve with the other human rights bodies in general and specialized agencies and programs in particular. Besides the International Labour Organization, the United Nations Educational, Scientific and Cultural Organization, the World Health Organization (WHO), and the United Nations Children's Fund (UNICEF), the Sub-Commission on the Prevention of Discrimination and Protection of Minorities, a unit of the Commission on Human Rights, was an important ally. Representatives of these bodies could sit in on the CSW meetings and vice versa. There was also provision for collaborative ventures—sharing of and commenting on reports, requests for preparation of studies, and so forth. This kind of interagency collaboration on the subject of women's rights broadened the perspective as well as the network of accountability. It sent a clear message that women's issues did not just relate to the CSW; in fact, it challenged the likelihood of ghettoization and predicted what feminists would say much later: "All issues are women's issues."

This period, then, saw two different sets of energies flowing simultaneously. Agencies worked together on various aspects dealing with women's status and women's rights without any functional link except collaboration and coordination on issue-based themes; their functional mandates included women and the presence of the CSW enabled the mandate to be dealt with in a better way. The other energy was in the creation and strengthening of women-only mechanisms—whether they were laws, secretariat units, or commissions. There was no sense of contradiction between these two strategies because at a pragmatic level both were needed and women in the UN believed that what worked well was what was needed rather than a theoretical formulation about how to deal with an issue.

Even though the new Commission on the Status of Women was a small group—it started with only fifteen members—its members used their institutional status wisely and effectively. Commission members regularly attended the meetings of the Commission on Human Rights as it worked through the long and arduous process of drafting the Universal Declaration of Human Rights (UDHR). Articles of the draft declaration were sent to the CSW for comment, and commission members insisted that the language of the declaration be gender specific and gender inclusive.[25] The Preamble to the UDHR refers to the Charter of the UN as reaffirming faith in the "equal rights of men and women."

The document uses language such as "members of the human family" (Preamble) and "all human beings" (Article I). Like the Charter, the UDHR uses the phrase "men and women."

This accomplishment did not come easily; women had to struggle with male drafters of the declaration to convince them to change "all men" to "all human beings." The UDHR enumerates basic rights and freedoms to which all men and women are entitled—among them the right to life, to work, to education, to liberty and nationality, to participate in government, to freedom of speech, to freedom of religion, to freedom of belief, and to freedom from fear. It describes rights as inalienable and indivisible. Yet the idea that these rights apply to every single human being was not clear in the draft formulation of its first article, which said, "All men are created equal." Hansa Mehta, an Indian delegate to the meeting of the human rights drafting committee, protested at the use of this gender-opaque language. "That would never do," she said. "'All men' might be interpreted to exclude women." Eleanor Roosevelt disagreed. She came from a long tradition of women's activism in the United States that based its actions on women's special needs as workers. She supported gender-inclusive language, but she tried to bridge the gap between "difference" feminism and "equality" feminism with the statement that she "wished to make it clear that equality did not mean identical treatment for men and women in all matters; there were certain cases, as for example the case of maternity benefits, where different treatment was essential."[26] She argued that the women of the United States had never felt they were left out of the Declaration of Independence because it said "all men." But she eventually had to agree with the other women, mostly from developing countries, who felt strongly on this point. Thirty-two countries voted in favor of the change; only two voted against it and three abstained. The language was changed from "all men" to "all human beings." While changing or adding words might look like an exercise in semantics, language as it describes phenomena has been a source of bias, of introducing hierarchies in values, of expressing prejudices and distortion. Introducing new language has been one of the tools the women's movement has used to readjust these hierarchies and be inclusive of difference; this effort continues from the past into the future throughout this historical narrative.

Early Notions of Women's Rights

The dialogues and discourses about women's equality reveal differences of opinion about how special measures intended to compensate for entrenched disadvantages or protect certain characteristics of a social group might deprive that group of the right to be treated equally. Such debates about difference had been present when the League of Nations was drafting an equal rights treaty in the 1930s.[27]

The issue of workers' rights provides the clearest example of this debate. Should women be treated as workers with special needs that require policies that gave them maternity benefits or prohibited them from working at night or on hazardous jobs? One argument was that special arrangements smacked of discrimination, albeit positive discrimination; this argument viewed the strategy as incompatible with the overall struggle by women to dismantle inequality. Agencies such as the ILO worked hard in this period to find a position that would accommodate both the difference argument (by providing protective legislation for women workers) and the equality position (by avoiding all protective legislation).[28]

Those who claimed to speak for the cause of women workers defined their needs in the context of competing social roles. They maintained that the position of women in society could be improved only if legislation addressed their special needs as workers, wives, and mothers in addition to the rights they were entitled to share with men. Sex-based legislation regarding working hours and working conditions, in their opinion, would improve the health and welfare of women, as would social policies to protect mothers and children. Trade unionists and reformers who had fought hard for paid maternity leave, minimum wages, and the regulation of working hours did not welcome initiatives that threatened protective legislation.[29]

Finding a way out of this knotted thicket is difficult, as the implications are vital for ensuring justice to women. That the right of women to equality with men is seen to be in opposition to women's rights to protection in certain areas arises from the fuzziness that surrounds the concept of equality itself. What does "equality" mean? Does it mean giving women exactly the same rights as men, even when men do not have adequate rights in the workplace and as citizens? Does it mean writing laws that give special consideration to women because they bear children in order to "level the playing field" for women workers? How can an international convention designed to give all the women of the world equality be reconciled with differences in political and economic spaces and opportunities, much less the cultural and religious practices of individual states that inhibit such ideas? What kind of ideology could be constructed that would encompass the seemingly opposed concepts that women are both different from and equal to men?

In the early period, the UN emphasized the equality of rights of both men and women; this was a crucial component of its founding principles. It placed a premium on the principle of equal access to resources (education, positions of power, etc.) and highlighted the importance of legislation as a way to bring equality to women in the areas of labor law, marriage, citizenship, and political participation. To the founders of the UN's seminal documents, special provisions to ensure equality for women seemed inevitable. It was much later that the UN learned from its experience of working with women that it is not equality of *treatment* but equality of *outcomes* that is crucial to ensuring women's equality.

At a normative and prescriptive level, the idea of men and women having equal rights was itself quite new. Until the Universal Declaration of Human Rights, no international treaty or legal instrument had expressed this value in clear and unambiguous terms. In parts of the world, as in old English law, women were not seen as capable of having legal rights to own property or cast a vote and were treated as chattel. The UN broke new ground by inscribing equality between men and women into its founding texts and creating a separate human rights body exclusively for women, even though a clear understanding of what equality meant was still elusive. Women did not speak with one voice, though they were all committed to the ideal of gender equality, and they were as divided as the men were in their opinions and statements.

A comparison of Eleanor Roosevelt's "Open Letter to the Women of the World" (February 1946), which she read at one of the first sessions of ECOSOC, with Bodil Begtrup's speech on the status of women in the second session of ECOSOC (May 1946) is instructive about the different strategies women pursued. Eleanor Roosevelt's "Open Letter" dwelled in depth on the role and contributions of women in the war effort as well as in other civic and citizenship fields, mainly peace and reconstruction. While the document emphasized women's capabilities and capacities and how they are to be used for national and international tasks, it gave equal weight to how their primary duty lies in childbearing and child rearing. It did not expend words on what "women's status" or "women's equality" meant. Bodil Begtrup's address was a forthright mapping of the road to equality "to raise the status of women to equality with men in all fields of human enterprise" through the agency of the new Sub-commission on the Status of Women. It was a summary of a charter for women's progress in political, civil, social, and economic fields based on the principle of equality of rights.

The difference in approach can be traced to the political traditions of the two camps. Eleanor Roosevelt came from a tradition of women activists who had fought long and hard for suffrage for women. In the extremely conservative political environment of the United States, and after eight decades of activism that tried every strategy, women were finally able to convince enough members of Congress to vote for women's suffrage because of the service they performed during World War I; they had proved their capacity to be good citizens. Roosevelt based her arguments for women's rights on what she was familiar with: women deserve rights because of their contributions to the world, because they have accomplished or proven certain things. On the other hand, the majority of the women at the subcommission had come from movements that struggled for freedom from colonialism, religious fundamentalism, and so forth, and so had an expanded view of rights that was more close to the right to be free of domination of various kinds. The mixed responses to the debate that followed the reading of the "Open Letter" reflected the lack of clarity about rights and equality. While all speakers asked for a better deal for women, some (both men and women, including Roosevelt) stressed the roles, responsibilities, and contributions of women, especially in the just-concluded war, and urged women to come forward and share in the work of peace and reconstruction. These individuals did not speak of women's rights or lack of rights. No one conjoined the two or spoke of rights and responsibilities going in tandem. Many underlined that in their countries men and women enjoyed the same rights and privileges, that they had already achieved equality, but that in other countries women "still walk[ed] in obscurity." Marie-Helen Lefaucheux, chair of the CSW in 1948, pointed out that these attitudes were divisive: the "habit so dear to some delegates, of dwelling complacently on the perfections of the systems in their own countries in reference to any subject brought up" hampered the work of defining equality and moving forward to achieve it.[30]

Political Rights

Within a year of its being founded in 1945, the UN took the imaginative step of advocating that women be given full political suffrage worldwide. This step was radical at the time; only thirty of the original fifty-one member states allowed women to vote.[31] The call for suffrage for women emanated from the Subcommission on the Status of Women. This daring act at once gave millions of women the world over access to what was till then distant, if not taboo, political territory. Bodil Begtrup asked ECOSOC to "direct an appeal to the governments of the United Nations that have not yet accorded suffrage to the women."[32] Suffrage meant "equal political rights with men, in particular in regard to the right to vote and to be elected to public office on equal terms with men."[33] The founding belief underlying work to bring suffrage to all women was that "political rights and development are fundamental."[34] This formulation was in itself pathbreaking and farsighted, as subsequent experience was to show.

During the first decade after its birth, the UN provided and sustained the drive for suffrage for women. In 1952, the UN put the campaign for women's suffrage on a legal footing. That year, the General Assembly adopted the Convention on Political Rights of Women "to implement the principle of equality of rights for men and women contained in the Charter of the United Nations." The convention was to bind the countries in contract to ensure that:

Article I: Women shall be entitled to vote in all elections on equal terms with men, without any discrimination.

Article II: Women shall be eligible for election to all publicly elected bodies, established by national law, on equal terms with men, without any discrimination.

Article III: Women shall be entitled to hold public office and to exercise all public functions, established by national law, on equal terms with men, without any discrimination.[35]

The process the UN adopted from the beginning was itself a crucial factor in the progress achieved in promoting suffrage for women. The Secretary-General put the issue of suffrage for women high on the agenda of all seventy-four UN member governments at the time and called upon them to furnish progress reports. The responses received were closely monitored by the CSW, and the results were periodically reported to the General Assembly.

In 1954, the UN Secretary-General complimented the CSW for "faithfully seeking to carry out its mandate." He added that "the Commission could note with pride that as a result of its activities, the United Nations, under the authority of the General Assembly, had sponsored the opening of an International Convention on Political Rights of Women under which women would have the right to vote, to be elected, to hold all public offices and to discharge all public functions." Thirty-five countries signed the Convention and three countries deposited instruments of ratification, the first being the Dominican Republic.[36]

However, there were serious impediments to achieving the UN's goal of universal suffrage. During the first decade of 1946–1955, when the UN was in the forefront of the campaign for suffrage, a number of member countries were still under colonial rule. They had no democratic regimes. In such countries there was no scope for suffrage for women. But from the 1950s onward, as the national liberation struggles succeeded in overthrowing colonial rule, the issue of suffrage for women received fresh impetus. The demand for women's right to vote was fueled by local political formations that included women who were active in the liberation and other social movements of their respective countries.

A View from the South

The composition of the UN was changing rapidly by the 1960s. From 1956 to 1963, almost all the new member states admitted to the UN were Third World countries and the newly liberated countries of Africa.[37] Many of them sent women as delegates. Women who represented the developing countries were often those who had participated in the struggles against colonial rule and in the many socioeconomic campaigns that accompanied them.[38] In many countries, these

Box 1.3. Women in Freedom Struggles

In developing countries . . . particularly in those under colonial rule, it had often been the struggle for independence in which women participated that had led to petitioning for equal political rights with men. This was the case, for example, in Mexico, but it was not until 1953 that women gained the right to vote in that country. In the early 1900s, Palestinian women had organized to protest against British occupation of Palestine and in 1919, Egyptian women had marched in the streets of Cairo. Women in India had their consciousness raised by the movement against colonialism and had played key political as well as military roles in a number of their own peasant uprisings. In the Philippines as early as 1904, the first public debates about gender equality had started and the first two formal women's organizations which were established in the early 1900s both carried the name *feministas.* The early suffragists in the Philippines in the media, in the Philippine Assembly, in schools, and in other public and private gatherings, advocated for women's right to vote. But the right to vote was not achieved by women in the Philippines until 1937. Women's movements have often been intertwined with broader movements for political and social change.

Source: Women Go Global.

movements had raised the banner of women's emancipation from their entrenched positions within patriarchal and feudal structures. Political freedom, democratic rights for the people, and women's emancipation were often interlinked themes for struggle in these countries. For example, Gandhi's leadership provided the incentive for large numbers of Indian women to take part in the freedom movement and in struggles for their rights as women.

These women extended the concept of women's equality beyond legal equality in civil and political rights to equal participation in nation-building, social and economic development, the strengthening of civic responsibilities, and the overall improvement of the status of women. Equality for women became increasingly transposed into the debates on development. The work of the Commission on the Status of Women in the 1960s took them "beyond the negotiating tables in New York and Geneva and into the fields and rice paddies of the developing world."[39]

The increase and change in the composition of UN members served to modify or enrich the issues. In addition to the issues of citizenship, nationality, property, suffrage, and civil and political rights that were already on board, other issues such as illiteracy, poor health, and the absence of professional and vocational education were put on the agenda.[40] Though female poverty, especially mass poverty, had not yet captured attention on the UN stage, the conventional belief was that the problems of underdevelopment or lack of development were the result of poverty, which in turn was the outcome of lack of economic growth.[41]

Box 1.4. Vijaya Lakshmi Pandit: The First Woman President of UN General Assembly

Born in 1900, Vijaya Lakshmi Pandit was the sister of Jawaharlal Nehru, the first prime minister of India. She herself had been active in the Independence Movement in her country and had been imprisoned many times in connection with the civil disobedience movement led by Mahatma Gandhi. Pandit campaigned for and was elected as a member of the Legislative Assembly of the United Provinces in 1937. She went on to become the Minister for Local Self-Government and Public Health. Pandit was linked to women's groups and served as the president of the All India Women's Conference from 1941 to 1943. She was also appointed as the Indian ambassador to the Soviet Union (1947) and to the United States (1949). She created history when she became the first woman to be elected president of the UN General Assembly at its eighth session in 1953. Her strong ideological moorings were reflected in her work. In an interview for the *United Nations Bulletin* in 1953, she spoke of her philosophy:

> Those of us who have been brought up under the shadow of Gandhi and trained under his leadership must inevitably approach international problems from his angle. It is for this reason that we are occasionally misunderstood. The great contribution that Mahatma Gandhi made was his insistence that means are as important as ends and that if the goal towards which we travel is a good one, we cannot employ means that are unworthy. In our own small way we attempt to apply this principle in our own work in the United Nations. . . . The United Nations' existence depends on its ability to translate the noble words and high ideals of the Charter into the lives of the humblest individuals in the smallest nations.

Sources: "A Famous Woman of India," available online at http://www.ozedesi.com/ News/NewsDetails.asp?NewsID=12; "The Growing Role of Women in the General Assembly," *United Nations Bulletin* 13, no. 10 (15 November 1952), 451.

The profile of women workers that was becoming visible was no longer composed only of the factory worker protected by labor laws of earlier decades or the professional or technical worker whose job was regulated by prescribed service conditions and written contracts. The new groupings were the masses of women in developing countries who lacked legal protection and worked as household or subsistence workers or workers in handicrafts or cottage industries. These women workers suffered daily exploitation, yet they contributed to their national economies through their productive and creative skills. They did not have a healthy or hygienic working environment, were not members of unions, had no social security benefits, were abused by their employers, and had to suffer from the malpractices of middlemen.[42]

The ILO's sphere of influence did not extend to these vast millions of women, many of whom were not even counted as workers in their country's or the UN's statistical systems. The invisibility of much of the work of poor women of the developing countries was a theme the UN system and the CSW would address in future decades. These types of women workers became the subject of all the UN agencies. They were the labor in the "unorganized sector," later named the "informal sector" and the "informal economy." But during this initial period, the reality of the world's majority of women workers succeeded in impinging on UN consciousness. The process of learning initiated in this period would take the UN far in succeeding decades when concepts of measurement and valuation of women's work would engage the minds and pens of women researchers and economists.

Grappling with "Customs"

As early as the 1950s, the UN confronted the prototypes of what later would be called human rights violations against women and children. There was the incident of the Greek mothers whose children had been abducted and had not been repatriated (1950).[43] There was the plight of women survivors of concentration camps who were subjected to so-called medical experiments during the Nazi regime. Many of these had become stateless persons who could not count on the legal protection of any state government and therefore could not obtain compensation for their sufferings.

The UN responded to all these abuses and violations of women's rights and equality on a case-by-case basis. In some cases, the response was through legislation—as, for example, in the case of child marriage. In the case of the abduction of the children of Greek mothers, all the CSW could do was to send a resolution to the General Assembly expressing the hope that the efforts of the UN Secretary-General and the Red Cross would put an end to the agony of the mothers.

In the case of the victims of Nazis, the CSW asked ECOSOC to ask the Social Commission and the WHO to attend to the plight of those affected by war.

One of the most contentious issues during this period was related to what was considered to be "personal" or in the realm of "customs and traditions." A process of evolution in naming the problem took place. First, "customs" were viewed as barbaric, then "barbaric" became "violence against women," and finally "violence against women" became "rights violations." The debates that led to these shifts offer a poignant illustration of the complexities of standard-setting. The case of what was later called "female genital mutilation" (FGM) in Africa (later changed to female genital cutting by the end of the twentieth century) first came to the attention of the UN in the early 1950s from the WHO in Africa. Within the UN, no precise name had been found for this violation. It was first referred to as "ritual operations," then "ritual practices," and then to "operations based on custom." The initial reaction was to ask the member states to abolish all such customs that violate the dignity and security of persons. In 1952, ECOSOC, acting on the recommendations of the CSW, asked member states to "abolish progressively . . . all customs that violate the physical integrity of women and which thereby violate the dignity and worth of the human person as proclaimed in the Charter and in the Universal Declaration of Human Rights."[44] The resolution pointed out that in the trust and non-self-governing territories, certain prevalent customs violated the physical integrity of women, thereby violating their human rights. There were no discriminatory or unequal laws, only the force of custom and tradition. Though FGM was the most publicized issue, several others fell under the general rubric of violations of the bodily integrity of women and girls, such as child marriage, bride price, and dowry.

In 1954, the General Assembly, despite some debate, approved a resolution to take appropriate measures to abolish practices that violated human rights. It did not include any specific references to FGM but cited issues such as eliminating child marriages, bride price, and dowry and guaranteeing widows the custody of children and the right to remarry. In 1958, the specific practice of FGM was taken up for discussion, and the CSW asked the WHO to conduct an "inquiry" into the "persistence of these practices." ECOSOC diluted the word "inquiry" by using a weaker substitute "study."[45] The WHO turned down the request, stating that it was outside its competence because the matter was "cultural, not medical, and was thus outside its jurisdiction."[46] The WHO's negative reply, which came from its Executive Board, was later confirmed by the WHO Health Assembly in 1959. Neither African women nor their communities were noticeable players on this issue in these early decades. African women's voices, especially, were not heard because they were still living under colonial rule.[47]

In this first period, there was already an imperceptible shift away from a judgmental approach to a more realistic and consultative one, with an underlying message that the countries concerned should "own" the problem. In 1960, although ECOSOC changed terminology from "ritual operations" to "operations based on customs," it noted with approval that countries were trying to work toward elimination of these practices. But it had already become a North-South issue based on questions such as who was entitled to define or to name a practice as a rights violation.

The concern that any type of intervention might be perceived as outsider interference in traditional practices and ways of life lay just beneath the surface at the UN. Some argued that education would change these deeply rooted customs and others worried about the possibility that following this policy would be construed as violation of the Charter, which forbids interference in domestic affairs. Even in this early part of the story, the difficulties of finding a universal norm or standard were apparent.

Rights Are Indivisible

In the "mainstream" UN—if one can call it that—human rights followed a set trajectory. The UDHR was followed by two international covenants—one on civil and political rights and the other on economic, social, and cultural rights. The former were termed "negative rights" and the latter "positive rights."[48] The positive rights were to be progressively achieved while the negative rights were to be immediately applied and achieved. This insistence on separation and prioritization of rights reflected the impact of Cold War ideological hostilities and anxieties.

During the Cold War, there was a strong difference of opinion about the ranking of the different types of rights. Western nations were arguing basically for civil and political rights, while the socialist countries, and some developing countries, were arguing for greater emphasis on social and economic rights. The West argued that there was a denial of civil and political rights in the East and the East argued that there was deep inequality in the West linked to economic injustice. It is said that in the General Assembly this was a dividing line that often thwarted the consensus that was necessary to pass various legislation. Since the developing countries had been colonized by countries who claimed to honor civil and political rights but had in fact violated those rights in their rule over them, and since their main concern was to find ways of overcoming widespread poverty, they were often in alliance with the socialists, and the Eastern bloc often supported the arguments of these countries.

But in the substream, or the women's stream, this division was neither accepted nor applied. In this holistic vision, the issues of human rights, the status of women, peace, and development were all linked. From the beginning of its work in 1946–1947, the CSW looked at the reality of women's lives on the ground and formatted its work plan to suit that reality. The conventions that moved through the CSW or in collaboration with the ILO related not only to political rights and nationality but also to issues of equal wages, suppression of trafficking and the exploitation of prostitution, consent to marriage, minimum age of marriage and registration of marriages, night work and women, discrimination in employment and occupation, and so forth. The CSW saw the links between the economic, the social, and the political and acted upon them. Responding to a report on discrimination in education against minorities, it observed that "equality in educational opportunities was closely linked to equality in political, economic, civil and social matters. Education for girls should be compulsory and the curricula for boys and girls should be identical."[49] In considering the issue of equal pay for equal work, the CSW made the refreshing observation that "equal pay for equal work was as important to the status of women as the right to vote."[50] The indivisibility of human rights has always been an article of faith with the women of the UN.

Women spoke out against the fragmentation of rights, even when it was women doing the fragmenting. When the CSW discussed the political rights of women separately in November 1946, Vijaya Lakshmi Pandit, a leader in the freedom movement, observed that it was wrong to speak of the rights of women apart from the rights of human beings as a whole. She believed that if it is necessary to single out the rights of women, all rights should be cited, not just political rights.[51] There was general support among the women of the commission for this point of view. But there was a variety of opinions about how to address the issue. They included mentioning economic and social rights in addition to political rights or dropping the word "political" from the resolution in question altogether so that the General Assembly's recommendations to member states did not focus on any one particular set of rights of women. The debates in the assembly indicated that there was support for widening the scope of the resolution, but in the end the resolution recommended that all member states grant women "the same political rights as men."[52]

Gathering Knowledge

One of the first tasks the CSW identified under its mandate was the collection of data about women. What was women's status worldwide? No one could answer this question because no comprehensive survey had ever been completed. The ILO had begun this work, as had the League of Nations, but the war had interrupted these efforts.[53] One thing was clear to commission members—there were very noticeable gaps between the letter of the law and the reality on the ground. In the UN, these were apparent right from the beginning. Yet initial debates and discussions saw equality as a legal issue and the abolition of legal disabilities as sufficient to iron out disparities. The first period of UN history is often referred to as the era of women's formal equality, but it is also the period when the difference between law and fact, between law and practice, became obvious. The down-to-earth working style of the early women institutional pioneers in the UN helped make these disparities clear because they were very concerned with practical outcomes. Bodil Begtrup once referred to the UN Charter as a "working paper requiring implementation."[54] The view of Begtrup and her colleagues on the CSW was that the earlier attempt of the League of Nations to study the question of women's status suffered from the defect that it "only dealt with laws and not application, which we think is fundamental."[55]

In 1947, the UN launched a worldwide information-gathering exercise using the questionnaire method. The survey form was called "Questionnaire on the Legal Status and Treatment of Women." Responses started flowing regularly to the UN, containing an "unprecedented wealth of information . . . from nearly every region of the world. The success of the questionnaire approach ensured its future use as a tool in the survey of women's issues."[56] The information from various countries reinforced what the UN was finding through other sources of data and information—denial of access of services to women was based more on cultural practices and religious customs than on laws.

In 1949, the UN sent another questionnaire to thirty-two countries concerning opportunities for women in education and the professions. It also launched a complementary study on how far these opportunities were actually realized in the field of women's education. The studies aimed to pinpoint the nature and causes of the obstacles that hindered full equality of educational opportunities for women. While statistics were collected from member countries, the UN used nongovernmental and intergovernmental organizations to get qualitative information. It set up a committee of experts that consisted of mostly women educators and social workers, including representatives from the Inter-American Commission of Women and the Moslem-Arab League. According to the Committee of Experts of UNESCO, "if women do not possess the same educational facilities as men, it is not for any psychological or pedagogical reason that could justify the existing qualitative and quantitative difference between the opportunities offered to boys and girls. The only established differences in intellectual aptitudes are differences between individuals and not differences between the sexes."[57]

In 1950, at the request of the CSW, the UN collected information from seventy-four countries on whether there were legal constraints to women's right to vote and to stand for public office on the same terms as men. The results of the survey showed that fifty-two countries provided equal political rights to men and women and twenty-two countries did not. In thirteen of the latter countries, women were not permitted to vote or hold office, whereas in the remaining nine, women's political rights were subject to conditions and requirements (such as owning property or educational qualifications) that were not required of men.[58] In 1958, the ILO conducted a survey in seven Asian countries to identify the most urgent problems with respect to female labor. This in turn resulted in more research and expert groups and attracted the attention of the members of the CSW and other UN bodies.[59]

The UN also tackled the "culture" argument. UNESCO conducted anthropological and sociological studies that questioned the assumptions of social scientists about the naturalness of sex differences. Sex roles were now seen not as mere indicators of differences between women and men but as markers of key social hierarchical divisions. These studies showed that culture and location, not only in terms of geographical space but also in terms of degrees or stages of economic development, played a critical role in determining the spaces women could use to move toward self-empowerment.[60]

UNESCO adopted a Convention Against Discrimination in Education in 1960, which the UN adopted in 1962.[61] During the initial period of the UN's existence, UNESCO studied and surveyed women in a large number of countries in Asia and Africa, including a pilot study on the political rights of women in Asia. The countries studied included: Mexico, Turkey, Nigeria and other countries in Sub-Saharan Africa, and Asian countries such as Burma, India, Pakistan, Indonesia, Malaysia, Singapore, and the Philippines. The CSW and UNESCO collaborated in work of mutual interest related to women, education, and social and cultural development revolving around questions of access, contribution, participation, roles, and opportunity.[62]

One of the most significant contributions of UNESCO was its support of the CSW's view that the existence of traditions and customs meant that mere legal equality was not sufficient to ensure equality. It was also necessary to change gender relations. Since gender relations were a part of the power structures in society, power could be claimed or leveled by the powerless only through political means.

Through these conduits, a wealth of information poured into the UN from all parts of the world on diverse issues relating to the status of women. This helped the UN in general and the CSW and other agencies in particular to move away from a purely law-based strategy toward policies that addressed issues of inequality, lack of access, and discrimination. This is not to say that the CSW no longer believed in law as the agent of social change. But it was no longer the sole or even the most important factor. In fact, at the instance of the CSW and

ECOSOC, the UN General Assembly adopted conventions seeking to establish equality for women in areas as diverse as political rights, marriage laws, laws relating to nationality, and trafficking/slavery.[63]

The UN learned to go beyond the confines of formal equality bestowed by laws and to investigate why, in spite of the political rights enjoyed by women in many countries through the instrument of the law, the actual situation of women did not correspond fully with the legal situation. Its research revealed that "legal equality" does not mean that women actually hold public offices proportionally. Even in a fairly progressive and liberal country such as Sweden, only 6.6 percent of the Riksdag (legislative assembly) were women. The data showed that "only exceptionally does the percentage of women in any legislative assembly exceed ten." The evolution of thinking at the UN about women's equality is illustrated in the organization of the report of the Secretary-General on political discrimination; it had two sections, one to address the "Situation in Law" and one to address the "Situation in Practice."[64] These were among the first efforts of the UN to recognize the gap between ideas as enshrined in doctrinal documents and the reality as it operates, a gap it would repeatedly seek to narrow.

Working Differently

The UN's strength lay in its capacity to serve as a global advocate for women so as to prevail over entrenched attitudes in member countries. Yet it was bound by the rules, norms, and ethos of international diplomacy. It could only suggest, recommend, show by example, and gently prod countries into action along desired paths. It had to think of new strategies and ways of working if it was to be a successful countervailing force for women in the community of nations. Women had to have distinctive working methods if they were to be effective within the UN. The seventeen women representatives in the first session of the UN General Assembly in London in 1946 quickly found a working style that was productive and creative. Eleanor Roosevelt had remarked during the UN General Assembly in 1946 that through informal meetings with her women colleagues, she achieved "more progress in reaching an understanding on some question before the United Nations than we had been able to achieve in the formal work of our committees." This discovery would influence her later work with the UN on human rights.[65]

The few women delegates in the General Assembly and the intergovernmental organizations—along with the few women in the Secretariat—were women on the "inside." But a much larger constituency of women on the "outside" backed them. These were women from the nongovernmental organizations, intergovernmental organizations, women's associations, trade unions, cooperatives, academia, professional bodies, and political parties. Without their help, the few women inside the UN would have had fewer opportunities and would have had to struggle harder to make their views heard in the predominantly male gatherings of the UN. As a tiny minority located in a huge organization that was part representative and part bureaucratic, they quickly realized the effectiveness of coming together on a common platform, whether that platform was issue-based or ideological.

Women who were planning to push their agenda through the complicated organizational systems of the UN needed special ways of working and needed to forge alliances to make use of special structures and configurations of space. If the UN was the theater, the women were the players who used various styles of acting to reach their objective. Ways of working with men had to be modulated, divides had to be bridged; they had to use informal methods to supplement formal patterns of interactions, lateral movements rather than hierarchical.

Strategic combinations of women located in different spaces in the system was a not-uncommon feature of these "acting styles." Often a triangular alliance formed between three sets of women: women delegates to UN bodies, women working in the Secretariat and other parts of the UN, and women working outside the UN, the representatives of nongovernmental organizations and academicians or other individuals who were working on the same issue. Such combinations, with some variations, have become an enduring feature of the style of women's work at the UN. This alliance of the CSW, the UN Secretariat's women's branch, and women in nongovernmental organizations became visible in the first debate in the UN General Assembly, when all three were referred to in the speeches. In 1950, Marie-Helene Lefaucheux, chair of the CSW, remarked that one of the "outstanding characteristics" of the CSW's sessions was "the excellent collaboration of the specialized agencies and the non-governmental organizations." She particularly mentioned the Inter-American Commission of Women, "a faithful ally and a great source of inspiration."[66]

The consultative arrangement whereby women working with nongovernmental organizations were accredited to sit in the meetings of ECOSOC was a device that promoted interaction. Many of the NGOs that had consultative status with ECOSOC and attended CSW meetings in the early years, such as the Women's International League for Peace and Freedom and the Inter-American Commission on Women, were active in the peace movement. Some of these organizations regularly sent a representative to the CSW meetings.

This different style of work and use of ingenious ways to promote the agenda of the CSW happened on many occasions. One example is women's strategic use of the Third Committee of the General Assembly as a way to bring issues to the larger body. The social committee of ECOSOC and the Third Committee of the

General Assembly were the most important representative bodies that dealt with the women's questions. They also dealt with issues such as racism and human rights. Many questions relating to women's views were raised in the Third Committee, which had more women members than the other committees, and then found their way to the plenary meetings of the General Assembly for final decision.[67]

It is interesting that at this time the specialists chosen to fill posts in the UN agencies or nominated to committees often were members of movements (including the women's movement) or had a background of public life. They brought a quality that merged outside resources and inside resources. They represented many voices and were powerful in their influence over the outcomes, affirming two features of the CSW's working style at the UN: one, the merging and welding of conventional dichotomies; and two, the use of the experience and strength of existing movements to overcome institutional and political barriers. The commission's holistic view of rights—its refusal to divide rights into separate categories—illustrates the first feature. The valuable experience in drafting conventions that women such as Jessie Street brought from the League of Nations illustrates the second.

Responding to Stereotypes of Early Development Thought

The declaration of the First Development Decade of 1961–1970 did not mention women specifically, but in 1962, the General Assembly instructed the CSW "to prepare a report on the role of women in the social and economic development plans of member governments." At that time most governments and NGOs assumed that economic and social development would bring about the desired changes for women, according to Margaret Bruce, who served as the head of the UN's Division for the Advancement of Women for many years.[68]

Within the CSW there was an opinion that development was not really a women's issue and that too much attention to economic development would divert the commission from its primary goal of securing women's equal rights. "They preferred to emphasize the human element in development and called for greater investment in women as human resources."[69] In a resolution to ECOSOC in 1962, the CSW called on UN bodies such as UNICEF to "expand and strengthen their efforts to assist women in developing countries,"[70] but the issue of women and development was not a major part of the CSW's agenda during these very early years of the decade.

Even though in the 1960s there was growing evidence that women "were affected disproportionately by poverty and inequality with men—including barriers to women's ownership of land and access to credit," and that "representatives from the former colonies were offering the profile of women as producers, as bread winners," the UN's approach hinged on stereotypical notions of femininity and issues that especially affected the women of the North.[71] UN agencies that dealt with development tended to view women primarily as mothers, homemakers, and the "frailer sex."[72] This can be illustrated by the approach and programs of agencies such as UNICEF, the WHO, and the Food and Agriculture Organization (FAO) at that time.

For example, in 1948, the WHO focused on maternity and child welfare as one of its primary areas of concern. It had set up a number of model maternity and child welfare centers by 1953. Gro Brundtland, the director-general of the WHO in 1999, spoke of that agency's attitudes toward women during this period:

> The first "reality" is that for long . . . the focus has been on the reproductive period of women's lives. Primarily women have been considered as synonymous with "mothers." However, the time has come to focus beyond the sexual and reproductive health of women and view the different needs in the entire life-span.[73]

In the 1950s and the 1960s, WHO programs typically grouped women with children, the elderly, or the "infirm." UNICEF also focused on women only as mothers in the 1960s to 1970s, assisting welfare-driven development policies and programs for maternal and child health such as mother-craft and home-craft.

This perpetuation of stereotypes was not limited to the UN; sometimes funding agencies exported it to their partners. For example, a program for India funded by the U.S. Agency for International Development (USAID) in the 1950s, which was later generalized by the Food and Agriculture Organization into its approach to rural women, selected a gendered schema that chose agricultural knowledge and inputs for men and home science for women. The episode illustrates how much the interventions were based on ideas of modernization and social relations in Western cultures. As Marianne Marchand and Jane Parpart characterize it: "The rationale for this progression was provided by colonial (and later neo-colonial) discourse which compared 'backward and primitive' Third World peoples unfavorably with the 'progressive' North."[74]

The United States exported its program of domestic science, pioneered in home economics programs in land-grant colleges at the turn of the twentieth century, to the developing world. The U.S. program was based on a set of assumptions about class, gender, race, and sexuality that were rendered invisible in the process of exportation to nations such as India and other nations of the South, even though the women in those nations did not focus their energies on housework or "homemaking"; they were too busy being the major growers, processors, and distributors of agricultural goods in the South. UN programs under the auspices of agencies such as the FAO presented "domestic science" as a tool of nation-building that was "modern" and "scientific."[75]

A 1947 report by the Indian National Congress's Sub-Committee on Women noted the inappropriateness of the cultural schema being imposed on the women of its nation and advocated development for women based on their roles as producers, not as consumers or home managers:

> The crux of the situation lies, indeed, in the economic position of woman, her right to own or hold or inherit or acquire property; carry on any trade, profession or vocation; or accept any remunerative employment. So long as this fundamental right is not fully conceded, and actually realized in daily life, all talk of relief, remedy or reform would be just hot wind.[76]

Yet Indian policymakers ignored these recommendations and instead adopted the American home-science approach the FAO promoted through the Community Development Programme in 1952. Interestingly, farm women in the United States had protested against a similar pattern of assistance that was being imposed on them at that time.[77] In later decades, as women networked across sectoral and regional interests, they could build solidarity against such ignorant and biased practices that pushed them back rather than forward.

Defining Work and the Worker

These perceptions of women's roles penetrated the expert discipline of quantification of the economy. Unpaid work—predominantly an aspect of women's domain—would not be included as a statistical measure until the mid-1990s. Nilüfer Çagatay notes that including this type of women's work in the accounts would not have been difficult: "Of the four components of work affected by undercounting—subsistence production, the informal sector, domestic work and voluntary activities—the inclusion of the first two in national income accounts did not require much of a conceptual reorientation."[78] The informal sector, by and large, includes paid activities that are not recorded, so the problem is more practical than conceptual. Likewise, subsistence production, though unpaid, produces marketable goods. Satisfactory ways of measuring subsistence agricultural production—that is, production that never reaches a market and may never involve an exchange of money—have been devised since the 1950s in most countries.[79] But many economists found it more difficult to include the value of domestic work and voluntary activities in the national income accounts. That these activities could have any economic significance, apart from considerations of gender equity, was not easily accepted.

In the 1950s, despite arguments over how to define production boundaries, there was a tacit agreement about the exclusion of housewives. In 1960, a working party of UN statisticians in Africa recommended that other nonmonetary activities such as processing raw materials, carrying water, and manufacture of clothing be included.[80] This broadened the scope of the national accounts and the understanding of the work women do; however, not all the suggestions made were accepted. Much of "women's" work—the roles and responsibilities allotted to women and even claimed by women—is still invisible.

In 1953, the UN System of National Accounts (UNSNA) was widely implemented as the international standard for the production of national accounts and labor force statistics. The UNSNA established a distinction between primary and other producers. It also defined what is called a "production boundary" that differentiates between those activities that have a market value and/or are paid for and those activities that are not paid for and are therefore not considered to be economic activities in this system. Feminists internationally have critiqued the UNSNA in particular and economists more generally for failing to recognize the socially necessary contribution of women's unpaid labor.[81]

Feminists have been arguing that unpaid household work is economically valuable since the turn of the twentieth century, when Charlotte Perkins Gilman wrote *Women and Economics* (1898). Margaret Gilpin Reid added to Gilman's work in 1934 with *Economics of Household Production*. The "third-person criteria" first articulated by Margaret Reid in 1934 proposed that if a third person could be paid to do the unpaid activity of a household member, it should be deemed work. Thus, cooking, childcare, and gardening are all work, since others could be paid to perform these tasks. Iulie Aslaksen and Charlotte Koren note that "awareness of the economic importance of unpaid household work, and of women's work in general, has led to the widespread acceptance that statistical measurements should be expanded to include unpaid work."[82]

However, the UNSNA was based on a market-based approach and emphasized that only goods and services that were traded or could be traded should be included. The bias is evident; the only exception is the inclusion of an imputed value for owner-occupied housing. This partial coverage of economics inevitably results in a serious gender bias because the allocation of human resources between the nonmonetized domestic sector and the monetized market sector in most societies is highly correlated with gender.[83]

The issue of how to value housework has continued to be a struggle. Women in developing countries engage in household production. Not only is this work not exchanged for money, it is hidden or invisible because it may be a part of a production process where only the end product reaches the market. The push to identify such labor as work and its operative as a worker continues to be an item on the agenda of the global women's movement because it has implications for

Box 1.5. Alva Myrdal: Pioneering Peacemaker

Alva Myrdal (1902–1986) was ahead of her time. Her life's work and writings touched on issues that women and peacemakers still grapple with today. She co-authored a book with Viola Klein, *Women's Two Roles: Home and Work* (1956), that broke the silence about women's double burden of work for wages and housework and drew attention to the state's responsibility to address the issue. She helped craft the Swedish welfare state and was an active supporter of women's liberation and equal rights. At the UN Secretariat in New York, she was the first woman to be appointed head of a department, in its section dealing with welfare policy (1949–1950). Subsequently, she chaired UNESCO's social science section (1950–1955).

As advisor to the Swedish minister of foreign affairs, she proposed a number of anti-nuclear plans, including the Undén Plan (a proposal for Swedish disarmament within the framework of the United Nations) and plans for nuclear-free zones and test-ban treaties. At the United Nations Disarmament Conference in Geneva (1962), she led a group of non-aligned nations that pressured the two superpowers to focus on concrete disarmament measures.

Myrdal played a key role in gathering support for a treaty that banned all nuclear testing during her years in Geneva as the head of the Swedish delegation to the UN Disarmament Committee (1962–1973). When she was awarded the Nobel Prize for Peace, she used the opportunity to speak bluntly about the need for disarmament: "At the disarmament negotiations and in the United Nations, rhetoric is by no means enough. . . . We must exert ourselves to break through the wall of silence which, unfortunately, the great powers have erected to ward off the small powers' influence in the international debate."

Sources: Alva Myrdal, "Disarmament, Technology and the Growth in Violence," available at http://nobelprize.org/peace/laureates/1982/myrdal-lecture.html; "Alva Myrdal—Biography," available at http://nobelprize.org/peace/laureates/1982/myrdal-bio.html; E. Stina Lyon, "Alva Myrdal and Viola Klein's *Women's Two Roles:* Women Writing about Women's Dilemmas," available at http://www.pcr.uu.se/conferenses/myrdal/pdf/Stina_Lyon.pdf; Maj-Britt Theoron, "Alva Myrdal and the Peace Movement," available at http://www.pcr.uu.se/conferenses/myrdal/pdf/maj_britt_theorin.pdf.

social security protection, wage fixation, and recognition of "value."[84] The resistance to "making the invisible visible" stems from the same mindset that operated in this period.

The Peace Tent

While peace has been a central objective of the UN—the world body was created out of a desire to avoid world wars and it figures very centrally in its Charter—it is women who have been the major players in the field of working for peace. Peace, or the absence of conflict, has been an issue that has bound women across the conventional divides of place, race, even class and age and has done so almost from time immemorial. We see the connection between women and peace in ancient Greek plays and in parables in India. The idea of the peace tent is used in this book to symbolize that women are the majority of those who work for peace and that such work was separated from the mainstream activities of the UN in these early years. Further, women continue to be excluded from the front lines of peace negotiations despite their universal and collective contributions and interest in and campaigns for peace.

Eleanor Roosevelt's "Open Letter" spoke of a new chance for peace that was won by the joint efforts of men and women and made a direct appeal to the women of the world, pointing out that women needed to be involved in peace efforts and that the UN provided that window of opportunity for women. However, initially the UN was preoccupied with refugees, repatriation, and genocide, all issues that were viewed as gender neutral. The Convention on the Prevention and Punishment of the Crime of Genocide (1948) spoke only of "members of the group" and not specifically of men and women. It did not refer to sexual crimes or rape, though it did mention "causing serious bodily or mental harm to members of the group."[85]

The 1951 Convention Relating to the Status of Refugees defined a refugee as a person who "owing to well-founded fear of persecution for reasons of race, religion, nationality, membership in a particular social group or political opinion, is outside the country of his nationality and is unable or, owing to such fear, is unwilling to avail himself of the protection of that country."[86] It is silent on the "ways in which gender may play a major role in how refugees are created, and how distinct the refugee experience can be for men and women."[87] Doreen Indra explains that the grounds for refugee status offered in the convention reflect the experiences of men within the public sphere, neglecting or obscuring altogether the private-sphere experiences of women. As a result, the convention reproduces the idea that oppression suffered in the private sphere is somehow neither political nor connected to the public sphere. This severs the connection between state responsibility and gender-related forms of persecution women suffer. Indra points out the irony of this false separation:

> It is remarkable that sex and gender oppression are not even mentioned, whereas oppression arising from parallel forms of invidious status distinction such as race or religious conviction are central. Thus an individual risking death at the hands of the majority group institutions for maintaining a minority religion (say Baha'i in Iran) fits the definition, where a woman (again, say in Iran) facing death by the same institutions for stepping out of her "appropriate role" or for deviating from misogynous sexual mores does not.[88]

However, within the UN, many delegates emphasized the need for women to work for peace. "It is important that women work on political questions. Even if war is mostly masculine, peace and peacemaking (through the United Nations)— ought not to be an entirely masculine job. In Sweden, about ten percent of the members of Parliament are women. It is a higher proportion than in most countries but of course it is not at all enough," said Ulla Lindstrom, representative of Sweden.[89] She later threatened to leave the Swedish government if Sweden became a nuclear weapon state. Dr. Elena N. Khokhol, representative of the Ukrainian Soviet Socialist Republic in the 1952 General Assembly remarked, "I am happy to participate in any international conference whose ultimate aim is peace. As a woman I am especially desirous of working for peace. More than half of the signatories of the Stockholm Peace Pact were women."[90]

On the outside, organized efforts by women, especially the group Women Strike for Peace, came together in 1961 to discuss the political and health effects of atmospheric nuclear testing.[91] This was prompted by the discovery of strontium-90 in women's breast milk and by other radioactive hazards of the fallout from atmospheric nuclear tests.[92] Jerome Wiesner, science advisor to President Kennedy, later admitted that women peace activists contributed to the conclusion of the Partial Test Ban Treaty in 1963.[93] However, the Partial Test Ban did something the pacifists had not envisioned: "We never had the scientific or political imagination to realize that taking testing out of the atmosphere would push them underground."[94] Cora Weiss, recounting that struggle, says, "We were not pacifists. We were frightened mothers who had sent our babies' teeth to Barry Commoner at the Washington University Medical School in St. Louis to be examined for the presence of strontium 90. But we clearly understood that the absence of women at all levels of decision making was part of the problem and therefore basic to our demands."[95]

The general attitude was that women's issues need not be taken seriously, that they were "the babble of women," as the leaders of the French Revolution described women's voices.[96] Peace work was seen as something obscure and at best naive when the Cold War was raging. In her account of Alva Myrdal, Maj-Britt Theorin talks about the constant struggle waged among the social democrats to put peace issues on the agenda. "In each meeting organized by local social democratic groups, women requested that the group would speak up against Swedish atomic weapons. The male members—who back then, even more than now, ran the organization—shook their heads saying 'My dear. These matters you don't understand. Let our elected representatives make these types of decisions!'" Women ignored this advice and persevered, insisting at every meeting that the issue of atomic weapons be discussed and that the social democrats take a clear stand against them.[97] And so the peace tent continues, revealing the connections between peace and development, between peace and unity of struggle—an ageless and timeless women's issue.

2

Inscribing Development into Rights, 1966–1975

> *Discrimination against any group of human beings is wrong, not because it hurts that particular group but because, in the final analysis, the fact of its existence hurts all groups of society.*
> —Minerva Bernardino[1]

- **Building the Institutional Architecture**
- **Learning to Integrate Women in Development**
- **Expanding Women's Rights: The CSW and the UN's Population Policy**
- **Finding Allies: UNESCO**
- **Expanding Women's Space: The International Women's Year Conference at Mexico City**
- **The Peace Tent**

The UN's First Development Decade (1960–1970) was based on the hypothesis that injections of capital into the economies of developing countries would "trickle down" to those placed low in the economic scale. The International Development Strategy (IDS) devised for the Second Development Decade (1970–1980) redefined the purpose of development as "bring[ing] about sustained improvement in the well-being of the individual and bestow[ing] benefits on all."[2] During the Second Development Decade, both women and men became important to the development process and the IDS specifically called for "the full integration of women in the total development effort."[3] This sentence was included in the Second Development Decade plan on the initiative of Gloria Scott of the Department of Economic and Social Affairs at the UN Secretariat.[4]

Women who entered the UN from the newly liberated countries added a new dimension to the deliberations, knowledge, and prioritization of issues in the organization. Many of these women had been participants in their countries' freedom struggles and in their national women's movements. Their presence and voice played a significant role in changing the knowledge base, the priorities of the UN, imperialistic and orientalist notions and images of themselves, and the choice of development paths. In 1961, the formation of a third political bloc, the Non-Aligned Movement, provided a political space from which women from the South could articulate and build consensus on development ideas. The values the NAM added to women's engagement with the UN and to changes in development ideas in the next decade would become more apparent in the International Women's Decade, 1975–1985.

During the decade of 1965–1975, events at the UN validated the inclusion of women on the agenda that had been initiated in the earlier era and women's adoption of the world body as a space in which they could do good work. Ideas women introduced into the UN in its earliest years were developed further during this period. They also added new concepts, such as the notion that rights are inseparable, or the indivisibility of rights, hence the idea of development, to the framework of rights. Despite the fact that there were very few women in policymaking positions in the UN, the women on the CSW used strategic alliances and the institutional mechanism of global conferences to further their agenda. The goals and rhetoric of the commission became strongly embedded into the UN system and the development discourse. In addition, the work of the CSW received a valuable injection of new ideas from the strong presence and voice of the newly liberated countries.[5] Interthematic connections were made. Intellect, energy, and commitment combined to create a new momentum that made it possible to construct a long-term plan for the advancement of women (resolution IX of 1968), the Declaration on the Elimination of Discrimination Against Women (DEDAW, 1967), and the first UN-sponsored world conference on women at Mexico City (1975). Development cooperation propelled the issue of women in development (WID) to the world stage. Ignited by the work of Ester Boserup, the profile of women as productive workers forced donor agencies to look at women's programs as a worthwhile area of investment, even if this view was instrumental and looked at including women in development programs as a means to an end.

Women continued to make skillful use of UN space to generate knowledge through inclusive processes and to garner support for campaigns. The existence of autonomous spaces for women in the world body helped them make crucial connections and underscored the integral link between ideas and appropriate institutions in the arena of social transformation. Women also drew responses and reactions to gendered aspects of war and peace from the UN for the first time in its history.

Building the Institutional Architecture

DEDAW

In 1950, the CSW began working with other UN specialized agencies, particularly the ILO, to collect data about employed women and to strategize about how to improve work opportunities for women and create policies that would result in equal pay for equal work.[6] This work bore fruit in 1951, when the ILO passed the Convention on Equal Remuneration.[7] In the 1960s, the commission began to respond to growing evidence that development benefits did not "trickle down" to women, that in fact women were "disproportionately affected by poverty" and that barriers such as lack of access to land ownership and credit "perpetuated their low status in many regions."[8] The issue of how the UN could assist women in developing countries became a focus of the commission's work. It networked extensively with ECOSOC and UN specialized agencies to advocate that development projects include programs for women. In 1970, these efforts were rewarded when the General Assembly's IDS for the Second Development Decade included women in a comprehensive plan for the first time; it endorsed the "full integration of women in the total development effort."[9] Programming for women received another boost that year when the General Assembly approved a Programme of Concerted International Action for the Advancement of Women designed to "advance the status of women and increase their effective participation in all sectors." The goals of the program were to eliminate illiteracy, bring about universal acceptance of the principle of equal pay for equal work, provide "health and maternity protection," and facilitate a "substantial increase" in the number of women participating in public life and government at all levels.[10]

These programs and plans built on the CSW's framework of equal rights for women. The commission's research over two decades had clearly outlined the problems: women around the world faced inequality and discrimination in education and employment. How to deal with the problem was another issue entirely. How could a small commission in a large organization work effectively to create change that would improve the status of half the world's population? Certainly the momentum generated by the Second Development Decade was something the commission could build on. But more was needed.

In December 1963, the General Assembly asked the CSW and ECOSOC to prepare a draft declaration on the elimination of discrimination against women. Four years later, in 1967, the UN General Assembly adopted the Declaration on the Elimination of Discrimination Against Women (DEDAW). This was a watershed in the UN's quest for women's equality. The work done in the area of law by the CSW and other bodies since 1945 in the shape of various conventions and declarations was now transformed into a single code—a progression in method, thought, and concept. The declaration, while it is not law, is directed to public opinion as much as to governments. It established international norms. It was a call to action.

DEDAW is the first comprehensive legal measure on women's rights. The term "discrimination" was an integral part of the UN vocabulary associated with equality and rights, not only in the context of gender but also in the context of race. Discrimination was widely perceived in the UN to be based on "difference," as in the case of religious or ethnic minorities, stigmatized groups such as unwed mothers, or those who for reasons of class differentiation are deprived of opportunities for advancement. Some analysts see equality and nondiscrimination as positive and negative formulations of the same principle. Other analysts see the principle of nondiscrimination as more limited than the principle of equality.

The timing of the request makes it more than probable that at least part of the inspiration for DEDAW came from the newly adopted Declaration on the Elimination of all Forms of Racial Discrimination. Since 1962, the UN Sub-Commission on the Prevention of Discrimination and the Protection of Minorities had been working on a draft declaration, which was adopted unanimously by the General Assembly on 20 November 1963. The theaters of ideas that constitute the UN facilitate such cross-pollination. The request that the CSW draft DEDAW was a defining point in the learning curve on women and equality in the UN. It was the first time the UN had accepted the need to deal with the phenomenon of discrimination from the women's perspective and to draft the principles on which the UN would deal with such a problem. The achievement reveals the relevance of the intersectionality of gendered experience and the value of a space, like the UN, which enables the cross-border solidarity and learning between groups facing similar challenges.

The resolutions drafted by the CSW between 1946 and 1962 focused individually on women's rights in special problem areas such as marriage, maternity, nationality, traditional practices with harmful impacts on young women, and exploitative practices such as trafficking and slavery. These issues were specific to women and related to the vulnerabilities females faced by virtue of biology, albeit accentuated by social norms and biases. The only exception was the Convention on Political Rights of Women (1952), which used the term "discrimination" in each of its three operative articles.[11] But its preamble still spoke of equality and equal access and did not speak of discrimination or the nature of discrimination even once. The declaration made the first attempt to define discrimination against women by referring to laws, customs, regulations, practices, and prejudice as being responsible for denying and limiting women's equality of rights with men. It viewed discrimination as incompatible with human dignity and the welfare of society.

DEDAW moved the idea of women's equality beyond the confines of a rigid legal construct by pointing out those extralegal barriers that were socially constructed and more resistant to change. It filled the gap that was left by the mere adoption of formal prescriptions based on the principle of equality of the sexes. The declaration required the abolition of traditional norms and practices that prevented equality, which was a step toward understanding the real roots of women's inequality. It also loosened the constraints that had earlier placed the family, the community, and the household beyond the pale of public interventions. With DEDAW, the UN opened up the private sphere for scrutiny as part of its commitment to upholding the values of the Charter and the human rights instruments.

During the drafting process, specialized agencies contributed to the identification of "discrimination," which they saw as the key barrier to enhancing women's status. The FAO focused attention on women in special situations (such as rural women), the value of rural women's work (especially in food production), and women's need for social and economic support. UNESCO tried to push through the idea of coeducation as a better choice than the already-approved norm of a uniform curriculum for boys and girls. The final product created a touchstone for testing the principle of equality as the absence of discrimination, but its substantive articles deal with positive measures to improve women's access to education, social security, social services, child care, and so forth (mostly "development" subjects) and themes of exploitation of women such as trafficking. The idea of affirmative action was posited during the drafting process but not included. NGOs were especially concerned about issues such as family laws, bias against single women and heads of households, and prostitution. Many of the ideas that were presented, discussed, and debated—such as the comprehensive definition of discrimination—but were not picked up entered the later Convention on the Elimination of All Forms of Discrimination Against Women in 1979.

The DEDAW process took four years—from 1963, when the proposal was first made that the CSW draft a declaration—to 1967, when the UN General Assembly adopted it. During these four years, the women of the CSW and the Third Committee of the General Assembly used a number of skilled approaches and working devices to finalize their work speedily.[12] Other major actors involved in the process included ECOSOC, the UN specialized agencies, the UN Secretariat's Section on the Status of Women, NGOs, and the UN General Assembly.[13]

During the process, especially at the end, there was an unspoken agreement that the process would have to go farther than a declaration, which is not a legally binding instrument. There were differences of opinion on sensitive issues such as custom, culture, and tradition that many countries felt were obstacles to women's advancement. The primacy of the family as an institution was stressed as a conservative viewpoint of some countries, as was the primary role of women as mothers. The choice between modifying or changing customs and abolishing customs—a point on which opinion was quite divided among the members—was made at the later stages when the CSW voted to overturn the recommendations of the drafting committee. Women bonded across identities to work toward the ideals of equality contained in the UN treaties. Conventional power blocs did not hold much sway because women used informal consultative methods even while holding formal positions in UN bodies.

One of the earliest manifestations of the weight DEDAW could carry internationally was the establishment of the eighteen-nation Arab Women's Commission of the Arab League in 1971, the first regional commission for women outside of the UN system since the birth of the world body. The new commission used DEDAW as its term of reference.[14]

The declaration was an important accomplishment for women in the UN. It laid crucial groundwork for arguments that would be useful to women in the development community. The General Assembly resolution accepting DEDAW contained language that specifically mentioned women in conjunction with development: "the full and complete development of a country, the welfare of the world[,] and the cause of peace require the maximum participation of women as well as men in all fields."[15] It could be suggested that this connecting of rights with development anticipated the later recognition across the spectrum of people's or social movements that access to development itself is a human right, resonating Sen's concept of development as freedom.[16]

The Unified Long-Term Plan

Another milestone in legal documents related to women in development was the unified long-term plan for the advancement of women that the General Assembly asked the CSW to formulate in 1962.[17] This took place in the context of the Second Development Decade and was the initiative of the Secretary-General, who wanted to consolidate the various piecemeal development efforts of the specialized agencies relating to women. As John Mathiason has noted, "It was recognized that the various United Nations programs providing development assistance were not coordinating their efforts to advance women and it was felt that placing them within a programmatic context would obtain 'more bang for a buck.'"[18] The CSW consulted the specialized agencies, the regional commissions, and member states. It also looked at existing UN programs and collected information about resources, mechanisms, women's involvement with community development, training opportunities for women, and current proposals for projects. Based on the assessment of these programs and documents and the output of a Regional Seminar on Advancement of Women held at Manila in 1966, the CSW framed a proposal for a Long-Term Program for the Advancement of Women.[19]

As a result of the hard work of the CSW, the UN's International Conference on Human Rights held at Teheran in 1968 adopted and endorsed the proposal and its objectives as suggested by the Secretary-General. Resolution IX, one of the twenty-nine resolutions adopted in Teheran, was titled "Measures to Promote Women's Rights in the Modern World" and contained a reference to the Secretary-General's proposal for a unified long-term program for women. Two of the three objectives of the long-term program emphasized women's participation in and contribution to the development of society.[20] At the conference, Margaret Bruce, head of the Section on the Status of Women, presented the resolution as well as the Declaration on the Elimination of Discrimination Against Women.[21]

The significance of the two documents, one on the achievement of women's right to equality through elimination of discrimination and the other on realization of women's potential for contributing to social development, lies in the conjoining of two ideas during this period—that legal rights were essential for women's participation in and contribution to national development. This magical amalgam of ideas was to frame work in the UN on issues relating to women throughout the years of the women's conferences.

Programme of Concerted International Action
for the Advancement of Women

Achievement of equality meant removal of discriminatory treatment of women vis-à-vis men and this meant setting standards that would serve as indicators for nondiscriminatory treatment of women. In 1970, the UN initiated a Programme of Concerted International Action for the Advancement of Women that put resolution IX in a development format.[22] The actions proposed and the goals of the program were woven into a rights framework. This is another instance of how the legacy of equal rights for women from the initial period of the UN was consciously intertwined with development interventions in the next period of the UN's history. The targets are divided into four segments—education, training and employment, health and maternity protection, and public life. A few of the important targets are listed below:

- Eliminate illiteracy and achieve equality of literacy between the sexes
- Facilitate universal acceptance of the principle of equal pay for equal work and the adoption of effective measures to implement it
- Provide maternity protection for all mothers
- Provide information and advice to enable all persons to decide freely and responsibly on the number and spacing of their children and to prepare them for responsible parenthood, including ways in which women can benefit from family planning
- Substantially increase the number of women participating in public and government life at all levels[23]

This resolution clearly emphasizes that the achievement of equality of women with men will enable them "to devote their energies, talents and abilities to the benefit of society." Most of the objectives are based on the simple principle of equality with men. Only one is based on the notion of protection, which has the subtext of inequality; protection connotes making special efforts.

Because development imperatives prevailed at the UN during this period, the CSW's earlier emphasis on individual realization of women's rights as the cornerstone of equality began to undergo changes. Preparing the Long-Term Program for the Advancement of Women helped the CSW make this shift in thinking.[24] Problems associated with underdevelopment, such as poverty, illiteracy, and lack of access to vocational training and employment, shifted the UN's focus to women's roles in economic and social development processes worldwide. The importance of overall policy prescriptions increased with the growing need to bring positive changes in the status of millions of persons rather than focusing only on individuals whose rights have been violated. Examining broad social trends enabled developing countries to highlight their problems and ask for resources to be allocated.

The shift to looking at problems of inequality in a broad development format is exemplified by the new focus on the issue of employment, which was propelled by the findings of the Interregional Meeting of Experts on the Integration of Women in Development in 1972 (see below). One of its main recommendations was the introduction of programs to create jobs, training, and vocational guidance. This came at a time when the ILO was moving from a narrower focus on labor to looking at strategies to create employment.[25] It also steered away from the narrow concept of vocational training and moved toward the wider and more dynamic concept of "human resource development" in its Convention No. 142 of 1975.[26] The ILO adopted the recommendation of the expert group and worked to ensure that women were included in the programs and projects that flowed out of this convention and the accompanying recommendations.

The ways of defining equality and discrimination also changed over time. For example, the initial concern about women's family responsibilities and their repercussions for employment led the ILO to adopt a nonbinding recommendation that promoted measures that allow women to harmonize their professional and family obligations, reduce their hours, and provide them with education and vocational training to facilitate entry into the workforce. The Employment (Women with Family Responsibilities) Recommendation of 1965 pointed out that these provisions would benefit all workers, not just women.[27] The recommendation was a response to the fear that action to promote women could not realize equality as long as family responsibilities forced them either to abandon their jobs or forego opportunities for advancement.

Learning to Integrate Women in Development

Because colonial masters saw their former colonies as backward, the development approach of this era is described as the modernization project. This approach, which predominated in economic and development thought in the 1940s and 1950s, held many dilemmas for women. On the one hand, modernization brought values such as liberation from constricting traditions that hid women from public space and deprived them of rights to equal citizenship. It meant that women could "play an active part in social life, especially in the struggle for safeguarding peace, availing themselves of their political, civil, economic, cultural and social rights."[28] On the other hand, modernization led to the neglect of some of the corridors of women's power, as an anonymous Tanzanian scholar once described such spaces. Many resistance movements mobilized around the issue of affirmation of culture to efface their histories of colonization; nations emerging from the era of colonization often tried to rebuild their nationhood through reinvoking their cultural and political histories, their epics, their traditions of creativity. Through this process, members of these movements re-created their identities and regained self-confidence. This placed women in a bind: if they resisted modernization, they could be seen as conservative by international development policymakers; if they supported it, they could be seen as unpatriotic by the "leadership" of their countries.

Questioning Paradigms

Perceptions about where women were located in the economies of the South began to change with Danish economist Ester Boserup's pathbreaking book *Women's Role in Economic Development* (1970).[29] Using data from official statistics, Boserup provided "clear evidence of women's contributions . . . to national economic productivity."[30] Boserup argued that in the past, women in Africa had enjoyed relative equality with men based on their roles as agricultural produc-ers. Her main contribution was her finding that with changes in technology as-sociated with modernization and patterns of land use, the status of women was reduced on account of their marginalization in agricultural systems. She pointed out that injections of development funding for agriculture usually focused on cash crops and ignored the subsistence farming that women typically engaged in. She wrote:

> As agriculture becomes less dependent upon human muscular power, the differ-ence in labor productivity between the two sexes might be expected to narrow. In actual fact . . . it is usually the men who learn to operate the new types of equip-ment while women continue to work with the old hand tools. . . . [T]he productiv-ity gap tends to widen because men monopolize the use of the new equipment and the modern agricultural methods. . . . Thus, in the course of agricultural de-velopment, men's labour productivity tends to increase while women's remains more or less static.[31]

Male monopoly over new technology and the new cash crops facilitated by de-velopment projects cost women status, power, and income and made their eco-nomic contributions invisible.[32] Boserup warned that ignoring women's pro-ductive work would retard the entire process of development, and she critiqued the welfare approach that saw women primarily as mothers and wives.

Boserup's work greatly influenced the UN's interest in Africa, not just on official policies on funding women's participation in agriculture but in all development programs in general, which no longer considered women to be "nonproductive" household members from an economic point of view. Though Boserup's argu-ments influenced a whole genre of development programs for women research-ers as well as the donor communities, her work has been criticized because it seems to suggest instrumentalism, the idea that identifying women's economic value would add to the productivity of investment. Her argument that women were creditworthy on account of their enormous contribution to agriculture seemed to indicate such a reasoning rather than the principle that women were entitled to recognition on the more basic grounds of rights, of women's equality. She also believed that productive economic roles automatically translated into higher status for women, a finding that has since been disproved in many con-texts. Nevertheless, her contribution cannot be underestimated or diluted on the basis of these arguments as it was extremely influential both on the design of development cooperation and in promoting further research to reveal the vital roles that women played in the economies of the South.[33]

Partly as a result of Boserup's publications and her location in the UN system as a researcher within the Economic Commission for Europe (ECE), UN specialized agencies and bilateral donors began funding country-based research on women as workers.[34] UN specialized agencies and bilateral donors were strong early supporters of this new work. The ILO enabled investigations into this area, not only supporting research but also holding several annual conferences and expert group meetings to understand and disseminate these facts. This was the beginning of the process of making the invisible visible in statistics on labor and employment. The burst of new knowledge about women's work led to the emergence of a "new" development definition called women in development, or WID. Advocates of this idea, many of whom were women researchers and women policymakers, rejected the welfare approach that saw women as "needy" recipients of assistance. Instead, they saw women as vital producers who were the missing link in development. They were a valuable resource that had not been recognized.[35]

Understanding Development

Women in the UN helped provide a format in which Boserup's research findings could be disseminated. In keeping with the goals of the UN's Second Development Decade, an Interregional Meeting of Experts on the Integration of Women in Development was held at the UN in 1972, co-sponsored by the CSW and the Commission on Social Development. The meeting was facilitated both by the large presence of developing countries in the UN and the weight Boserup's book carried within influential circles. Boserup wrote the working document for the meeting. The women who organized and attended this meeting would later become key figures in the international women and development movement. They included organizer Aida Gindy (Egypt, chief of the UN Social Affairs Section and a former staff member of the Economic Commission for Africa) and experts Aziza Hussein (Egypt), Justice Annie Jiagge (Ghana), Vida Tomšič (Yugoslavia), Leticia Shahani (Philippines), and Inga Thorsson (Sweden).[36]

The purpose of the meeting was to "advise on broad policy measures regarding women's role in economic and social development."[37] The interregional meeting emphasized the integration of planning for women in overall policy formulation at national and regional levels rather than dealing with women's development issues in isolation. The topics discussed included the role of women in rural societies, women in small-scale business, employment of women in modern industry, employment of women with family responsibilities, women's education in relation to their participation in development, and ways to improve the integration of women in development. The expert group recommended programs to create jobs for women and programs to provide education and vocational training, a clear departure from the way the welfare approach saw its beneficiaries.

Box 2.1. Ester Boserup:
Launching the Field of Women in Development

Ester Boserup (1910–1999) devoted more than two decades of her life to civil service, first in economic administration in Denmark and then as a researcher in the United Nations and its agencies.

Her book *Women's Role in Economic Development* (1970) launched the field of women in development. Boserup pointed out that the introduction of modern technologies and the increase of the number of men engaged in cash cropping for the market often increased the work burden of women with regard to both family and casual labor. This was an indictment of prevailing assumptions of economic planners that their efforts benefited everyone. She also argued that recruiting women into the modern sector of society accelerates economic growth, a viewpoint that was new to most policymakers.

The major multilateral and bilateral donor agencies adopted the theme of integration of women in development, the earliest among them being Sweden. Later, the UN established offices within the Food and Agriculture Organization, the United Nations Development Programme, and other agencies to look after women's development programs. Integration of women in development became the reigning approach.

Women's Role in Economic Development became what one scholar described as "the fundamental text of the U.N. Decade for Women." Her thesis had many implications, including how women's work was counted and evaluated, how work was allocated between genders, what constituted work, and what type of education women needed. Her view that women's contributions, both domestic and in the paid workforce, constituted crucial contributions to national economies electrified women scholars and birthed a new development approach at the UN and other global development agencies.

Boserup's last book, *My Professional Life and Publications 1929–1998* (1999), documents her own intellectual history, explaining that her personal encounters with events and places were the inspiration for her conceptualization and guided the policy recommendations she made.

Sources: Tinker, "A Context for the Field and for the Book," 8; Snyder, "The Politics of Women and Development," 97; Boserup, *My Professional Life and Publications 1929–1998,* 24.

At its 1973 session, the UN's Commission on Social Development considered the report of the Secretary-General on the meeting and heard the viewpoints that:

- Participation of women in development should form an integral part of planning and policy formulation at national and regional levels rather than being dealt with in isolation.
- Promoting national strategies for identifying needs and problems related to women's role in economic development was important.
- More women should participate in policy formulation and decision-making at all levels.
- An appropriate machinery should be provided for identifying and assessing women's contribution to development.
- Strategies and programs should be closely related to the stage of development of a country and to the economic, social, and cultural factors and trends existing in specific countries.[38]

The report reflected the work the CSW had been doing since 1968 to construct a plan that would put women on the development agenda. Even though the Commission on Social Development did not implement these recommendations,[39] the synergy of women academics—in this case, Boserup—and women within the UN helped create a new way of thinking at the organization:

> The experts' findings helped buttress a growing perception at the United Nations and elsewhere that the low status of women, especially in developing countries, was a major factor in such increasingly globalized problems as poverty, rapid population growth, illiteracy, malnutrition, migration and forced urbanization, and poor health conditions.[40]

The use of the term "low" in describing the status of women in the developing world has been challenged. Often the cultural and political histories of these countries gave women status, but economic underdevelopment—the conditions of poverty and lack of resources for education and health care—inhibited their participation.

One of the issues the experts highlighted was the value of bringing in the regional dimension. Attention was drawn to Africa, where the All Africa Women's Conference had been formed during the struggle for freedom in Kenya in 1962. Margaret Kenyatta had organized the first Women's Seminar in Kenya in the same year. The recommendations of the African intergovernmental conferences influenced the UN regional commission for Africa—the Economic Commission for Africa (ECA)—to open a window for women. The ECA's work program for 1968–1969 included an item on women and development; this led to the creation of a women's program at the ECA secretariat in 1972. The ECA became the first regional commission to start such a program.[41]

UN world conferences played an important role in knitting together the strands of the incipient international women's movement during the early 1970s, which in turn reinforced the new thinking about development that was emerging at the UN. Two world conferences in 1974—the World Population Conference in Bucharest and the World Food Conference in Rome—affirmed the key roles that women play in population matters and the production of food.[42] These events saw a modest start in women's participation in world conferences, both during the preparatory phase and at the actual events. The method through which women influenced these conferences reaffirms both the importance of having women in leadership positions in institutions such as the UN and the capacity of the few to influence the many through mobilization of allies on the outside, techniques women used during the birth of the UN.

The CSW took on the new challenges of women and development in its stride, but it still kept faith with its commitment to the legal foundation of women's equality and rights. When the UN entered the new development track, the commission was able to include women's economic contributions in its conceptualization of equality for women. For example, in 1972, the commission embraced the new development goals of ECOSOC, but in its own language; it urged member states

> in planning and implementing their programmes of action to promote the advancement of women, to take account of the varying needs of women in their countries, with a view to enabling women to achieve their maximum potential, not only as wives and mothers but also as citizens and full participants in the development of their countries.[43]

This was a clear departure from the earlier modernization approach to women's role in development; the CSW envisioned women in developing countries as co-partners in policymaking and governance.

Adding women to development programs at the UN attracted funds from many sources. The newly created United Nations Fund for Population Activities (UNFPA) supported the efforts of specialized agencies such as UNICEF and the FAO and the regional commission in Africa to underwrite programs for women. Among the multilateral donors, Sweden passed legislation that earmarked development cooperation funds for women in 1964. In 1975, the Organisation for Economic Co-Operation and Development (OECD) began convening expert group meetings on women and development to promote cooperation among donors. These groups set criteria for funding by bilateral agencies that included a policy requiring women's involvement in preparing both women-only and general projects and laid down guidelines regarding the type of projects that would be funded.[44]

Programming for women became a focus of work at the UN in the 1970s. Irene Tinker notes that a report on women and development that Gloria Scott wrote for the International Women's Year conference at Mexico "resulted in resolutions for integrating women into development programs being introduced into the working plans of most of the UN agencies in addition to the General Assembly."[45] Desks for WID were set up in lending agencies. Agency administrators began to understand that women's programs required a special, separate component of programming. Women-specific development priorities such as programs to eradicate illiteracy, provide equal pay, provide health and maternity protection, provide access to family planning, and increase participation in national and public life were articulated.

Between 1978 and 1989, the United Nations Development Programme (UNDP) launched sixty-five projects involving women in the areas of agriculture and rural development, education, population, health, nutrition, small-scale enterprises, technical assistance, water supply, and urban development.[46] The projects fell into three categories: projects that did not include women in the design of the project but benefited women; projects that provided resources and access to education; and projects that targeted women. The projects that targeted women had the highest rates of participation by women (43 percent, as compared to 32 percent participation for the first type of project and 25 percent participation for the second type of project); these projects tended to have a strong focus on increasing women's income-earning potential. For example, a project in the United Arab Emirates designed to help women develop their productive roles enabled over 1,850 women in twelve villages to increase their earnings by an average of 30 percent.[47] Women in developing countries demonstrated a preference for projects that would directly increase family income over projects that aided them in more indirect ways such as through education and other resources.

Proponents of the WID approach argued that women should be given equality with men and granted the same privileges and rights as men had. This is sometimes referred to as the equity approach. It is easy to see why such arguments appealed to the women on the CSW; these were similar to the arguments they had been making for years.[48] But though development cooperation took note of gender differentiation, such an approach led to deep flaws in impact, as there was little rigorous gender analysis or exploration into gender relations at this time. The research being conducted was done to provide a baseline and to identify the gender division of labor at all levels as a first step.[49]

Part of the problem was that there were very few women in policymaking positions at the specialized agencies, programs, and funds (see table 2.1). Projects for women were not typically part of the planning process at the early stages; a later evaluation of women in development at the UNDP noted that women's projects in the 1970s and 1980s seemed tacked on to already-developed programs.[50] The UNDP had a total professional staff of 643 in 1976; only five were women at the D-1 and D-2 (middle and senior management) levels.[51] A United Nations Institute for Training and Research (UNITAR) study of women in the specialized agencies in the mid-1970s noted that WID programs often fell short because of the way they were conceived. There was a strong belief that development was gender neutral, though there was some understanding that it was not class neutral. The UNITAR investigators blamed this attitude for the failure of many WID projects: "In some instances the measures adopted have, in fact, worsened the situation of women."[52] This uncovering of the inequality and discriminations within class and other traditional social and economic categories of people, as well as the difference in priorities in services, would be one of the great values of the research that was developing at that time and that influenced the programming in later years.

Despite its shortcomings, UN involvement with the development theme brought about changes in ideas about women's equality. Equality of women with men became a sine qua non for their greater and more effective participation in development—a brick in the edifice of the nation-building enterprise. UN agencies undertook investigations into women's roles, women's contributions, and women's participation within a wider societal framework. Women's unequal status was identified as the reason for their poor participation in social processes, whether political or economic. Conversely, the advancement of a nation and the advancement of its women were recognized as positively correlated.

Expanding Women's Rights: The CSW and the UN's Population Policy

By the 1950s and 1960s, as Michael Ward points out, the success of specialized agencies such as the WHO and the FAO in improving human nutrition led to "rapid expansion of the world's population, especially in the poorer areas."[53] Management of population was seen in the "the broad perspective of human progress in modern societies, which increasingly recognizes the need to provide the citizen with the means of controlling the size of his family."[54] Richard Jolly and colleagues point out that many nations had not yet conducted national-level statistical surveys of their population and thus had no clear sense of the scope of the population growth.[55]

A few countries such as India and Pakistan saw an exploding population as a barrier to economic growth and development and had launched government-

Table 2.1. Percent Female Staff at the FAO, the ILO, UNESCO, and the WHO by Grade, 1976

	P-1	P-2	P-3	P-4	P-5	D-1	D-2	ADG/ASG and Above
FAO	47.8	33.9	19.7	7.5	2.7	1.8	—	—
ILO	66.7	38.8	24.9	8.5	3.4	3.6	5.0	8.3
UNESCO	36.0	56.4	36.9	15.7	7.1	5.7	—	12.5
WHO	40.0	49.1	35.0	13.4	5.1	4.4	—	—

Note: P-1 and P-2 are entry-level grades; P-3 and P-4 are journeyman grades; P-5 and D-1 correspond to middle management; D-2 corresponds to senior management. ADG is assistant director-general; ASG is assistant secretary-general. *

Source: Earl D. Sohm, *Report on Women in the Professional Category and Above in the United Nations System*, JIU/REP/77/7, December 1977, 12. Numbers have been rounded up.

sponsored family planning programs early in the 1950s. These programs required external funding, and the two nations proactively pushed for donor assistance. In the same decade, the Family Planning Council of Nigeria began setting up clinics on a small scale.[56]

In the 1960s and 1970s, solving the population issue was promoted as the answer to the widespread hunger and poverty that was prevalent at the time. The UN's Population Commission was dominated by the demographic approach at that time rather than the broader perspective of social development, gender justice, and rights that was to emerge as more wholesome in later years.[57]

In 1965 the CSW suggested that nongovernmental organizations with consultative status should study the possibility of "making available the increasing fund of knowledge in this field as a source of assistance to married couples in fulfilling their parental responsibilities."[58] Although the CSW clearly understood that the spacing of births was a women's issue, their frame of analysis was women workers in industrialized countries.

However, a turning point that enabled the CSW to reclaim its ethos was the 1974 World Conference on Population in Bucharest. The initiatives by which this became the turning point illustrates what was possible when women were appointed to policymaking positions and how women mobilize support from the outside—in this case, members of the women's movement as lobbies and knowledge providers—while making a dent in a patriarchal system. They also illustrate how one woman's determination can provide the platform for a space such as the CSW.

Helvi Sipilä had been a member of the CSW for many years. In 1971, she had chaired the Third Committee of the General Assembly. In 1972, a report of a survey of women at the UN Secretariat revealed that there were no women at the under-secretary-general or assistant secretary-general levels and that there were only seven women of a total of 240 employees at the D-1 and D-2 levels. The report also noted "with satisfaction" the recent appointment of a woman as assistant secretary-general.[59] That woman was Sipilä, who had just been named assistant secretary-general for social development and humanitarian affairs, a post she would hold for the next ten years.

Sipilä was concerned about the lack of attention to women in the background papers being prepared for the Population Conference. She was able to fill the gap by organizing an unofficial preparatory meeting, the International Forum on the Role of Women and Population. The meeting was attended by 116 prominent women and focused on international lobbying strategies to help ensure that women were included in government delegations and that the importance of population policies to women was highlighted in the Population Conference proceedings. She also promoted a series of regional seminars on women and population as part of the preparations for the Bucharest conference.[60] Women used such opportunities to disseminate information and raise consciousness about women's deep interest in population policies. Her efforts, it could be suggested, set in motion the inclusion of women's participation in this subject and helped in the evolution of ideas about women's rights, empowerment, power relations, and structures in succeeding world conferences. They also acted as a stimulus to research, including gendered data collection, on this key topic.

Sipilä's report on the connections between family planning and the status of women demonstrated the intellectual growth of the commission over time. For nearly twenty years, the CSW had used the phrase "status of women" to discuss the rights of women; this was the language previous generations of activists in the ILO and the League of Nations had used in their surveys. The CSW had used the phrase as a talisman and a road map to indicate the direction of its work. But the phrase itself had never been defined. It was a composite term that was difficult to pin down. Sipilä wrote "the direct measurement of status is a difficult and complex problem. . . . Over-emphasis on the legal status of women . . . fails to reflect the frequently very wide discrepancies between law and everyday practice." She perceptively remarked that

> women in some societies may participate fully and equally in the process of economic production, but find themselves constrained by traditional expectations as to the division of labour at home. Or they may wield considerable power within the family but very little in the governance of the community or country.[61]

The cultural context made defining women's status even more difficult. Western researchers might judge the status of a woman who bore ten children as low because she did not have "personal autonomy" in child spacing. But in her own culture, that woman's status might be very high because in the "eyes of her family and community" her prestige "rises with every child she bears."[62] Sipilä concluded that the concept of "status" could not be reduced to single variables such as employment or political rights or low fertility. This report enabled the CSW to broaden the scope of its inquiry beyond political and legal rights. Now cultural and social factors were on the table as well.

Sipilä's report also moved the issue of family planning out of the realm of macroeconomics and into the realm of women's rights. From the new venue it was only one short step to human rights. She wrote:

> Viewing the status of women in the context of family planning as a fundamental human right reminds us that the time has passed when human rights could be discussed on a purely theoretical level. The question now becomes one of specifying the conditions under which individual women can truly decide, both freely and responsibly, on the number and spacing of their children. . . . It is a question of ensuring the actual conditions under which women may exercise the full range of human rights to which they are entitled.[63]

With this report, the groundwork was laid for the CSW to make a firm claim on the field of development. Women from developing countries would have much to say on this issue, of course, but this early instance of women claiming new political turf at the UN demonstrated what was possible when women were appointed to policymaking positions.

Family planning, or birth control, as it was explicitly called in this era, came to occupy a major place on the agenda of many women's organizations. Hilkka Pietilä notes that "women activists saw this as a major issue for women in general and not just in the developing countries."[64] Although it was and continues to be a much-contested issue, many nations eagerly embraced the new agenda, particularly in Asia.

Pivotal figures such as Sipilä were sometimes able to merge the male-dominated areas of the UN with the research skills and expertise of the CSW for specific projects, and such temporary unions sometimes led to lasting influence. For example, the leading UN body in the promotion of population programs, UNFPA, which had been established as a trust fund for work on population by the Secretary-General in 1967, has emerged as a forerunner in the engagement of the UN in women's rights, albeit slowly. UNFPA funds helped pay for the national surveys on which Helvi Sipilä based her report on the links between women's status and family planning. In the early 1970s, Executive Director Rafael Salas used UNFPA funds to finance regional conferences and underwrite activities related to women and population in other UN bodies, including UNICEF, the ECA, and the FAO.[65]

Despite the uncovering of women's knowledge and this nuancing and affirmation of women's rights, the dominance of demographers continued with
neo-Malthusian approaches to population programs. It would take another two
decades and the expertise of the women's lobbies that were built up over the
decade 1985–1995, operating at international conferences, before the centrality
of women in shaping their reproductive rights would be restored on the UN
agenda in 1994 at the UN International Conference on Population and Development in Cairo.

In many ways, the engagement of women and the UN during this period on
the issue of birth control was a failed attempt. In spite of the best efforts of
women, the links between the main discipline of population studies and women's
status did not emerge clearly. And in spite of the prodigious work UNESCO did
on women's capacity to access rights and other enabling ideas from the UN system, the location of women in international dialogue remained firmly in the
realm of geography and politics. On the issue of population, women had to reinvent the wheel (again). They would score a more definite victory in Cairo in
1994. To transpose Boserup's dictum that excluding women hurts development,
it would be fair to say excluding women's agency from population discourse and
practice has hurt the population issue itself as much as it has hurt women.

Finding Allies: UNESCO

UNESCO played a crucial role in revealing women's particular location within
various sociopolitical contexts and identifying the levers required to emancipate
them. It became a strong ally of the CSW in these early years. Its studies extended to the role of social sciences in population activities and provided inputs
both to the UN conference on population in Bucharest and the UN conference
on women in Mexico City. It prepared documents on population and education, population and environment, population and family planning activities,
population and human rights, and population and the family for the Bucharest
conference. UNESCO's view was that population as a subject was important not
just because of its human rights aspects but also because it pointed to the social,
cultural, and economic framework within which demographic factors should
be perceived. By the end of the 1970s, UNESCO was emphasizing research on
the status of women in relation to development and demographic behavior with
a special emphasis on family structures and the household.

Through its studies UNESCO argued that the only way women can tear
through the screen of "preserving tradition and culture" was to put them in
places of formal power, in public and political spaces. This argument foreshadowed realizations of the worldwide women's movement several decades later,
clearly claimed at the UN world conference in Beijing in 1995. UNESCO went

farther than promoting the familiar cause of education for women; it revealed the layers beneath the word "status." UNESCO not only uncovered women's cultural values through anthropological studies, it linked equality to power. The agency continuously drew attention to power and politics and how crucial political power is for recasting gender relations, landing equality, removing discrimination, and overpowering cultural inhibitions.

The new integration idea stimulated questions that were emerging from studies done elsewhere during this period, such as projects that revealed that the standards for education of girls were lower than those for boys in Africa. It was not just a question of ensuring equal access by enabling girls to "catch up" with boys in recruitment. Both gaps—in access to and in quality of education—had to be tackled. In 1960, women teachers from Africa met to discuss this problem. The Department of Social Sciences of UNESCO contributed to a socioeconomic analysis of women's access to education in Sub-Saharan Africa, prepared by African experts, published in 1962. Other studies included socio-anthropological studies (South and Southeast Asia), a study of the changing social position of women (Japan), and a study of the emancipation of women (Turkey). Many of these studies were carried out by women from the countries being studied or were syntheses of reports already published in the country. Cross-country studies promoted mutual appreciation of different value systems.

A 1966 recommendation by UNESCO concerning the status of teachers referred to discrimination against women. It asked that the subject of women's status be incorporated in the national educational curricula so that public education could carry the campaign for women's equality forward.

Well before the Women's Decade was even planned, UNESCO devised a set of institutional mechanisms to deal with the women's question in education in particular and on the larger canvas of social sciences and culture. While the Department of Social Sciences was the main agency, in 1965 it also set up a special unit to oversee the mandate of equality in education for women. Two years later, this unit was given the responsibility to coordinate a ten-year program to promote women's equality of access to education. UNESCO's Department of Mass Media Communication had the mandate to disseminate information about education linked to women's rights and equality.

In the area of programming, like many other agencies, UNESCO followed a more conventional approach in the early 1960s; it emphasized activities such as home economics and welfare services touching upon women's familial roles and needs. But somewhat along the lines of the CSW, UNESCO's perspective changed in the latter part of the 1960s, when it increasingly stressed women's contribution to the social and economic development of their countries. The role of educational planning as a means toward this end also came into prominence.[66]

In his report of 1968, UNESCO's director-general expressed that "it is impossible to conceive of development, absurd to imagine the building of peace in minds and hearts, without the active co-operation of women." UNESCO's unique positioning and mandate enabled its staff to look at women's intellectual and cultural contributions as well. The Division of Philosophy prepared a collection of "Comparative Studies on the Cultural and Intellectual Role of Women" in 1975.[67]

As part of this work, scholars undertook a series of UNESCO studies on the social, cultural, political, and economic roles of African women in traditional precolonial society in Benin, Guinea, Kenya, Madagascar, Mali, and Niger. In 1976, the director-general reported that "women also have to contend with more specific obstacles relating to customs, ways of life and the traditional distribution of labor in male-dominated societies, and with the isolation of women which is often desired by the men, whether consciously or unconsciously."[68] The agency emphasized that women in many societies are required to maintain traditions that exclude them from spheres of power and participation. Because cultural practices have always marked sexual differences and gender structures the division of labor, gender discrimination has both political-economic dimensions and cultural values. This leads to a conflict between the struggle against gender differentiation and the recognition of cultural specificity.[69]

Studies showed that problems such as girls' higher rates of school-leaving were connected with structural changes overtaking national economies, such as urbanization. UNESCO realized that it was necessary to look at all women's roles in tandem—social, cultural, political, and economic. Women's status within the family was a strong indicator of their ability to perform extrafamilial roles. For African women, specific obstacles revealed were customs, way of life, sexual division of labor, male-dominated society, and the isolation of women. UNESCO's study *Women and Racial Discrimination in Rhodesia,* one of the 1975 series, showed that race was an axis of discrimination that could affect the process of development for women.[70]

While it was in 1977–1982 that UNESCO first considered women as a social group and declared the improvement of their status as an objective, the ground for this defining moment had been prepared much earlier. In 1974, a study entitled *UNESCO's Contribution toward Improving the Status of Women* was presented to the Executive Board.[71] In 1976, the General Conference proclaimed that an aim of the next program was to enable women to take part in economic and social development on an equal footing with men. As areas of specialization became more strictly defined within the UN family of agencies, UNESCO did not seem to figure in the interactions of women's movements with the UN as much as the UNDP, UNFPA, UNICEF, or the ILO. But in those early years it was at the vanguard of breaking open the concept of status and bringing value through research into the CSW's work; it was the most critical handmaiden to the commission.

Expanding Women's Space: The International Women's Year Conference at Mexico City

The UN held numerous regional seminars and forums and global conferences during the late 1960s and 1970s on thematic issues of development and rights, including the International Conference on Human Rights in Tehran (1968), the World Population Conference in Bucharest (1974), and the World Food Conference in Rome (1974). The seminars and forums drew on the work of the CSW, especially DEDAW, and linked development issues with women's status.[72]

During the 1970s, conferences did not take women into account very well, but some of the agencies had sections that were predominantly managed by women, and these individuals became the "activators." For example, the FAO had an efficient nutrition section that was staffed mainly by women. It ensured that women's roles in food production, especially in Africa, were covered in the conference documents. When the World Food Conference was taking place, an NGO group was organizing a parallel conference at Rome that succeeded in influencing the official conference.[73] Members of this group had been active in their own countries well before the conference, influencing the preparations for the world event (it is now called the NGO/CSO Forum for Food Sovereignty).

The CSW was a major presence at some of these conferences. For example, at the International Conference on Human Rights in Teheran women won the endorsement of the General Assembly for the unified long-term UN program for the advancement of women in the conference's resolution IX. Their special skill of combining their focus on women's rights with emerging issues at the UN in order to strengthen both issues was also evident; although the resolution promoted "women's rights in the modern world," it was basically a development plan. This sleight of hand shows how equality and development were both important concepts for women's advancement and status and occupied a legitimate place in a human rights document. As John Mathiason has noted, "While [the unified long-term plan for the advancement of women] maintained its human rights base, its focus was heavily on issues related to economic and social development, especially on education."[74]

The long-term plan asked for education for women and compulsory elementary education for girls, economic plans that would enable women to contribute to national development, the establishment of national commissions on the status of women, and the development of human resources and community services that incorporate women's skills. It also affirmed the need for all member states to ratify the various conventions on women's equality, rights, equal remuneration, discrimination, and protection against abuses such as trafficking.[75]

Despite its positive features, the long-term plan for women approved in Teheran can be faulted for not having successfully integrated women into the mainstream regime of human rights. It did not stipulate that all human rights conventions and UN system-wide activities had to reflect concerns of women (e.g., on torture, in armed conflict situations, etc.). For example, the Proclamation of Teheran mentions women only once. It states:

> The discrimination of which women are still victims in various regions of the world must be eliminated. An inferior status for women is contrary to the Charter of the United Nations as well as the provisions of the Universal Declaration of Human Rights. The full implementation of the Declaration on the Elimination of Discrimination Against Women is a necessity for the progress of mankind.[76]

The proclamation does not mention women in the context of war. However, looked at from a more evolutionary point of view, the plan represents an early and synergistic exercise in planning for women on a multisectoral basis. The lesson is that women's needs are not divisible. They represent half of humanity and cannot be confined to one set of rights or needs. By locating the plan in the intersection of development and rights, the resolution set the format that would be used in later women's conferences.

At a very basic level, the UN world conferences of this period were informative and useful because they mapped broad trends across the world and presented plans of action that were multisectoral and had a long-term perspective. The themes that were chosen related to pressing problems such as food and population, both of which were widely seen as portents of future global crises. At another level, the conferences triggered a mobilization of groups and individuals who learned to use conferences as opportunities to lobby for changes at national and local levels. This aspect led to a strengthening of national, regional, and global networks taking up particular causes or fighting for changes in laws and policies in general. They also opened up the hitherto-little-realized matter of women's roles and contributions in sectors such as agriculture and industry, which led to new searches for knowledge and ways to disseminate new information.

The convergence of the momentum created by development mandates created by the goals of the Second Development Decade and the growing visibility of the issue of women's rights in the UN made new initiatives possible. The international women's movement provided an external context for these initiatives. The CSW had always welcomed representatives from women's NGOs as observers at its meetings, and in 1972, the Women's International Democratic

Federation used its observer status to ask the commission to proclaim an International Women's Year (IWY) to mark its twenty-fifth anniversary.[77] The commission took the proposal to ECOSOC, which approved it in 1974. Many at the UN felt that this would be just another theme year among many and that not much would come of it; previous theme years had accomplished little. But the IWY of 1975 proved to be a watershed in the history of women around the world.[78]

By the time of the IWY, the women's question had become complex and multifaceted. Women's integration in development had been raised as a policy imperative within and outside the UN. The WID perspective enhanced the understanding of women's development needs and the need to improve statistical measures of women's work. That women influenced the course of development was more or less accepted, whether the subject was the production of food, population, education, rights, contribution to rural development, petty trading, home-based work, sweatshop work, or domestic workers.[79]

The initial goal of the IWY was to "devote that year to intensified action to promote equality between men and women and to increase women's contribution to national and international development."[80] Gloria Scott of the Secretariat was assigned the task of collecting what data existed in preparation for the conference; her report, "Integration of Women in the Development Process as Equal Partners with Men" was submitted as an official document of the conference in Mexico City.[81] In 1974, ECOSOC asked the Secretary-General to convene an international conference during the IWY that focused on these goals, which women had linked to the goal of peace. The world conference on women in Mexico City was a defining moment for the internal/external partnerships women had crafted because it was the start of the most vibrant and influential phase of the worldwide women's movement. The NGO Forum idea changed the nature of the participation of women in all future UN conferences on development, rights, children, women, environment, population, and social development. The Mexico conference set the procedures not only for wide participation but also for monitoring follow-up on UN pledges.

The period leading to the Mexico conference set the stage for the International Women's Decade to build and expand on many ideas and structures from the early years of the United Nations. Since the modernization project's concern was to "uplift" the newly liberated nations out of their poverty and "backwardness," development cooperation attempted to integrate women into development as part of their "humanitarian" approach. Development policymakers realized that women needed to be included in development projects, but they saw them incorrectly as mirror images of housewives in developed countries. A gap developed between development projects from the North and the research on the ground about the realities of women's lives in the South. The distances wid-

Box 2.2. Annie Jiagge: Driving Force in the CSW

Annie Jiagge (Ghana) was a member of the CSW from 1962 to 1972 and served as chairperson in 1968. She was one of the participants in the 1972 UN Interregional Meeting of Experts on the Integration of Women in Development and played an active role in drafting the Declaration, and later the Convention, on the Elimination of All Forms of Discrimination Against Women. She founded and was the first chairperson of the Ghana National Council on Women and Development initiated in 1974. She attributed her idea for the council to her experience with the CSW. Under her leadership, the council made increasing women's incomes its priority. She headed Ghana's delegation to the Mexico City conference in 1975, where she was one of the delegates who proposed a draft resolution that became the basis for Women's World Banking. At Mexico City, she remarked, "What we have put in motion is a revolution from which there is no turning back. If we succeed, all humanity has a chance." For ten years she was a driving force on the commission and helped shape its programs and develop its unwavering focus on women's rights. At her death, Secretary-General Boutros-Ghali noted that "she employed her vision of full equal rights for all women in the shaping of the draft Declaration on the Elimination of Discrimination against Women. . . . The process required determination and ingenuity. Annie Jiagge had those attributes."

Sources: Women Go Global; http://www.poorservants.com/links.htm; tribute by UN Secretary-General Boutros Boutros-Ghali on the occasion of the memorial for Justice Annie Ruth Jiagge, 3 August 1996.

ened as the decades proceeded and the women of the South consolidated their perspective.

More than 130 nations sent delegates to the World Conference of the International Women's Year in Mexico City; 75 percent were women. The conference served to open the UN to many more NGOs. While earlier it was the bigger, more established NGOs that attended international conferences, at Mexico City, many smaller, South-based nontraditional NGOs found a meaningful space for themselves that went beyond tokenism. The networking of women from many movements at these conferences led to the birth of a worldwide women's movement that steadily gained in strength, visibility, and clout over the next decades. Women from within the governments turned out to be important allies of women's groups in pushing through changes. Women were able to forge a political identity on the basis of the discrimination they faced universally, in spite of diversity and divisions. They emerged as a global social entity.

The conference brought about a crucial change in the area of data collection and analysis. The recommendations of the conference led to efforts through the UN Decade for Women to "map" women better. Hilkka Pietilä writes that "[d]uring the Decade the UN system collected an enormous amount of information, facts and figures on the lives, problems and conditions of women in different countries. However, this highlighted the problem that, as a rule, national and international statistics did not provide gender-disaggregated data."[82] This became the basis for a demand that member states review their procedure of data collection, which helped reduce some of the invisibility of women's work and contributions to society.

Another measure of the impact of the conference is seen in the adoption of its World Plan of Action (WPA), which acknowledged that women did not have equal access to resources. Its goal was to secure this access for women in education, employment opportunities, political participation, health services, housing, nutrition, and family planning. It also set minimum targets to be met by 1980. It paid attention to social issues such as migrant women, female prisoners, prostitution, and trafficking. One of the strengths of the WPA was that it allowed each country to decide its own strategy and identify its own targets and priorities. It also suggested that the UN General Assembly establish mechanisms for regular review of recommendations.

Another outcome of the conference was that 127 member states decided to establish what were called "national machinery/institutions" dealing with policy, research, and programs on WID (many other member states already had these in place). Leticia Shahani, who had chaired the Commission on the Status of Women in 1974, recalls that "the Philippine delegation had to create a national machinery before it went to Mexico because we wanted to announce to the world that we had a national machinery in accordance with General Assembly resolutions. That's one of the wonderful things which the UN can do—to put pressure on national governments to think and act on global issues which also affect domestic policies."[83]

The Plan of Action that the Mexico conference generated changed perceptions of women at the United Nations. Instead of seeing women as mere recipients of support and assistance, the plan acknowledged women's contributions to development and peace. It included significant departures from earlier notions of women and development. While earlier it was thought that development served women (and men), a new consensus emerged that development was not possible without women.[84]

However, the conference was not problem-free. No consensus could be reached on the Declaration of Mexico, partly because conference organizers had not had enough time to follow the usual procedure of reaching consensus during a several-years'-long preparation process. Cold War tensions were apparent in the positions countries took on various issues, slowing down the progress that could be made; G-77 countries came to the conference with a draft declaration, which prompted Germany, the United States, and the United Kingdom to quickly draft a "Western" declaration. The G-77 version's references to Zionism as a form of racism proved to be contentious. Furthermore, the three themes of the conference drew different responses from women from different regions. Former UNIFEM director Margaret Snyder recalls that "the question of the scope of women's issues caused a serious rift among delegates at Mexico City. The major concern of women of the North, where feminism was taking hold, was male-female relations and opportunities. For women of the South, fresh from colonial domination, issues such as apartheid, the global economy, and Palestinian rights were integral to improving the status and situation of women."[85] And Eddah Gachukia, who led the Kenyan delegation to the conference, has written that "although the themes of the conference—equality, development, and peace— were and remain important, our priorities in Kenya were different. While for women from developed countries the issue that resonated most was equality, in most provinces of Kenya the priority was bringing water closer to homes."[86]

A parallel meeting for women in NGOs called the Women's Tribune was held by NGOs, activists, and academics at a venue near Mexico City.[87] The Tribune was useful in creating cross-linkages between middle-class and poor women in Mexico and elsewhere in Latin America.[88] For many of the women who attended, many of whom were from developing countries, it was the first time they realized that women around the world struggled with the same issues and had similar interests. Women and development emerged as an important commonality: the UN Division for the Advancement of Women's history notes that "discussions concerning the male bias of development policies focused on how they worsened women's situations rather than ameliorated them."[89] The Tribune set in motion a new wave of the international women's movement, one that brought new ideas from women from developing countries that expanded and enriched feminist thought, especially regarding development issues.

The Mexico City conference and the Decade for Women set in motion a long-term campaign for the advancement of women. Numerous NGOs, informal groups, and national and international programs were spawned by these efforts. For example, the Women's Feature Service (WFS), which seeks to provide print and audiovisual service on development from progressive women's perspectives to mainstream media, was launched after the first world conference on women as a UNESCO-UNFPA initiative. The conference itself meant that women's concerns had received some attention, and this enabled the WFS to gain ground. Today it has writers from forty countries and media clients around the world.[90] Many of the women who attended the Mexico City conference from far-flung countries encountered the UN for the first time, as they did the diversity and energy of women's groups from all over the world. The exposure strengthened their sense of identity as well as their capacity and desire to engage with the UN. Thus, Mexico City provided more than a document called the Plan of Action; it was the jumping board for a new phase of the UN's partnership with the women's constituency.

The Peace Tent

Until 1975, UN discussions on aspects of security and defense almost never referred to women; in the postwar conventions, male nouns and pronouns were used to represent both men and women.[91] The themes of the International Women's Year of equality, development, and peace brought women into the official references to peace. The delegations from Greece and Guatemala had suggested that the word "peace" be added to the themes, arguing that women, as much as men, should be encouraged to join in the search for solutions to two of the most urgent issues of the period, peace and disarmament. It is no coincidence that in 1975 women were called upon by a General Assembly resolution to participate in the process of strengthening international peace and security.[92] The assembly was beginning to perceive women not just as victims but also as potential contributors to the peacemaking process. It also called for an expansion of the "process of international détente" to ensure that it was irreversible. The Mexico City conference conclusively demonstrated that the absence of peace deeply affects the effectiveness of development initiatives and the efforts to build equality that will mitigate structural violence.

The CSW's thinking about women in wartime was evolving during this period. The issue of protection of women and children in armed conflicts and emergencies had touched off a strong debate in 1969. Some of the members of the commission argued that women and children were not entitled to more protection than any other civilians caught in dangerous situations. Nevertheless, the CSW decided that women and children should be considered the most vulnerable members of the population who were too often the victims of inhuman acts. In a resolution adopted on 14 December 1974, the General Assembly urged governments to do everything possible "to spare women and children from the ravages of war." It reminded them of their obligations under the 1925 Geneva Protocol and the 1949 Geneva Conventions and affirmed that all forms of repression and cruel and inhuman treatment of women and children were criminal acts.[93] The collapsing of women and children into a single category that required safeguarding can be seen as the beginning of a move away from a nongendered discourse on the issue, but it is debatable whether that linguistic choice shows a sufficient understanding of women and war.

Before Mexico City, women participated in the arenas of war and peace as victims of military action. At the conference, Leticia Shahani says, "governments accepted the issue of women, the status of women, as a governmental concern. It wasn't just a social welfare [issue] handled only by NGOs. Now governments took a serious look at how half of the population in their societies live."[94] Governments that signed the Declaration of Mexico pledged to eliminate all obstacles that stood in the way of women's full integration into national development and peace. The declaration stressed the important role that women had to play not only in the achievement and maintenance of international peace but in "peace in all spheres of life: in the family, the community, the nation and the world. . . . Women must participate equally with men in the decision-making processes which help to promote peace at all levels."[95] This was an important breakthrough that expanded the formal definition of peace used in international relations.

3

Questioning Development Paradigms, 1976–1985

> *An unattainable goal is as meaningless as a right that cannot be exercised. Equality of opportunities cannot be achieved in the face of tremendous disabilities and obstacles which the social system imposes on all those sectors whom traditional India treated as second class . . . citizens. . . . The application of the theoretical principle of equality in the context of unequal situations only intensifies inequalities, because equality in such situations merely means privileges for those who have them already and not for those who need them.*
> —Lotika Sarkar and Vina Mazumdar, 1974[1]

- **Questioning Knowledge**
- **Questioning Development Models**
- **Adding to the Institutional Architecture**
- **Cultivating Networks: DAWN Mobilizes for Nairobi**
- **Applying New Knowledge: The ATRCW and the Lagos Plan of Action**

During the period 1976–1985, tensions between the East and the West, the two ideological blocs that dominated the global landscape, were intense. The playing out of this adversarial politics in the UN stimulated the emergence of a lively third bloc that did not get swept into either camp but carved out its own trajectory. The third bloc was interested in follow-up work on permanent sovereignty issues, especially as they related to the ownership of physical and intellectual assets and the control over their use. This work led to the Declaration on a New International Economic Order (NIEO) and the Charter of Economic Rights and Duties of States in 1974.

In a shift related to the emerging power of the third bloc, the scope of development widened to include equity considerations. The concept of equity covered the economic dimension as well as a larger concern for the well-being of peoples, to use a latter-day term, through provisioning of key material and social requirements of daily life. A contradictory trend was the reappearance of the modernization enterprise as the dominant idea for development—a new avatar of trickle-down economics, inappropriately labeled neoliberal, instead of *ill*-liberal, as in fact it turned out to be. Louis Emmerij has noted that "[n]ot only did this new orthodoxy become the economic strategy of the West but, through its adoption by the World Bank and the IMF (International Monetary Fund), it became the conventional wisdom of practically the entire globe, whether voluntarily or not."[2] The pains of structural adjustment appeared and along with them the critique of this ill-liberal paradigm. This energized research and stimulated debates on development.

The process of understanding what equality means to women continued; significant new contributions such as embedding development in rights and exposing and dealing with culture and its relationship to the affirmation of women's rights came together—a convergence of thought that is an attribute of women's intellect. Collective strategizing—notably in the shape of alliances between the "inside" and the "outside"—transmuted UN spaces, including UN conferences, turning them into sites of struggles and campaigns as well as settings for solidarity-building through shared knowledge.

As a result of the world conference held in Mexico City in 1975, the UN formally declared 1976–1985 as the Decade for Women. Almost all development agencies—international, regional, national, and UN specialized agencies—had to engage with the woman question. This system-wide mandate created enormous demands for information, which produced an explosion of knowledge. Information on the particulars of women's position in the political economy was made clearer both within and outside the UN, which prepared several global reviews of development in relation to women's position.

In development terms, both the welfare approach—one that sought to bring women into development as better mothers who could improve the lives of family members through better birth spacing and nutrition—and the emancipation approach—the socialist model that sought to improve women's status through state provision of goods and services—continued to be applied.[3] The purpose of the original women in development approach, which emerged in the 1970s, was to gain equity for women in the development process and to seek to reduce inequality with men. New research during this decade emphasized the inequalities between women and men, and the earlier concerns or perceptions based on sex roles were replaced by new concepts, in particular the concept of gender, a relational understanding of the difference between men and women in structures of power. Debates about whether gender or biological sex was the best way to conceptualize women's inequality continued throughout this decade, not only in relationship to femininity and masculinity but also regarding other differences and inequalities related to class and race.[4]

The Non-Aligned Movement provided an opportunity for women from the countries that had been liberated or had liberated themselves from imperial powers. Several entered the UN in the era 1946–1974, and eight more joined at the time under consideration in this chapter.[5] They brought their own collective view on inequality between men and women and its relation to the overall struggle for justice. They emerged as a credible presence in the UN world conferences on women because of the linkage the NAM made between women's struggle and the struggle against other forms of domination and with the global economic power regimes. Women from the developing countries or the South emerged as intellectual and political beings no longer "behind a veil," uncovering knowledge, emphasizing diversity. Networks and caucuses emerged with specialized interests and politics, moving along their own learning curve.

Questioning Knowledge

Redefining Women's Work

One of the issues where provisioning of knowledge had an impact was on the measurement and understanding of the work women do. Research within the ILO, the UNDP, and the FAO as well as by scholars and organizers revealed that there were deep flaws in the tools used to measure female labor because of the nature and style of women's work. There was recognition that the work styles of women are determined by history, biology, and cultural attitudes—a whole package. These work styles are characterized by intermittent participation over the life cycle or even over a day or week; contribution to productive activities at the processing/premarketing stage, which is less visible and less likely to involve cash; and intermingling of production for self-consumption and production for sale. They are not easy to disentangle, and the existing designs did not capture them. Furthermore, household structures as well as religion/culture, size of family, and number of infants all affected female labor force participation more than they affected male labor force participation.

The existence of these flaws in the premises of measures was systematically uncovered by the experience from the ground as well as the work of women academics.[6] In 1981, the ILO took a deeper look at unpaid work and discussed several ways in which it could be measured. Measuring women's unpaid work was important for several reasons: if it was measured it could be included in national accounts, and quantifying such work would help point policymakers to an understanding of inequalities between paid and unpaid work.[7] To facilitate comparison with market-oriented activities, UN agencies, especially the ILO, attempted to measure non-market household work in terms of volume of inputs and outputs or by attaching a monetary value to these outputs.[8] In 1983, even as studies were emerging from the continents of Latin America and Africa on the failure of measurement techniques to capture women's employment and work typologies, the ILO, led by Richard Anker, undertook a study of "Female Labour-Force Participation: An ILO Research on Conceptual and Measurement Issues."[9]

One of the values that emerged from time-use studies—for example, one done in India in 1976–1977—was the revelation that poor women (women from land-less households) were more deeply engaged in work than their men.[10] This study found that the female work participation rate was inversely related to class and that not only were children of the poor working in fields, farms, and firms but that in rural areas little girls worked as mother surrogates for up to eighteen hours a day.[11] It suggested that the methodologies used by statistical systems not only neglect housework and its value, they do not even measure the economic activity of the kind the majority of women in developing countries engage in. It revealed that even when housework is brought into recognition in systems of national accounts, breaking down housework into its components such as house-hold production (as different from cooking, cleaning, and caring) across ages, classes, occupations, and seasons in agriculture would help to identify the kind of responses programs and policies needed to make. The study also showed ways in which time disposition in hours can be incorporated into large-scale house-hold surveys, thus rectifying the inaccuracy of the national data.[12]

These suggestions were made to the national and international data systems, and the variable of household production as different from household chores was incorporated in some of the official household surveys in India. In this mea-surement scheme, the major departure was the use of the variable of time (espe-cially hours of drudgery and hard labor) rather than the variable of money as the unit of measurement. For the poor, especially women, measuring labor in this way would reorder the hierarchies embedded in measures and values. In a world dominated by economics, putting a monetary value as well as a time mea-sure on women's work is seen by many as a strategic—even though insufficient—action. Time as a measure of value would reverse the values of men and women's work—women would always come on top because they spend more hours work-ing than men.

Ideas fly across regions and balloon into interregional advocacy. Women in the labor force became a primary area of investigation and policymaking during the women's decade. The Instituto Universitário de Pesquisas do Rio de Janeiro (IUPERJ), a Brazilian research institute, called a Seminar on Women in the Labour Force in Latin America in 1979. This seminar brought together demographers and women's rights activists from the whole region, who carved out an agenda both for improving the quality of data collected and for understanding women's work in a broader context of work and regional economic impulses and problems. The seminar also invited representatives from other regions such as Africa and Asia, cross-fertilizing the analytical exercises. This seminar triggered seminars in other regions on the same set of issues. The interregional links made at IUPERJ laid the first "brick" for the building of the network Development Alternatives with Women for a New Era; both the convener of the seminar, Neuma Aguiar, and the representative of the African continent, Marie-Angelique Savané, were to become founding members of DAWN. Indian work on household survey design to take into account women's role in the economy transformed the first Conference on Household Survey convened by the UN Statistical Office at the Economic and Social Commission for Asia and the Pacific (ESCAP.) in Bangkok in 1980.[13] Later that decade, the United Nations International Research and Training Institute for the Advancement of Women held its international conference on the invisibility and visibility of women in statistics in India[14] and UNIFEM undertook pilot interventions in the questionnaire the Indian census used in 1991. UNIFEM demonstrated that the method used led to the underenumeration of workers, drawing from the recommendations of an Indian time-use study's argument and suggestions for methodology.[15] A seminar on Women in the Labour Force in South Asia was convened by the Asian Regional Team for Employment Promotion, an offshoot of the ILO in the ESCAP region with offices in Bangkok.

Each of these seminars brought together data on women's labor force participation and location in the economy and the special features of their location in the labor force. They drew attention to the fact that women were deeply embedded in the economic zones but were not recognized or enabled to sustain or enhance their positions. They clustered in the more poorly paid, more arduous, and less recognized areas of the occupational landscape. For example, women in Latin America were clustered in the urban domestic work sector because their livelihoods were disappearing in rural areas as a result of production choices and policies on land use. Such work emerged as a vital special field of feminist exploration that found an ally in the ILO, the UNDP, the FAO, UNIFEM, and INSTRAW—all of which held regional as well as global conferences on women and work, on women's visibility and invisibility in statistics. National data systems also responded and improved their gender-differentiated data on labor force participation.

Most of this work was done through women's studies centers and by women in applied social science centers who learned from and interacted with grassroots organizations and field-based research. Women's studies entities, whether located in universities as women's studies departments and programs or as inde-

pendent nongovernmental women's resource centers, became spaces for discourse, analysis, and building linkages across traditional political divides, be they
North and South or other. They enabled the building of theory and mobilization across distances in geographical and political spaces to back up the theory.
Chang Pilwha, a leading feminist from Korea, notes that in that country, where
women's studies came into being in the mid-1970s, "one of the remarkable
achievements of women's studies education is that it has produced many of the
leaders in the women's movements."[16]

UN agencies such as UNESCO, the UNDP, and the United Nations Environment Programme also carried out microanalyses of specific events or situations
in both industrialized and developing countries to fill the gap in data that was
identified at the beginning of the 1980s. Microanalysis was initiated in the early
1980s by the United Nations University based on a series of meetings held in
Tokyo in 1979, Oslo in 1980, and Dartmouth and Rome in 1981.[17] The seminar
participants met again in 1982 to establish a methodological framework that would
emphasize the role of women in development. The goal of such analysis was
both to show how women are affected by change and to challenge stereotypes
about development. It sought to bring women's participation in social change
into focus and to indicate to decision-makers how this participation could be
enhanced by policies designed to support households and women in the present
and the future. A life-course approach was used.[18] In the early 1990s, the seminar
group published their findings in a report by Eleonora Barbieri Masini called
"The Household, Gender, and Age Project." The audience for this report was
international and national level decision-makers, including the various UN specialized agencies.[19]

During the ten-year period between the world conferences on women in
Mexico and Nairobi, the tenor and content of the development discourse on
women changed significantly. The emergence and growth of a self-identified
worldwide women's movement stimulated curiosity, enthusiasm, and the demand for more information, not only about the difference between men and
women but also about the condition and aspirations of women and the larger
picture. The UN and its agencies, governments, and organizations and scholars
within the women's movement were the chief consumers and producers of the
new information about women generated during this decade. ECOSOC also took
note in 1977 of the progress report by the Secretary-General on action "to establish a system-wide UN research program on the role and position of women in
development."[20] The new research was one of the priorities that had emerged
from the UN world conference on women in Mexico in 1975, which had identified
gaps between men and women in the quantitative profile of inequalities in their
economic activities. Stalwarts such as Ester Boserup and Nafis Sadik were members of a panel on women and work at that conference, where the importance of

employment for poor women and the need to understand its nature and its existence through better measurement techniques were highlighted.

The research on women and development included analysis of what is now called best practices: micro studies, explorations of cultural practices, sectoral and regional studies, and analytical reports examining the links between the realities on the ground and the policy impulses from the top on topics such as women, poverty, natural resources, and employment. The women's lobby—women's movement activists both inside and outside the United Nations—helped legitimize a new methodology that combined knowledge created by professional research and knowledge created by experience on the ground.

The new research about women as workers entered the development discourse. During the women's decade, the UN held several regional seminars on women's participation in development, in particular with its regional economic and social commissions: in Buenos Aires (1976); in Kathmandu, Havana, and Mauritania (1977); in Amman (1978); and in the Mediterranean region (1984). This theme was also echoed in a Conference of the Non-Aligned and Other Developing Countries in Baghdad in 1979. In July 1981, the First Encuentro Feminista Latinoamericano y del Caribe was held in Bogotá, Colombia, with more than 250 participants. The Second Encuentro Feminista followed in Lima, Peru, in July 1983, where more than 600 women discussed manifestations of patriarchy in the region as it affected women workers. They looked at such practices as listing women engaged in domestic work as unemployed, unequal wages, discrimination against women in the workplace, women's double burden of work for wages and work at home, and the absence of social security for women who perform unpaid labor at home.

By 1980, researchers, academics, and activists from the developing countries had become a communicating club, meeting frequently in various international forums, largely those convened by the specialized agencies such as the ILO, UNESCO, and the FAO; funds such as UNICEF and UNIFEM; and regional commissions such as ESCAP, the ECA, the Economic Commission for Latin America (ECLA), and the Economic Commission for Western Asia (ECWA). The entire system came alive through the knowledge base that was being provided by the combination of activists, writers, researchers, and the UN family of organizations. Such gatherings added to the understanding of gender, showing both the differences in values arising out of location and political systems and the universality of the nettles in gender relations. It also enabled those who were designing policies in the South to use critical lenses to examine the policy approaches and programs of the Eastern and Western blocs.

During the UN Decade for Women, the ILO outlined the actions it would undertake vis-à-vis women workers and identified key areas of discrimination against women to fight. Irene Tinker notes that studies carried out by funding agencies were "pragmatic studies" on the actual conditions of various women workers, but they tended to operate within the "liberal economic theory" of the funding agency. The UN on the other hand, "supported research on women from a broad, theoretical perspective." Studies such as the one done for the Rural Development Program of the ILO and the background document that was prepared for the mid-decade conference of the UN in Copenhagen, Tinker says, perceived women's problems as "emanating from colonialism and the current capitalistic structure of global society."[21] The ILO has also influenced regional or subregional initiatives. For example, the Caribbean Community (CARICOM) has used the ILO Conventions to draw up model laws on equal opportunity and treatment for men and women. A number of countries have also introduced enforcement agencies as part of the national machinery.

The ten-year interval between Mexico and Nairobi was unique in that women's intellectual contributions on development became a major force, albeit slowly. These voices brought new information and knowledge along with a new mindset. From a more narrow and focused approach on women's status vis-à-vis men, they enlarged the scope of investigation to look at the broader implications of global economic, political, and social changes and their impact on women's lives in their entirety. These voices came from coalitions of developing countries that did not want their development agenda to be hijacked by the need to align with any particular big power or simply from networks of women researchers and activists who came together as a result of the world conferences and kept the communication grids humming with new information. As these outside voices became louder, they began to claim larger spaces and audiences within the UN.

Questioning Development Models

Women and the NAM

By the 1960s, the majority of the members in the General Assembly were from the newly liberated countries and these nations and the Eastern bloc countries had become a strong presence in the UN. They supported the stand taken by developing countries on various issues surrounding development, identity, political participation, and economic policies. New political alignments among developing countries were forged in the early 1960s as a result of the need to build, preserve, and exhibit a new identity both within and outside the UN. One such group was the G-77, the Group of 77 developing countries, which came into being in 1964 and became a formidable power bloc at the UN. These alliances, which constituted a substantive majority of membership, came to effectively influence UN policies.[22]

Another such alliance was the Non-Aligned Movement, which was formed in 1961 by a group of twenty-five states that were concerned about the accelerating arms race. The members were not aligned with either of the Cold War great powers. Many developing countries joined the NAM, and by 1964 a key component of the movement was criticism of Western colonialism. The NAM uses a nontraditional organization style in which each member state, regardless of size, has an equal voice in decision-making about global issues and politics. It provided a strong platform from which developing states could discuss a range of issues having to do with equality, including women's equality.

The NAM was a strong and supportive presence, though physically invisible, in the UN conferences on women. Its attention to women's contributions to economic development was sparked by the UN's International Women's Year. The Ministerial Conference of the Non-Aligned Countries that was held in Lima in August 1975, which took place right after the Mexico City conference, strongly supported and reiterated the Plan of Action, the document that emerged from the Mexico conference.[23] This support was reaffirmed in the many conferences that followed, including the Fifth Summit Conference of Heads of State of Government of Non-Aligned Countries in Colombo in 1976 and the Conference of Foreign Ministers of Non-Aligned Countries in Belgrade in 1978.[24]

The NAM passed a series of resolutions on the issue of economic development in succeeding conferences, culminating in its Conference of Non-Aligned and Other Developing Countries on the Role of Women in Baghdad in 1979. Representatives from forty-five developing nations attended the conference, and the UN sent observers from the ILO, ECWA, the UNDP, the United Nations Industrial Development Organization (UNIDO), and the WHO. As a result of dialogues in conference venues, the NAM saw women's role in development as an international and political issue, in contrast to its earlier conceptualization of issues relating to women's status as social or cultural phenomena. By the time of the UN's Mid-Decade Review Conference in Copenhagen, the movement's analysis of women in development had sharpened to a complex understanding of "the interconnection between trends in women's roles and status in their societies and the nature and pattern of the development processes, including the latter's dependence on international, economic, and political relations."[25] This model of development grew from a deep understanding of the realities of women's lives in developing countries.

The NAM approach was based on the principle of self-reliance, the idea that each country would determine what development policies would best serve its people. It "presuppose[d] the autonomy of each country in deciding on its own development, stemming from its full awareness of its own resources and development needs."[26] In its attempt to usher in a New International Economic Order, the NAM sought "a new system of world economic relations based on equality and common interests of all countries."[27] This worldview saw all nations as interdependent entities with resources—intellectual, technological, and economic—to be exchanged cooperatively in a way that would benefit all parties. It envisioned that governments would share both research findings that included studies of women's status and economic contributions, particularly those of rural women, and their experiences with programs for women relating to development.[28] Members of the movement believed that "[w]hat is particularly important to understand is that [the] self-reliant development pattern has the welfare of the people and not growth of GDP [gross domestic product] as its principal objective."[29] The NAM approach to development grew policy from the reality on the ground and changed policies when realities changed. It featured a cooperative sharing of resources between men and women, community members, and states. It did not see growth as a zero-sum game.

The Baghdad conference document acknowledged that promoting women's status and their role in development would yield other benefits, including "a more humane life, . . . peace and more equitable economic and political relations in the world, as well as . . . progressive socio-economic changes in each country."[30] Conference participants located the roots of women's oppression in two factors: 1) "poverty, iniquitous unequal utilization and distribution of resources and power that characterise the present world order," and 2) "obsolete, irrational attitudes that thrive on inequalities of all types." Although they acknowledged that development had benefited some women, they firmly stated that "for the majority, development has meant little more than stagnation, or increasing misery, greater vulnerability to exploitation and sometimes even a decline in opportunities and status in certain sectors."[31] The conference participants were unequivocal about the cause of women's decline in status after development; the roots lay in development policymakers' poor understanding of women's roles in their societies and the low priority they gave to women. The Baghdad Recommendations were endorsed at the Sixth Conference of the Non-Aligned Movement in Havana in 1979 and at the UN's world conference on women in Copenhagen in 1980.

The NAM's Conference on the Role of Women in Development in New Delhi in 1985, which was attended by 224 delegates from 65 countries, illustrated the value of some level of political homogeneity for arriving at consensus before attending UN events. In many of the newly liberated or former colony countries, leaders saw struggles by women for their rights either as not of high priority or as stimulated by Western notions, Western "culture." But for the women of those countries, acquiring space in the NAM gave their concerns legitimacy in the political space of the South.[32]

The NAM's New Delhi conference on women was a key to the success of the UN World Conference on Women in Nairobi held a few months later. Leticia Shahani, the secretary-general of the Nairobi conference, has stated that the consensus-building across the NAM countries on several important progressive propositions in New Delhi made possible the progress of and passing of a consensus declaration in Nairobi.[33] Vida Tomšič commented that the New Delhi NAM conference enabled the formation of a group of women across the traditional global political blocs that was able to forge a unified position on contentious issues. They used the forum to debate and absorb difficult topics and present a cogent proposal on women's issues, which they then carried to Nairobi.[34]

The NAM's model of the path to women's equality departed from UN strategies; the UN system at this time saw "women's status" as a social development issue that was not connected to the larger context of international development.[35] Within the UN women were still viewed as resources whose potential could be tapped, not as political and economic agents in the development of their countries. But the NAM movement and gatherings offered a space where the women from these former colonies could reassert the standpoint that they were active agents in their nations, contributors to their country's progress, not just consumers of social services. The NAM consultations introduced a more nuanced understanding of concepts that had seemed fairly straightforward, for example the idea of discrimination. Delegates from developing countries saw discrimination as "part of a system of exploitation in every country as well as within the international economic and political order." In contrast, delegates from developed countries tended to see it only in the context of male dominance.[36] This new view of the source of discrimination was the contribution the women of the NAM made to the statements of the mid-decade UN world conference on women held in Copenhagen. The conference report stated that "the inequality of women in most countries stems to a very large extent from mass poverty and general backwardness of the majority of the world's population caused by underdevelopment which is a product of imperialism, colonialism, neo-colonialism and also of unjust international economic relations."[37] This was a very different statement than the one in the report of the Mexico City conference just five years before, which had focused on equality with men through legal means.

Since the NAM was in many ways a collective resistance against domination by either world power, East or West, socialist or capitalist, women's engagement with it enabled them to locate their struggle as one against domination, against subordination. The fading out of the Cold War led to the dimming and reduction of value of this third space, which in later years removed a vital political umbrella that had sheltered the women of the South, given them a legitimacy to stake a claim for justice as part of the movements to redress domination. It could

Box 3.1. Vida Tomšič: Woman Leader in the NAM

As a young woman, Vida Tomšič stood against injustice and oppression in pre–World War II Yugoslavia, which later led her to actively participate in the antifascist liberation movement of the country. She continued to promote the role and status of women in society throughout her active public and political life (she was the first president of the Federal Women's Organisation and president of the Federal Council for Family Planning). She substantially contributed to developing the concept of "socialism with a human face," which implied full participation of women in social and economic life. (She published several books on the subject, among them *Women, Work, Family, Society* in 1976 and *Women in Development of Socialist Self-Managing Yugoslavia* in 1980.) Tomšič was the first woman minister (for social policy) in the government of Slovenia, also serving as president of the parliament of Slovenia and president of the People's Assembly of Yugoslavia. Her concern for the improvement of the status of women resulted in a number of positive measures in legal, health, educational and other policies in a country with heterogeneous social and cultural backgrounds. These policies remain valid today, especially in Slovenia, her home country.

Inspired by the goal of the United Nations to build a better world, she actively participated in discussions on social and humanitarian issues in the UN. She shared commitments with other prominent women of the time, such as Eleanor Roosevelt, particularly with regard to the implementation

be suggested that strong conservative alliances against women's rights were able to set back the UN's work between 1995 and 2005 in part because of the absence of this political space. The worldwide women's movement could not rebuild a similar space to counter these reconfigurations of the membership of the UN as conservative and progressive rather than North and South.

Women's Views on Development at Copenhagen

The UN's worldwide conferences for women are rightly celebrated as instruments that brought key issues of concern to women to the attention of the world body and thus to the governments of its member states. Through the worldwide conferences, the momentum was created to convert DEDAW into a convention that was then signed by member states. Networks across race, class, and geography were formed that took agendas such as women's human rights into the UN of the UN Universal Declaration of Human Rights. She argued that the status of women is not just a question of their legal, social, and political position but also an important development issue for each country in particular and the world as a whole. These ideas were pursued and further developed by the United Nations through the World Conference of the International Women's Year in 1975 in Mexico City, the United Nations Decade for Women (1975–1985), and the 1985 Nairobi World Conference on Women, in which she actively participated. Her work contributed to the prevalence of the concept that women are an integral part of all aspects of development. She played an important role in the establishment of the United Nations International Research and Training Institute for the Advancement of Women; the Secretary-General nominated her as one of the ten eminent members of its first Board of Trustees.

Inspired by the Indian leader Indira Gandhi, Tomšič promoted South-South cooperation, especially through the Non-Aligned Movement, where she was a pioneer in bringing gender issues to the fore. She played an important part in preparing the common position of the nonaligned countries for the UN world conferences on women through substantial contributions at NAM meetings on women in development (Baghdad 1979, New Delhi 1985, and Havana 1991). The study *The Role of Women in Development* was prepared under her leadership for the New Delhi meeting.

Source: Gorana Sipic.

mainstream, that ensured that women shaped UN policy regarding reproductive rights, and that successfully convinced the Security Council that their concerns regarding peace and security needed to be codified in a resolution. These accomplishments have set international standards that benefit all human beings, not just women.

Yet in some sense, the world conferences for women did not give equal weight to their three issues of equality, peace, and development. Perhaps this is because it was easier for women from the developed countries to relate to concepts of equality and peace and more difficult for them to understand development issues. For women from developing countries, it was impossible to separate the three. They came to conferences to speak about their perspectives and stories in the hope that women would begin to see their vision of what development could be.

Women at the NGO Forum in Copenhagen brought some of the earliest reports of the harmful effects of globalization on their bodies and economies.[38] The Women's International Democratic Federation had completed a study of the position of women in seventy-one countries and reported that the first years of the International Decade for Women had been marked by "a further worsening of women's situation," citing the growth of unemployment, inflation, the high cost of medical assistance, an aggravation of the housing crisis, an acute shortage of preschool childcare institutions, and feelings of insecurity.[39] One woman eloquently noted that in the developing world, the burden of both worlds fell on women.[40]

Forum participants who wanted to focus on development came well organized. With the help of governments and northern foundations, a group called Exchange, which included representatives from Third World women's networks, had planned daily workshops and events focusing on women and development. Topics ranged from ways to generate income to learning how to organize. The director of Exchange explained: "We had a feeling that the kinds of exchanges we wanted weren't being built into the structure [of the conference]." Four hundred women registered for the workshops, approximately 10 percent of the NGO Forum.[41] The workshops generated calls for regional organizing and women's participation in development policymaking.[42]

At Copenhagen, women from developing countries came with much to say and many ideas about how to move forward with a woman-centered development, but their voices were muted by the geopolitical conflicts of the Cold War era.[43] Issues such as Palestine and apartheid were intensely visible at the conference, which led to a lack of consensus on the draft conference document. But as the daily *Forum 80* reminded its readers, the issue of development was just as political as apartheid or the occupation of Palestine, and it objected to the way that "particular regional concerns have shaded out the global ones, and the special problems of development strategies in relation to women."[44] It became even more clear than it had been at Mexico City that location shaped consciousness; one participant writes, "I found North American feminists surprised to discover that not everyone shared their view that patriarchy was the major cause of women's oppression, and that Third World women held views closer to Marx than Friedan."[45]

The links between development and peace were strengthened at Copenhagen. By the end of the 1970s, the links between peace, equality, and development had been acknowledged. The UN General Assembly had passed a resolution in 1979 "affirming that the strengthening of international peace and security, the relaxation of international tension, general and complete disarmament, in particular nuclear disarmament under strict, effective international control will promote social progress and development and as a consequence will contribute to the attainment of full equality between men and women."[46] It also requested the Office of UN High Commissioner for Refugees (UNHCR) to review the situation of women refugees and make recommendations to the Preparatory Committee for the Copenhagen conference.

Forum 80 at Copenhagen highlighted the issue of the use of scarce resources for war. The head of CONGO (the Conference of Non-Governmental Organizations), Edith Ballantyne from Czechoslovakia, stressed the incompatibility of the goals of the Women's Decade with military expenditure. The NGO Forum discussed the arms race; the relationship between women, peace, and mass media; and the implications for peace arising from the fact that most national heroes were heroes of war rather than of peace. The final report emphasized peace as a prerequisite for development and the need to express peace in more positive terms than merely as the absence of war.

In 1982, the recommendations of the Copenhagen conference were taken up by the General Assembly, which adopted the Declaration on the Participation of Women in Promoting International Peace and Cooperation.[47] While Article 1 spoke of women and men having "an equal and vital interest in contributing to international peace and cooperation," Article 12 suggested measures to "provide practical opportunities for the effective participation of women" in peace processes. These included steps to encourage women to enter diplomatic service; to appoint or nominate women on an equal basis with men as members of delegations to national, regional, or international meetings; and increased employment of women at all levels in the secretariats of the United Nations. By calling for an increase in women's political participation, the article linked politics and peace.

One of the highlights of the otherwise politically fraught Copenhagen conference was the opening of the Convention on the Elimination of All Forms of Discrimination Against Women. Fifty-seven nations signed the new Convention during the opening ceremonies of the Nairobi conference, a gratifying acknowledgment of the new international consensus women were slowly building about women's rights.[48]

Adding to the Institutional Architecture

CEDAW

The typical procedure in the field of human rights at the UN is for a declaration to move to convention status. The CSW waited until 1972 for the Secretary-General's report on provisions in existing conventions that related to DEDAW, by which time it was working on plans for the International Women's Year. Helvi

Sipilä had presented her report on the connections between family planning and the status of women, and the CSW wanted to include that issue in the Convention. Although time was short, women within the UN who had worked on the Declaration could be counted on for their commitment, their political sense, and their sense of timing. The CSW was racing against time; the mid-decade conference was slated for 1980 and it was necessary to forestall the delaying tactics employed by certain member states.[49] Because time was of the essence, the CSW decided to put together a "well-connected, politically effective group of women" and allow them the anonymity they needed to withstand external pressures from member states so the Convention could be ready by the second world conference on women in Copenhagen.[50]

The process of drafting CEDAW (1979), provides a vivid illustration of women's alchemy, or their capacity to gather in diverse elements and make them into an intelligible and practical whole. CEDAW has been called the Women's Bill of Rights. Its brilliance lies in its capturing of a wide range of elements, however awkward, into a standard. The awkwardness arises out of the complex nature of the inequality experienced by women. The core idea of CEDAW was discrimination. Equality had mostly been seen in terms of physical or quantifiable elements such as age or income or other such numbers. But discrimination operates within other categories such as race and class. It is an unquantifiable element that exists in the mind as a perception. So it was a quantum leap forward that the CSW could find a term and a concept that encompassed all inequalities and could be universalized across all other categories or classifications. As Diane Otto explains:

> [F]ormal or de jure equality, which involves simply "adding women" to the existing paradigm, is an inadequate response to women's inequality. Realizing women's substantive or de facto equality involves addressing the institutionalized nature of women's disadvantage and changing the cultural, religious, and traditional beliefs that typecast women as inferior to men. It also involves recognizing that notions of masculinity and femininity are interdependent, so that changing women's secondary status also means challenging accepted wisdom about dominant masculinities. Rethinking equality as a substantive concept is therefore the major challenge facing the human rights treaty committees in their attempts to fully integrate women's human rights.[51]

During the International Women's Decade there was a continuation of the process of improving on the breadth and depth of understanding of what discrimination means. CEDAW improved on DEDAW by including attention to rural women; women's health, especially reproductive rights; and the treatment of customs and cultural practices. As African scholar Filomina Chioma Steady noted in 1985, "One of the Decade's greatest achievements has been the creation

Box 3.2. Lucille Mair: Scholar, Diplomat, Activist

Dr. Lucille Mair (Trinidad and Tobago) was secretary-general to the politically fraught Copenhagen conference in 1980. In 1983, she served as secretary-general of the United Nations Conference on the Question of Palestine—again a politically charged post. She brought to these posts experience from both within and outside the UN. She served as her country's deputy and permanent representative to the UN, chairperson to the General Assembly's Third Committee (Social, Humanitarian and Cultural), and special adviser to UNICEF on women's development.

She was in many ways as committed to Third World concerns as she was to those of women. She was able to link quite explicitly macro issues of imperialism and the "violence of development" with the violence women face within more intimate spaces. She wrote: "This [economic crisis] exists in a climate of mounting violence and militarism. . . . [V]iolence follows an ideological continuum, starting from the domestic sphere where it is tolerated, if not positively accepted. It then moves to the public political arena where it is glamorized and even celebrated. . . . Women and children are the prime victims of this cult of aggression."

Mair's engagement with the UN was not an uncritical one; even as she welcomed the progress made to secure equality for women she was acutely aware of the limitations. In her stocktaking of the Women's Decade, Mair pointed to the gains of the explosion of new knowledge that served to destroy many old myths but also underlined that Third World women have little control over policies due to a lack of political power. While they play important roles in the economic production process, they are hostage to the micro and macro forces they are struggling to influence.

She is credited with saying, "If development doesn't work for women, it doesn't work."

Sources: Karlene Faith, "Seven Days in India," *Lucille Mair Journal of Distance Education Revue de l'enseignement à distance* (1990); Lucille Mair, "Women in the World: The Challenge of the Nineties," Occasional Paper, WAND, University of West Indies, Barbados, 1987; *Women Go Global.*

of awareness about the injustices and negative effects of discriminatory practices against women."[52] Indeed, defining discrimination and setting up normative standards and mechanisms to identify and remedy it is considered the "greatest accomplishment of the UN system regarding human rights law relating to women."[53]

Although Article 2 of the 1967 Declaration had proclaimed that not only would all laws and regulations that discriminated against women be abolished but "all [such] customs and practices" would also be abolished, this idea finds a stronger exposition in CEDAW (Article 5a), which commits the state parties "to modify the social and cultural patterns of conduct of men and women." National governments who have ratified the Convention are responsible for altering private conduct if it infringes on women's rights. State agencies are to eliminate prejudices, customs, and all other practices "based on the idea of the inferiority or the superiority of either of the sexes or on stereotyped roles of men and women."[54]

During the process of drafting DEDAW, some of the developing countries had expressed their support for affirmative action, given their history of inherited laws, traditions, and customs that stood against women's advancement.[55] While DEDAW did not respond to this issue, CEDAW did. Article 4 of the Convention holds that the adoption by state parties of temporary special measures

---

Box 3.3. A Pioneering Human Rights Instrument

The Women's Convention (CEDAW) is a departure from the other human rights treaties and conventions (except to some extent those on racial discrimination). What makes the Convention a pioneering human rights instrument for women are the following:

- The centrality of the concept of nondiscrimination to the equality of women
- The inclusion of private acts in the definition of discrimination
- The accompanying articulation of prejudices, customary practices, and stereotyped roles of men and women as features to be eliminated by state parties to comply with the Convention
- The overturning of the formal approach to equality and establishment of the norm of equality of results or equality of outcomes—in other words, equality in real terms

The Convention defines the phrase "discrimination against women" as "any distinction, exclusion or restriction made on the basis of sex which has the effect or purpose of impairing or nullifying the recognition, enjoyment or exercise by women irrespective of their marital status, on a basis of equality of men and women, of human rights and fundamental freedoms in the political, economic, social, cultural, civil or any other field."

Source: "Convention on the Elimination of All Forms of Discrimination Against Women," Art. 1, GA document A/34/830, 18 December 1979.

aimed at accelerating de facto equality between men and women shall not be considered discrimination. The safeguard the Convention introduced was that these special measures shall not "entail, as a consequence, the maintenance of unequal or separate standards."[56] A further safeguard in Article 4 was that these measures would be discontinued as soon as the objectives of equality of opportunity and treatment are achieved.

UN agencies had not finalized a common view on this issue. UNESCO, for example, had explored the difference between de jure and de facto equality and posed some of the dilemmas of "special measures." In 1978, it said,

> Some differences of interpretation have emerged in regard to defining the concept of equality between the sexes. Although in certain cases special measures on behalf of women were necessary, care has had to be taken not to exceed certain limits beyond which the notion of discrimination might have re-emerged, bringing in its train new inequalities or prejudices.[57]

UNESCO envisaged its role as facilitating women's access to and participation in political, economic, and social life and in decision-making bodies through what it called "pragmatic action" (i.e., training women and taking other measures to enable women to participate) rather than "special measures on behalf of women unless such measures were the only way of ensuring the progress of certain very disadvantaged or peripheral groups."[58]

In many parts of the world, the principles underlying affirmative action are not new. It is used in many countries (in the United States for blacks, in Canada for disadvantaged groups and individuals, in the European Union for women, in South Africa for blacks and women) and is variously named affirmative action, compensatory action, or special measures, quotas. In these countries, such measures have been given full constitutional or legislative protection by national laws (as well as local laws in some cases). The courts have also largely been supportive of the legal soundness of the principle and the operational mechanisms involved.

In the UN, there has always been thinly veiled opposition to affirmative action in principle, especially for women,[59] though it is present in some of the human rights treaties such as the Convention on the Elimination of Racial Discrimination and the International Convention on Economic, Social and Cultural Rights. UNESCO, for example, openly rejected affirmative action on the ground that it preferred to work for gender equality by looking at the problems of women's education and advancement in different sociocultural contexts rather than by pinpointing specific activities to be undertaken on behalf of a single category such as women. An insider notes that as late as 1992, the theme of "temporary special measures" was still controversial. The underlying fear was that these measures for women would mean discrimination against men as "reverse discrimination" or as unethically or politically loaded practices. There is also an inability on the part of the rank and file in the UN civil service to connect or see the linkages between "temporary special measures" and women's equality.

CEDAW takes special care to distinguish the notion of "temporary special measures" from that of "protective measures," although it stipulates that women workers cannot be discriminated against on the grounds of maternity or pregnancy or marital status and calls for "special protection during pregnancy" vis-à-vis harmful work.[60] But the Convention does not consider these measures to be "temporary" because of their very nature, and it stipulates that such protective legislation has to be reviewed periodically "in the light of scientific and technological knowledge" for revision, repeal, or extension.[61] Temporary special measures, on the other hand, are corrective measures that are meant to correct historical imbalances and structural disadvantages.[62] While questions arose during the drafting about whether there should be a complaints procedure, this issue was not taken up. Some delegates argued that complaints procedures should be reserved for "serious international crimes" such as apartheid and racial discrimination rather than discrimination against women.[63]

The ILO provides a valuable example of how to deal with women's workplace issues, specifically how to resolve the conflict between protective measures and equality. The first world conference on women held in Mexico and the declaration of 1975 as International Women's Year prompted the ILO to issue the Declaration on Equality of Opportunity and Treatment for Women Workers[64] and the Resolution concerning a Plan of Action. The Declaration, while acknowledging that discrimination against women workers was rampant, asserted that "all forms of discrimination on the grounds of sex which deny or restrict equality of opportunity and treatment are unacceptable and must be eliminated."[65] It also said that "positive special treatment during a transitional period, aimed at effective equality between the sexes, shall not be regarded as discriminatory."[66] By differentiating "protective measures" from "special temporary measures" and tying the latter to the larger goal of achievement of de facto equality for women, CEDAW has made a commendable contribution to evolving new approaches to women's substantive equality.

CEDAW does not confine the protection of Article 4.1 to any particular group of women who are specially vulnerable or marginalized. The whole constituency of women is treated as an eligible group for the benefits of affirmative action. But feminist lawyers, activists, and researchers have highlighted the necessity of targeting women facing multiple barriers from structural and other types of discrimination and the obstacles they face in realizing their economic and social rights. It is not enough for special measures to be in position on the ground.

It is also necessary to make sure that conditions are in place that enable women to access these measures and to protect themselves against backlash and unintended adverse effects. Monitoring the effectiveness of such policies and putting in place complaint mechanisms are also essential.

It has been argued that these measures need to be sensitive to two possibilities: one, that values of a dominant culture will be imposed on another culture; and two, that the less-dominant culture will adapt to the dominant culture by assimilating to it. It has also been argued that these measures should cover legal aid and sympathetic counseling especially designed for non-citizens wherever needed. Since discrimination in such cases is multiple, the solutions must also lie in simultaneous, multilevel, and converging interventions so that the combination of support given to the women is able to mutually reinforce their access to relief.

CEDAW has been credited with evolving the concept of *substantive* equality, a foil to the conventional model of *formal* equality. The underlying basis of formal equality is that like should be treated alike—that those who are similarly situated be treated similarly. Formal equality denotes that among equals, laws should be equal and equally administered. Consequently, the argument would continue, that when groups are not similarly situated, they do not qualify for equality even if the differences among them are the product of historic or systemic discrimination. That women can be different from men but still equal to them is one way of looking at the new idea of equality the Convention tries to establish. A manual on how to use CEDAW illustrated how far thinking among women of the UN had come since the early days: "It is no longer possible to say that there is no discrimination against women if laws or policies do not overtly exclude women. Under the regime of the CEDAW Convention, neutrality has no legitimacy. Positive actions are required of the State to promote and protect the rights of women."[67]

Yet the Convention was beleaguered by large numbers of reservations entered into by the member states on basic provisions in spite of public education campaigns carried out by the international women's movement, national women's organizations, and other women's networks. Some sections of the women's movement, too, felt it reflected the concerns of the developed countries only. As Vida Tomšič noted,

> The acceptance of this Declaration can be seen as a summary of the period of defining women's rights in relation to men and society; the period when it could be felt from the subtexts of the discussions on women as if all men already possess the rights which are denied to women either by the state or—by men. Thus the Declaration concentrated primarily on the personal and civil rights of women, following the criterion of the legal status of men to whom women should become

equal. The general socio-economic and social status of men, class differences in society as well as the conditions for the enjoyment of human rights by both sexes, are to be hardly noticed. This notion was influenced in many respects by the struggle for women's equality in developed countries.[68]

UNIFEM and INSTRAW

UNIFEM and INSTRAW, two components of the UN's institutional architecture for women, were born as a result of the UN's first worldwide conference on women in Mexico City. They were the first global institutions within the world body assigned to women since the birth of the CSW.[69] Women within the UN and in the worldwide women's movement saw these bodies as two halves of a dual strategy to empower the poorest women of the world and enable them to become active partners in development policymaking and planning. What would later become INSTRAW was envisioned at the conference as a place where women could acquire the "skills, training and opportunities necessary to improve their situation and enable them to participate fully and effectively in the development effort."[70] UNIFEM was formed partly in response to women's realization that "the huge amount of productive work performed by women in agriculture, fuel supply, self-help community improvements and the like, remained nearly invisible to most development co-operation organizations."[71]

UNIFEM began its operations as the Voluntary Fund for the United Nations Decade for Women in 1976. During its first decade, it focused on getting financial and other resources into the hands of women in developing countries using the project approach. In its first year, it administered fewer than fifty projects; by 1984, it was managing more than 400.[72] In 1981, projects fell into the categories of employment (31 percent), planning (24 percent), human development (30 percent), and information and energy (15 percent).[73] Although the Voluntary Fund was originally intended to operate only through the International Decade for Women, the UN General Assembly was persuaded of the value of its work and made it an autonomous fund in 1984; although it was associated with the United Nations Development Programme, it had control over its funds and programming.[74]

INSTRAW began its operations from UN headquarters in 1980; in 1983 it was relocated to its permanent home in the Dominican Republic.[75] According to Irene Tinker, the momentum behind INSTRAW was gathered at a seminar on women in development in preparation for the annual meeting of the American Association for the Advancement of Science: "[T]he seminar made delegates aware of the need for further research on women."[76] Seminar delegates took this agenda to the Mexico City conference, where they gathered support for their idea of a research institute on women in the developing world. In its early years, INSTRAW worked closely with the UN Statistical Office to collect gender-specific statistics relating to women in development. It also cooperated with the OECD and Eurostat in revising the ways women's work is valued in the informal sector of the economy; this work supported a revision of the System of National Accounts at the UN regarding the valuation of women's work.[77]

The goals of both entities were congruent with the UN's initiatives during the Second Development Decade. The ECOSOC resolution establishing INSTRAW noted that "the promotion of development objectives and the solution of crucial world economic and social problems should contribute significantly to the improvement of the situation of women,"[78] mentioning poor women and rural women particularly, illustrating a perhaps naive belief that if macrolevel socioeconomic problems could be solved, women's situations would improve as a matter of course. The General Assembly resolution making UNIFEM a permanent fund stressed that improving women's access to development resources would "create conditions which will improve the quality of life for all" and noted the fund's "innovative and experimental activities" that had led to "highly specialized professional competence . . . in the area of development activities for women."[79]

Cultivating Networks: DAWN Mobilizes for Nairobi

DAWN was born as part of the preparations for the 1985 UN conference on women in Nairobi. During the preparation period for the conference, donor groups and the UN looked for ideas to incorporate at the conference that reflected Third World women's experience-derived critique of the UN development cooperation program. To coincide with their meeting in preparation for Nairobi, the Women in Development group of the Organisation for Economic Co-Operation and Development/Development Assistance Committee (OECD/DAC) commissioned a review of more than forty-eight evaluations done by UN and donor agencies of development transfers as part of the search for ideas to discuss at Nairobi. The report "Development as if Women Mattered: Can Women Build a New Paradigm?" was discussed at the review meeting of the WID group in 1983 in Paris. The study encouraged donors to consider supporting a furthering of such analysis and led the WID group to later support the DAWN process in many ways. It revealed, as other national studies had done,[80] that apart from not relieving the burdens of hunger and poverty, the transfers of development cooperation assistance to developing countries were often actually worsening the economic as well as social and political situation of women, especially poor women.[81]

The analysis was shared with a group of women selected to represent each continent but also representing a broader landscape, be it a regional network or the voice of a region through writing. The unanimous positive response revealed that the anxiety that all was not well with development cooperation initiatives was an experience that cut across the regions and women's experiences. This led to the initiative to call a meeting of these regional actors in Bangalore to think the analysis through and consider taking a program to Nairobi.

The UN had sent a questionnaire to help countries prepare for Nairobi that was based on what feminists called the "ladders approach," one that measures the disparities between men and women in a select set of indicators such as education, employment, and health and works to bring women up to the same level as men as a way of achieving equality.[82] It was a linear framework and did not engage in any analysis of the links between status and macro policies; it was not related to the reality on the ground or the downflow of the macro forces. The Bangalore group struggled to fit their issues within the framework for Nairobi, finally rejecting the entire questionnaire outright. As one participant said: "This is not the way to think—against someone else's framework." The group brainstormed about what factors were hurting women and arrived at identification of regional crises as the peg on which to hang the analysis of women's situations: Africa's food crisis, Latin America's debt, South Asia's poverty, and the militarization of the Pacific Islands. Poor women in these regions were not only totally engaged in the economies of these countries but were suffering from and responding creatively to these onslaughts. A new framework began to emerge.

The Bangalore group prepared a plan for a Nairobi presentation and named their new group Development Alternatives with Women for a New Era. The analysis that was born in these meetings was later published as a book, *Development, Crises, and Alternative Visions,* that has been widely used in university courses and development agencies.

DAWN's analysis noted that only a few countries that had pursued export-led strategies for growth had gained systematic results. In fact, countries that had experienced economic booms were the same ones that had a record of growing inequality. It located the structural roots of poverty not in insufficient economic growth but in "unequal access to resources, control over production, trade, finance, and money and across nations, genders, regions, and classes." DAWN's philosophy was that development planning needed to change so that meeting the needs of the poor became the central goal; if this happened, the work of poor women would become central to development and those women would become essential to the planning and implementation of development programs.

It called for a worldwide reduction in military spending and control over the activities of multinational corporations.[83]

DAWN linked its analysis to action and the potential in the women's movement for change and suggested that women's organizations form coalitions with other women's groups and organizations and across political affiliations to help it build a broad-based local and national movement.[84] DAWN's "manifesto" was a combination of political analysis and practical advice for women's organizations seeking change at the local, national, and international levels.

DAWN's efforts to build South-South reflections on development were recognized by another attempt at South-South economic cooperation, the South Commission. Representatives from two women's networks were asked to join the South Commission: myself as a founder of DAWN and Marie-Angelique Savané as the founder of the Association of African Women for Research and Development (AAWORD). Such linkages facilitated cross-fertilization between South or G-77 types of approaches and women's experiences of and demands for development. DAWN's preliminary outline was used in drafting the NAM declaration for its conference on women and development (New Delhi 1985). The NAM conference declaration of 1985 illustrates the exchange of ideas:

> Women from developing countries reject the separatist approach of some Western feminists. The Decade has certainly increased the awareness among many women and men of the gross violations of women's basic rights and needs. . . . Women have sought to establish links within and outside their countries and regions to increase solidarity on these issues.
>
> Approaches will have to be two-pronged: first to take programs which will directly affect women and lead to their growth and confer on them equal rights and administrative actions and second that society moves in a direction which will assist and support women's progress rather than be a hindrance. The UN organisations have been dealing with these issues mainly by establishing special bureaus, units and focal points.
>
> However, *this has not been sufficient,* since they tend to operate in isolation. It is, therefore necessary to widen the scope and objectives of the women's desks to incorporate women into an on-going and planned program. . . . The Governments, which recognize this potential force (Women's movement) as a positive one, could harness it to promote the aims of development and peace. Governments which reject this force may crush the movement for the time being but may find themselves weaker as a result.[85]

DAWN's new framework initiated a shift in development analysis characterized by the central location of poor women in development planning, the merging of "women's issues" with macroeconomic structures and global crises, and the linkage of local organizing efforts with global themes and networks.

> **Box 3.4. DAWN's First Meeting, Bangalore, India:**
> **The Group, August 1984**
>
> | | |
> |---|---|
> | Neuma Aguiar (Latin America) | Zubeida Ahmad (South Asia) |
> | Peggy Antrobus (Caribbean) | Tone Bleie (Europe) |
> | Nirmala Banerjee (South Asia) | Ragnhild Lund (Europe) |
> | Devaki Jain (South Asia) | Fatema Mernissi (Africa) |
> | Geertje Lycklama (Europe) | Marie-Angelique Savané (Africa) |
> | Katharine McKee (North America) | Claire Slatter (Pacific) |
> | Gita Sen (South Asia) | |

Applying New Knowledge: The ATRCW and the Lagos Plan of Action

Margaret Snyder and Mary Tadesse point out that "women-specific organizations and institutions are critical to an effective women and development concept and movement."[86] The African Training and Research Centre for Women (ATRCW) offers an example of how women's institutions can create the solid base from which women can build theory and shape policy. It is also an example of the importance of UN spaces for women's empowerment.

The UN's Economic Commission for Africa was formed in 1958. Its member states had been shaped by their recent experiences of fighting for independence, in which women played prominent roles. As a result, the ECA almost from the first recognized women's contributions to their nations and provided venues such as the seminar "East African Women Look Ahead" in the mid-1960s.[87] Understanding that independence would not automatically benefit them, African women created institutions in the 1960s through which they could address their concerns, such as the All Africa Women's Conference and Pan-African Women's Organization.

Women's concerns were taken up by the ECA. In 1967, it published its study *The Status and Role of Women in East Africa,* which documented that women "often carried a major portion of the economic burden."[88] Furthering its commitment to women and development, the ECA published *The Data Base for Discussion on the Interrelations between the Integration of Women and Development, Their Situation and Population Factors in Africa* in 1974.[89] The information provided in the *Data Base* was used in many publications for years to come; it was the first development study to focus on women. The basis for women-centered policymaking was being created through the collection of this knowledge. These studies predated other UN data-gathering about women and development by a decade.

The ECA created a stable base from which women could transfer the skills they had honed in independence activism to advocacy for women's development issues. Through the knowledge it gathered, women and development became a core concern of the commission. In 1975, after several years of planning, it established the ATRCW, "the realization of what many African women had aspired to."[90] They believed that the research the center would provide a path to solutions to their economic obstacles. The information gathered at the center was distributed throughout Africa, creating a common base of information for women.

The ATRCW quickly became a space where women leaders and members of women's organizations could meet to share knowledge and discuss strategies for the future. Strategies for change emerged from the data the ECA and the center had collected. It developed institutional architecture through which policy could be disseminated, subregional committees through which women could make recommendations to their governments. The location of the center as part of the UN's ECA "was a distinct asset for women, one that prompted a willingness on the part of national politicians and civil servants to co-operate."[91]

The center worked on several levels to foster the crafting of an African policy on women and development. It sustained research projects that led to policy documents. It successfully persuaded government ministers to establish women's bureaus in African countries. It offered training workshops funded by UNIFEM to rural women designed to develop Africa's human resources. Its nonhierarchical style of operation enabled it to learn what skills or programs would help African women on the ground and then translate that knowledge to policies that were taken on board by national governments.

As a result, when the ECA began work with the Organization of African Unity (OAU) and the African Development Bank in the mid-1970s to design a regional trade agreement to cultivate an African economic community, the ATRCW was ready with policy recommendations for women. The Lagos Plan of Action was part of a hoped-for New International Economic Order in which developing countries worked to build economic self-reliance and interdependence with each other rather than dependence on trade with developing countries. Adebayo Adedeji, who headed the ECA during this period, recalls

> We emphasized self-sustaining internal development, rather than producing primary commodities for export and depending on food imports and aid. We felt developing intra-African trade is very important for the continent, rather than

continuing this vertical trade in terms of export commodities, and that the future
of the continent did not lie in depending on mono-cultural production, even when
you have included oil, but on diversification.[92]

African women were prepared with draft proposals about women and development. In a regional conference in Lusaka in preparation for the 1980 world
conference on women in Copenhagen, they had crafted detailed policy recommendations for women in African development based on the knowledge they
had gained from their own lives and from the research done by the ATRCW. The
draft proposals were merged into the Lagos Plan of Action, an acknowledgment
by heads of state and government that women were critical to the development
of the continent. The secretary-general of the OAU noted that the Lagos Plan of
Action emphasized "the imperative need to move the African women . . . to the
mainstream of our social planning."[93]

The "Women and Development" chapter of the Lagos Plan of Action is a detailed blueprint for women's economic empowerment, calling for education for
women to prepare them for employment in business, commerce, industry, and
handicrafts and small-scale industries; greater participation of women in higher
administrative and policymaking positions; and seminars to train women in
marketing and running cooperatives. It notes that women, as agriculturalists,
held the key to the solution of the food crisis and asked that women's agricultural contributions be included as a productive activity in national statistics. It
envisioned that governments, international agencies, women's NGOs such as
AAWORD, and the ECA's ATRCW would cooperate to produce "research on
changing attitudes towards full participation of women in all aspects of society,"
especially "the exchange of information on economic changes and their impact
on women."[94]

The story of women's contributions to development thought in Africa leads
in a direct line from women's political activism for independence to mobilization into networks to use of the institutional spaces the United Nations provided in both the ECA and the world conferences on women. African women
were several steps ahead of the rest of the world's women during the 1960s and
the 1970s; as they politely noted in the Lagos Plan, "actions taken during the first
half of the Women's Decade were not enough."[95] As women at Mexico City and
Copenhagen were making their initial demands for research on women, and
before the United Nations engaged in any comprehensive research on women
and development, African women were not only conducting that research but
also translating the results into policy recommendations that were embraced by
male government officials and administrators of regional bodies. They were entering the mainstream decades before the term became the watchword for

women's empowerment. Women-centered spaces were crucial in the process, as Jacqueline Ki-Zerbo, a governmental delegate to the ECA in 1960, noted: "We need to keep a double stream, to have specific support for women while at the same time trying to involve them in the mainstream of decisions and actions. . . . You cannot mainstream from scratch."[96]

Several weeks after the Lagos Plan of Action was adopted, the World Bank released its own plan for the economic development of the Third World. Characterized by structural adjustment programs and growth-led economic development, the World Bank's plan soon became the dominant economic force among developing countries. In Africa, structural adjustment replaced the Lagos Plan's vision of self-sustaining and collective regional self-reliance with "an efficient monocultural system," what former ECA head Adebayo Adedeji calls "a neo-colonial development strategy."[97] It was the shape of things to come.

4

Development as if Women Mattered, 1986–1995

Song of an African Woman

I have only one request.
I do not ask for money
Although I have need of it,
I do not ask for meat . . .
I have only one request,

And all I ask is
That you remove
The roadblock
From my path.

—Okot p'Bitek, *Song of Lawino*

- **The Impact of Modernization**
- **Understanding the Contours of the Economy**
- **Taming Development**
- **Changing Conduits to Power**
- **New Wings in the Architecture: The UN's Women-Only Spaces**

The decade **1986–1995** was one of unusual turbulence. From the early 1980s, laissez-faire policies and "free market" capitalism were prescribed as panaceas for the ills of development by a range of advocates that included Margaret Thatcher in Britain, Ronald Reagan in the United States, and institutions such as the World Bank and the IMF.[1] The prescription was to "get the prices right" and open markets.[2] Structural adjustment policies required decreased government spending and made loans to the less developed countries and the transition countries of Eastern Europe and Central Asia only on acceptance of these policies; this clustering of policies is often referred to as the Washington Consensus.

These policies were spectacularly unsuccessful. In the "mainstream," the 1980s and 1990s were seen as "lost decades" for development. The predicted rate of per capita growth for developing countries in the 1980s was 2.5 percent, but the median growth rate was less than 0.5 percent. The 1990s were even more dismal; the predicted rate of per capita growth was 3 percent, but the median growth rate was 0 percent.[3] One commentator, in what is perhaps the understatement of the decade, noted that the economic performance of countries that agreed to adopt Washington Consensus policies was "distinctly disappointing."[4]

Another significant change was the end of the Cold War, symbolized by the fall of the Berlin Wall in 1989, which changed configurations of power within the UN.[5] The disintegration of the East and West blocs critically impacted the approach to development. The Socialist bloc had supported approaches that required a strong state, a thrust toward public provision of basic services, and a more equitable global economic program such as the New International Economic Order. It was often an ally of the newly liberated states as they attempted to forge coalitions such as the NAM or the Group of 77 to negotiate with their former colonial masters.

The increasing role of the Bretton Woods institutions in global economic governance was accompanied by a decline in the role of the UN and its structures in negotiating global economic justice. The neoliberal paradigm, the market-led approach, weakened the role of the state, and since the UN is a parliament of states its access to influence was reduced.

Changes such as the entry of twenty-eight new states into the UN between 1990 and 1993, which could have initiated the emergence of an era of smaller states and added to the strength of the South, were clouded by new coalitions and clubs. "Unions of states" such as the European Union (1992), the Commonwealth of Independent States (1991), and the North American Free Trade Association (1991) emerged at this time.

Women's journey with the UN in this period in many ways marked a watershed. The momentum built up in the International Women's Decade continued, and women continued their work of engaging with the intricacies of inequality, critiquing development design (both at the overall level and with particular reference to women), and enlarging grassroots networks. The explosion of knowledge continued and women's studies was recognized as a discipline. It provided one more space, this time an intellectual space, for women to develop their understanding and their advocacy. Alternative measures of progress emerged, the most vivid being the human development indices. Attention to position in the economy increased. The informal sector moved from being a residual and undesirable sector of the economy to a vital economic force.

A dominant characteristic of the UN during the decade was the mobilization of women to influence policy and the emergence of women as leaders. For example, women took over leadership of six important agencies: Nafis Sadik was the first woman to head a major agency, UNFPA (1987–2000); Catherine Bertini headed the World Food Programme (1992–2002); Gro Harlem Brundtland headed the WHO (1998–2003); Mary Robinson was the UN High Commissioner for Human Rights (1997–2002); Sadako Ogata was the UN High Commissioner for Refugees (1991–2000); Carol Bellamy headed UNICEF (1995–); and Louise Fréchette was named the organization's first deputy secretary-general (1998–).

This decade is also associated with a flood of UN conferences and achievements in terms of incorporating women's advice on issues and sectors other than those identified as "women's" issues. Women, both inside and outside the UN, no longer attended world conferences as members of marginal groups or as last-minute additions to conference preparations; their advice and participation was sought from the outset and their leadership in intellectual and policy arenas emerged. They used the conferences as platforms to highlight the areas where discrimination and domination still continued. There was a shift here in priorities; a renewal of the recognition, an affirmation of an earlier UNESCO finding that it was through entry into formal power structures that the age-old barriers to equality can be broken. The influence of women's NGOs has been particularly manifest at the global conferences of the United Nations, where women's groups gained recognition at the 1992 Earth Summit in Rio de Janeiro and shaped the agenda at the World Conference on Human Rights in Vienna in 1993, the International Conference on Population and Development in Cairo in 1994, and the World Summit for Social Development in Copenhagen in 1995.

There was also a significant change in the relative position of the institutional structures operating on behalf of women and the conduits women used to reach the international negotiating spaces/structures. National women's bureaus and UN focal points came into greater play as a result of the mandates of the Nairobi Forward-Looking Strategies.

What was disturbing was that outside of this corridor of power within the UN, things were falling apart, to invoke Chinua Achebe.[6] While women fought to create space for themselves within the UN and worked to improve the understanding of women's location in their economies, inequality, poverty, and conflict and its injuries were rising and women were the worst hit—a painful disjunction.

The Impact of Modernization

Poor Women's Increasing Poverty

Many reports in the 1980s and 1990s pointed out the persistence and perpetuation of inequalities.[7] These critiques called into question mainstream thinking about how to proceed with development plans. One of the most significant was that of the South Commission, composed of twenty-eight economists from the developing countries. In 1990, after three years of research and consultations, the commission published its report *Challenge to the South,* which bluntly stated the problem: "While the developed countries began a recovery from 1983, for the South the crucial point was that this recovery in the North was not accompanied by a significant improvement in the external economic environment for most developing countries."[8]

Information about the increase in poverty and inequality also emerged from the regions. Between 1985 and 1998, the poverty rate rose in Africa, the transition economies of Eastern Europe, and the countries of the former Soviet Union.[9] With the exception of the People's Republic of China, the number of those living in poverty in the less developed countries rose steadily during the last two decades of the twentieth century. This increase in number of the poor was part of the phenomenon of growing global economic inequality, both among countries and within countries.[10] Susan Moller Okin concludes that "within most countries, the less-well-off became poorer even by the conventional measures of household income or consumption (which miss some crucial aspects of their impoverishment), while the rich got richer."[11] Overall, "for many countries over long periods of time, inequality has been surprisingly persistent, and where inequality has changed rapidly, it has increased."[12]

A series of reports from within the UN and from outside institutions pointed to the ways women suffered under the increasing inequality caused by structural adjustment and neoliberal economic programs. An ILO review noted the impact of the external context on women, which it describes as marked on the one hand by

> economic crisis, industrial restructuring and escalating unemployment in the industrialized countries; by the negative effects of debt and structural adjustment programmes on women's employment, earnings, and living conditions in the Third World and, on the other hand, by the process of economic globalization and liberalization. These trends have influenced the employment, earnings and living conditions of women who were particularly exposed to unemployment, precarious situations, reduced career prospects, downgrading to informal activities, diminished social protection, economic exploitation.[13]

By some measures, women's status was improving by the 1980s in ways that could conceivably be attributed to the influence of CEDAW. The enrollment ratio of girls to boys in secondary-level education in 1989 was 0.86 in countries that had signed the convention, as opposed to 0.80 for all countries and 0.71 for countries that had not signed. Similarly, the percentage of women in decision-making positions was higher than that for countries that had not signed and the average for all countries, although those numbers were still very low: in countries that had signed the convention, parliaments had 10.6 percent women, governments had 4.9 percent women ministers, and women filled top-level government positions at a rate of 5.6 percent. (The numbers for countries that had not signed were approximately half of these percentages.)[14] The UN's Division for the Advancement of Women wrote that the ratio of women to men in the labor force was an "indicator of equality," noting that women in CEDAW countries had a higher level of economic participation than women in non-CEDAW countries.[15]

Yet this movement toward "equality" was uneven; the UN's *World's Women 1970–1990* noted that with the onset of structural adjustment programs, "women [had] been disproportionately squeezed out of public sector employment."[16] Reductions in government spending for health, child care, family planning, and education hit women particularly hard. Wage freezes and the high cost of imported goods meant that women worked longer hours. In 1994, Gertrude Mongella, UN secretary-general for the Fourth World Conference on Women in Beijing, highlighted this differential situation: "Women have less influence in the market because they do not have control over their labour and have limited access to other means of production."[17]

For many of those concerned with development, the notion that women had their own particular experience of poverty was new, and there was a learning curve as research generated more and more new insights. Those who looked at gender within poverty began to understand the many hidden aspects of inequality and flaws in the understanding of poverty, the way it was measured, and its intersections with macropolicies. They also began to understand some of the potential for turning the process of development toward the stated goals of equality and justice. They began to look at such issues as inequality within households, the coping mechanisms women in poverty used, and the built-in discrimination in the poverty removal strategies directed toward women.

These new explorations led to an understanding that the way statisticians measured women's roles and contributions within economies was flawed. Previous analytical frameworks saw women as a subset of the poor who need special measures for relief. These ideas did not seem adequate any longer. The lack of data on individuals within households is due not only to lack of attention to gender but also to the difficulties of separating some of these indicators such as income, consumption, or nutrition by individuals in households, especially where individuals do not earn salaries or wages but nevertheless do work that contributes to family income, a typical characteristic of South economics. For example, food consumption is difficult to disaggregate as male and female, even though this variable is crucial to inequalities between men and women in some regions.

Table 4.1. Total Number of Rural People Living below the Poverty Line by Sex (estimated in millions), 1965–1970 and 1988

	1965–1970	1988	Percentage change
Women	383,673	564,000	+47.0
Men	288,832	375,481	+30.0
TOTAL	672,505	939,481	+39.7

Source: ILO, *Gender Poverty and Employment: Turning Capabilities into Entitlements* (Geneva: ILO, 1995), 9.

The Feminization of Poverty

One of the phenomena that emerged from new research was the increase of women among the poor, to the point where there were more women among the poor than men. This was described as the feminization of poverty.[18] The term originated in U.S. debates about single mothers and welfare dating from the 1970s. In the context of global economics, it was linked to a perceived increase in the proportion of female-headed households and the rise of female participation in low-return, informal-sector activities in urban areas, particularly in the context of the 1980s economic crises and structural adjustment programs in Sub-Saharan Africa and Latin America. The term "feminization of poverty" was used to describe three distinct elements:

- that women have a higher incidence of poverty than men
- that women's poverty is more severe than that of men
- that a trend toward greater poverty among women is associated with rising rates of female-headed households[19]

One way to measure women as a subset of the poor was to count the number of households that were headed by women on the assumption that these households were the poorest households within a universe of households. This seemed to fit the reality in some regions, but not in all.[20] Research on female-headed households conducted in many other regions of the world revealed that female-headedness emerged not only because of abandonment by men or deprivation but because of such factors as outmigration of male heads of households seeking work. These men sent remittances home on a regular basis, and these households, even if considered as female headed for a census or other surveys, were not necessarily poor. In fact, they were often better off due to the cash remittances they received in otherwise subsistence-type households. Other causes were identified for female-headedness that were not necessarily associated with poverty. For example, certain cultural practices or traditions such as matriliny declared or reported the oldest woman as "head" of the household. In these households, property could be owned by women, as in parts of South India.[21] Thus, it is argued that the variable "female-headed household" cannot universally be used as a proxy for women's poverty and that there are "dangers of assuming that female headship always represents disadvantage."[22]

The idea of the feminization of poverty introduced other analytical difficulties. Cecile Jackson points out that "the subordination of women is not caused by poverty," that "a poverty focus misses the range of interconnected gender issues across classes and socioeconomic strata." She advocates rescuing the concept of gender from what she calls the "poverty trap."[23] Another critique is that the formulation conceals the reasons why women are being pushed into poverty and is thus too simplistic. In many countries, inappropriate development policies have pushed women out of the place they earlier occupied in the economic and political landscape and have pauperized them. In other words, it is not that poverty has been feminized, it is women who have been pauperized. Anne Marie Goetz agrees and argues that focusing on women in isolation from their social relationships does little to address the power imbalances rooted in these social relations that lead to women's greater vulnerability to poverty.[24]

However, the concept of feminization continues to be used. For example, the term "feminization of work" is used to describe the trend when an increasing proportion of workers are women. Similarly, the term "feminization of agriculture" is entering the field, a term used when a high (perhaps even a dominant) proportion of women in agriculture is clustered in the worst corners of that sector. World Bank economist Valerie Kozel's study of Uttar Pradesh, which, with 160 million people, is India's most populous state, reveals that a higher proportion of female workers than male workers is involved in low-paid casual work, primarily in the agriculture sector.[25] Consequently, she says,

> [T]here has been a *feminisation* of the agricultural workforce, as the relative proportions of both female cultivators and female agricultural labourers have grown. Three quarters of women's employment days were in agriculture, as compared to only 40% of men's. Women were also three times more likely than men to work as agriculture labourers—work that is backbreaking, insecure, and low status. In contrast to men, women rarely held regular jobs or jobs in the non-farm sector, while these activities were left to the men. When they did obtain such employment, women were again relatively underpaid and confined to unskilled activities.[26]

In using this term there is a suggestion that feminization also connotes a low value and unpleasant situation. Feminization of work is seen both in terms of numbers entering the workforce and in terms of the quality of the work, which is usually poorly paid, physically demanding, and dirty. The UN's *1999 World Survey on the Role of Women in Development* noted that although the term was sometimes used loosely, it generally was used to describe two changes in women's labor force participation: "the rapid and substantial increase in the share of women in paid employment" and "the changing nature of employment, where irregular conditions that were once thought to be a hallmark of women's secondary employment have become widespread for both sexes."[27]

The word "feminization" thus includes a connotation of demeaning work or a diminishment of the nature of employment. Since increased participation of women in any field can enhance the culture and value of the field and is often the main demand of the women's movement, using the term to describe what is basically a proportionate increase in numbers does not seem appropriate. It gives negative values to the increased presence of women. The word "feminization" should be removed from such descriptions of trends.

World Surveys on the Role of Women in Development and the 1995 Human Development Report

Documents produced by the UN such as the 1986 and 1994 World Surveys on the Role of Women in Development also chronicled the unfolding crisis. The 1986 survey was done when the impact of the Washington Consensus was not yet clear. It recorded early warning signals of the harmful effects of structural adjustment policies, yet it also included hopeful notes in its analysis, a clinging to the belief that development must surely be good for women even if in the short term the impact seemed unduly harsh.

For example, under the section entitled "Benefits Accruing to Women from Development and Effects on Women of Economic Trends," the survey reported that "[modernization] failed to affect women's productivity in agriculture because it bypassed them, or even pushed them out of jobs by mechanizing the work traditionally done by them."[28] It stated that "women seldom participate in designing new technologies and are seldom consulted before one is introduced."[29] It noted that although women's labor force participation was increasing at a faster rate than men's, they were crowded in low-paying jobs and informal employment. It reported that women seldom were able to participate in decision-making at any level, household, local, or national.

Yet the survey's analysis had hope for the future and pointed to development policies that might improve women's situations. The chapter on women and agriculture suggested that when women agricultural producers also have access to control over marketing, they gain enough power within households to be seen as co-producers. It recommended women's cooperatives and production credit schemes for rural women.[30] The chapter on industry noted that "in those [countries and areas] where export processing zones have been set up, women have become the main beneficiaries of industrial employment creation."[31] Women with access to industrial employment realized the concrete benefits of improved health and nutrition and lower rates of infant mortality, which in turn would lead to a lower birth rate, or so the author of that chapter hoped. These hopeful projections did not match the evidence conference attendees at Copenhagen had heard in 1980 from women living in poverty around the world.

By 1994, the survey's analysis of each indicator of forward momentum for women was much sharper. It argued that poverty represented a failure of development because its policies did not invest in women's capacities as a way out. It pointed out that women's participation is integral to the transformation of the labor force and that the absence of women at the top of large corporate bureaucracies and their growing presence in a dynamic middle sector affected development policies. The survey clearly stated that developments over the past decade, especially global economic restructuring, had proven that economic change is not gender neutral. Despite the visibility of the gendered nature of the inequality of poverty, policymakers had failed to consider "gender as a key variable in their policy making." Some of the report's key recommendations on steps to address poverty among women were to give women equal access to employment opportunities and ensure that women participate fully in economic decision-making.[32] As these two surveys chronicled the growing crisis of the world's poor women, the understanding of their compilers changed; from a somewhat naive belief that development would eventually help women, the learning curve took them to the realization that this would not happen unless women participated fully in development policymaking.

In the 1970s, economists began critiquing development models by examining measures of progress or change and choosing new statistical indicators for that measure. The "indicator movement" began with Morris David Morris's Physical Quality of Life Index (PQLI, mid-1970s)[33] which was soon followed by Manfred Max-Neef's *Barefoot Economics* (1983),[34] The Other Economic Summit (TOES, 1984),[35] and Hazel Henderson's *Paradigms in Progress: Life Beyond Economics* (1991).[36] Each of these ideas was about "new" indicators or measures of economic and social transformation, about alternative economics.

The idea of human development followed these earlier explorations. The historical origins of the human development idea and its implementation into annual reports has been narrated by Amartya Sen:

The Human Development Reports started being published by the United Nations Development Programme from 1990. The initiation of the approach and the beginning of the annual series of Human Development Reports occurred under the remarkable leadership of Mahbub ul Haq, the great Pakistani economist. Even though Mahbub's primary focus was on the evaluative aspect of the human development approach (he questioned, in particular, the commonly used measures of economic success, such as the gross domestic product, on which so much of the development literature had tended to concentrate), he also had deep interest in the agency aspect. Even as he was hammering home the need to judge progress differently, Mahbub was also scrutinizing the ways and means of enhancing—through commitment and determination—the "life chances" that people enjoy in the miserable world in which we live.[37]

The Human Development Reports (HDRs) drew attention to the poor in ways that were persuasive, ranking countries according to the Human Development Index. During the course of the next twenty years, the HDR engaged in dramatic illustrations of disjunctions.[38] For example, in 1996, the HDR revealed by careful juxtaposition of data that countries that had high and rapidly growing rates of growth of GDP often had a reverse trend in human development and in economic and other disparities.[39]

The *Human Development Report 1995,* subtitled *Gender and human development,* was brought out by the UNDP Human Development Bureau in honor of the UN world conference in Beijing 1995 and was released at the conference. It reported that although gains had been made in women's education, illiterate women still outnumbered illiterate men by two to one. "Poverty has a woman's face," it announced, noting that women's labor force participation had increased by only 4 percent in the previous two decades, women lacked access to credit from formal banking institutions, there were more unemployed women than men in all regions, and women received lower wages than men. The report concluded that "despite considerable progress in developing women's capabilities, their participation in economic and political decision making remains very limited."[40] The 1995 HDR made it clear that the world's women were on two trajectories—as women activists, academics, and policymakers worked to increase knowledge and change policy both in the UN and at home, female poverty was increasing and the quest for equality was proceeding at an excruciatingly slow pace.

The report stirred up widespread interest, especially among those who are preoccupied with disparities. In unfolding discrimination against women worldwide, the report mobilized the women's constituency not only to use it for advocacy work but also to critique it for its inadequacies—both in the framework it used and in the quantities that went into composing the indices.

For example, the 1995 report innovated and developed two special indices for measuring gendered inequality, the GEM (Gender Empowerment Measure) and the GDI (Gender Development Index). The GEM seeks to determine the degree to which women and men participate actively in economic, professional, and political activity and take part in decision-making. This is measured on the basis of indices pertaining to three variables: power over economic resources depicted by per capita income; access to professional activities and participation in economic decision-making based on share of jobs in the professional, technical, managerial, and administrative categories; and political opportunities and decision-making reflected by share of parliamentary seats.

The GEM was criticized because its components were related to characteristics of power more appropriate to the developed countries.[41] The argument was that there would not be professional associations of women or many women in parliament in developing countries; instead, there were other types of organizations such as cooperatives and trade associations that would indicate empowerment. Community organizations and institutions provide corridors of power between classes and structures, and these are not reflected in the North-derived statistics. Also, the GDI was built around per capita income and work participation rates and since these figures were derived from the mainstream male-defined world of work, they also, it was argued, were not accurate measures for the developing countries. The majority of workers in these countries are doing what is called unwaged work, work that is invisible to valuation. Most, if not all, poor women are "workers."

The human development idea, however, was taken forward by the UN through the UNDP and became one of the most visible conscience-keeper tools of the UN. A number of HDRs have been prepared at the global level as well as at regional and national levels and many of them use women or gender as the theme. Because the HDRs describe the situation of the poor with special reference to basic elements of well-being such as health and education, they often influence allocation of resources. They hold up a mirror that reflects injustice, places where the UN's vision of economic and of social justice are not implemented. The HDRs challenge policies that do not reflect or fulfill this vision.

In 1986, the main UN document on women and development (the first *World Survey on the Role of Women in Development*) reflected untested assumptions about the relationship between those two subjects. The 1995 HDR, in contrast, despite its shortcomings, reflected the UN's learning from women's intellectual contributions to development thought. It noted the "fierce questioning" of the dominant development paradigm and stated that "the goal of development must be justice, not charity. . . . Investing in women's capabilities and empowering them to exercise their choices is the surest way to economic development."[42] It incorporated time-use data in its data collection about women's work, pointing out that "if the unpaid contributions by both women and men were recognized, there would be far-reaching consequences for social and economic policy and for social norms and institutions."[43] Its analysis of the quest to land equality for women was sophisticated and nuanced: "There should be no attempt to offer a universal model of gender equality. . . . Each society . . . must debate whether the outcome is what the society really desires or a reflection of structural barriers that ought to be removed."[44] Where nine years before, the UN could only gather disparate strands of data and try to fit the numbers into old models that were no longer relevant, now both the data collection and the analysis were rich and complex. The combination of the institutional resources of the UN and the new knowledge women had produced was powerful and compelling.

Understanding the Contours of the Economy

The Informal Economy

One of the major ideas that appeared in the 1970s and 1980s and then took center stage in the 1990s is the recognition of the value and characteristics of the informal sector. Starting as attention to workers in what was called the unorganized sector—suggesting both that the workers were not organized into unions and that production and trade was unstructured, "informal"—the attention and nomenclature changed to "informal sector," that "loosely defined structure of unorganized, often mobile, diverse, and flexible economic activity that . . . allow[s] casual workers to interact on an occasional basis with the market."[45] However, as the understanding of such economic activities developed and as the proportion of both workers and production and trade activities increased in this zone, this sector of activity gained in attention. Some networks and agencies, including Women in Informal Employment: Globalizing and Organizing (WIEGO), recommend an employment-based definition of the informal sector that would include all nonstandard wage workers who work without a minimum wage, assured work, or benefits, whether they work for formal or informal firms. These groups have begun to use the terms "informal employment" and "informal economy" rather than the term "informal sector."[46]

What was seen in the 1960s as not modern, as work that represented failure and was marginal,[47] was seen in the 1990s as a sector that had untapped development potential, and later concepts have stressed the idea of this sector as an opportunity rather than a failure (especially in the face of stagnating growth and rising unemployment).[48]

The macroeconomic regime—the reigning paradigm of liberalization, privatization, and globalization, or LPG, as several South-based networks call it— also changed the location of employment, the location of some part of production, from the formal to the informal economy. The informal economy became

particularly critical as employers in the formal economy began to shed workers. Retrenched workers were replaced by part-timers, temporary workers, leased
employees, and independent labor contractors, all of which are part of the informal economy.[49] Modern high-earning sectors also adopted outsourcing, or
home-based services, adding to the concentration of workers in the informal
economy. This new group of workers often lost the protection of labor laws. As
attention to the informal economy grew because of the sheer volume of its workers, home-based workers emerged as a significant proportion of workers in the
informal economy in need of study and analysis.

The nature of the expansion in employment opportunities was such that
women began to be preferred as workers in many of the fast-growing sectors of
production and export. A UNICEF study of five Asian countries found that often the job slots that emerge for home-based women workers are a result of the
retrenchment of men from what is called the low end of the production pyra-
mid. Informal occupations provide the livelihood (paid or otherwise) of more
than 80 percent of women in low-income countries and 40 percent of those in
middle-income countries; these countries combined account for 85 percent of
the world's population.[50] The UN (through the ILO and UN Statistical Office)
began to respond to this clustering and to understand the role and scope of the
informal sector.

Measuring the informal sector was difficult, though it was clear that it was
growing in many countries in the face of stagnant or contracting employment
opportunities in both manufacturing and agriculture. In 1991, the ILO focused
on the informal sector at its 14th International Labour Conference; this was the
first time the issue was an explicit agenda item for a major international conference. Labor statisticians at the conference concluded that "the 'economic unit'
was the most appropriate measurement unit for defining the informal sector."[51]

The ILO's 1992 *World Labour Report* estimated that in Asia, while the organized sector grew at 2 percent per year through the 1980s, the urban informal
sector managed 4 percent growth and more, providing between 40 and 66 percent of employment.[52] UNESCO has also published studies that focus on the
informal sector.[53]

In this new era of outsourcing and the rise of the informal labor economy,
women's work as outworkers in the garment industry in India and in the
maquiladoras of Mexico, as pieceworkers in their homes for Nike and Reebok in
Bangladesh and Indonesia, and as part-time workers inspired new responses.
They began to organize as workers to build alternative styles of trade unions;
Mujeres en Solidaridad in Guatemala and the Labor Federation of Independent
Unions in Taiwan are two examples of such unions. These new unions are more
like NGOs and the old craft associations; they are lobbies rather than legally

binding agencies. Women's labor unions sometimes began as cooperatives or associations and then grew into registered unions. SEWA, the trade union of women self-employed workers in India, evolved out of such a process. Other forms of collectivities such as cooperatives emerged to empower workers in the informal economy (K'inal Antzetik in Mexico is a good example).[54]

Conventional trade unions and their leaders felt that these workers did not belong to the working class as traditionally understood and thus that worker protection laws did not apply to them. They were thought to be without skill and without much scope for challenging "social relations of production" as they had no identifiable employer. Further, the feeling was that such workers gave employers a way to circumvent emerging factory laws, an anxiety that was not entirely unfounded. Workers in this sector were paid less than minimum wage, and they were not paid at all when they had no orders. The gendered aspect of the argument was that work at home was usually marginal, that women's work was of lower value, and that such work threatened the work of the male bread-winners. The factory that is the manufacturing center was considered the male domain and the home, the domestic, was seen as the domain of the female.

These perceptions changed, even if slowly, due to many reasons. One, the collection and dissemination of data made the issue of home work visible,[55] revealing the enormous scale of its occurrence. It became apparent that this was not a "fringe" activity. The database also highlighted the complexity of the situation: it revealed that the category called home workers was not homogenous, either in the diversity of the activities its members took up or in terms of categories. The classification system enlarged to include own-account workers and self-employed or unpaid family workers, categories that were not mutually exclusive.

Second, women workers organized themselves. Home-based workers worldwide engaged in a campaign that did much to expand the meaning of the term "worker."[56] An effective lobby of women who were self-employed or home-based workers, HomeNet, emerged that bridged North and South, highly paid information technology workers and low-income street vendors. The lobby led to a new convention, the ILO's Home-Based Workers Convention, which was signed in Geneva in 1996.[57] The convention carefully defined "homework" and "home worker" in ways that included women and defined "employer" in a way that included family members. It specified that signatories agree to national laws that give home workers "equality of treatment," which included equality with other workers regarding the right to organize, protection against discrimination, protection in the fields of occupational safety and health, wages, social security protection, and maternity protection. It also mandated that national statistics had to include home workers. SEWA was prominent in the lobbying process; it suc-

Box 4.1. SEWA Uses the Informal Economy
as a Source of Empowerment

SEWA, which means "service" in most Indian languages but is also an acronym for the Self-Employed Women's Association, is a trade union of economically active poor rural and urban women with a membership of 720,000 spread in six states of India. The organization grew from an idea that suggested itself to poor self-employed women workers in the city of Ahmedabad as a way to collectively bargain with exploitative suppliers of the materials they collected—waste from the textile mills (*chindi,* or rags and fents) or used newspapers (*raddi*) from wholesale vendors to remake into shopping bags. The organization has bloomed and now occupies global space. SEWA members have their own 200,000-member cooperative bank, eighty industrial and service cooperatives, thirteen producers' associations, its own insurance for women's risk coverage, and an academy to prepare organizers, managers, and researchers at the grassroots level. Its most recent and challenging effort is the SEWA Trade Facilitation Centre for artisans and marginal farmers, which accesses and influences local and global markets. SEWA has emerged as a globally recognized voice for poor women and illustrates their power to organize and their capabilities to pull themselves out of poverty.

SEWA's evolution over the last four decades follows the shift in thinking among economists from identifying workers (and a form of production) as unorganized to seeing them as part of the informal economy. The experience has generated innumerable models for designing development with justice across the spectrum—from economic activity to social awakening. SEWA's banking experience reveals the capacity of poor women to finance themselves even as it reveals the exclusion of the poorest from mainstream financial services. SEWA supports street or pavement vendors because city governments and urban planners do not take into account the need of poor people to earn a livelihood. Each aspect of SEWA's activities reveals new insights about how to remove poverty, challenge laws, and deliver service systems. In the process it uncovers perceptions of the poor, hierarchies in valuation, and new ideas about marketing systems and their management. Its core lesson is start with the poor, organize them, and let them move themselves forward. SEWA's method resonates with Gandhi's thought and demonstrates that an idea backed by mass mobilization can transform a situation or a location.

SEWA is the world hub for many movements associated with women workers in poverty zones. It is recognized as the teacher on method by the

ILO, the World Bank, UNIFEM, and many other UN and multilateral agencies. SEWA is a founding partner of many transnational agencies, such as Women's World Banking, DAWN, WIEGO, and HomeNet, to mention only a few. It is also a member of national, regional, and international trade unions and a member of the worldwide women's movement. Its founder, Ela Bhatt, has been recognized nationally and internationally with many awards for her contribution to this revolutionary movement. Bhatt has said, "This vast working population is the biggest, single most significant force in removing poverty, the fact that must not be ignored by any society or Government."

Sources: Jain, Singh, and Chand, *Women's Quest for Power,* 20; Kalima Rose, *Where Women Are Leaders: The SEWA Movement in India* (New Delhi: Vistaar Publications, 1992); Ela Bhatt and Renana Jhabvala, "The Idea of Work," paper prepared for an ILO conference on work, Geneva, 2003; Ela R. Bhatt, "Globalisation and Rural Women: SEWA Experience—A Plea for Non-Violent Reforms," lecture in honor of the Lal Bahadur Shastri National Award for Excellence in Public Administration, Academics and Management, New Delhi, 8 October 2004.

ceeded in gaining the support of the International Union of Food and Allied Workers and the International Confederation of Free Trade Unions. It also helped created bridges between home worker advocacy groups in Europe, Southeast Asia, and Africa.[58] The 1996 convention was the product of an international alliance of women workers and their feminist allies in the ILO.[59]

As deeper understanding and acceptance of the value of the informal economy and women within it emerged, interest moved toward claiming social security for these workers. South Africa floated the idea of the Basic Income Grant in 2001 to fill the gaps in its four-part social security system of voluntary savings, joint contributions by workers and employers, non-contributory benefits, and government relief in crisis situations. It advocated universal provision of a minimum income that would be indexed to the rate of inflation.[60] While new programs are still being negotiated, the problems they face are the same as those of the 1970s: lack of resources, diversion of resources in developing countries to pay for military expenditure, and high-profile infrastructure projects that benefit private capital at the expense of other social sectors.

One of the most significant achievements of the partnership between UN agencies and the outside is the improvement in the understanding of work, of who is a worker. National studies and research efforts made these new definitions much clearer and brought them into the domain of the UN's mainstream. The networking and lobbying of the women's movement furthered this shift in thinking. Studies by the ILO and the FAO helped consolidate the new understandings and definitions.

Convincing international agencies to include women's work in their accounting systems took some time. The concepts of valuing unpaid gainful activity, identifying a woman worker, or recognizing a home as a workplace were new. A great deal was at stake; these ways of quantifying women's contributions to national economies had important policy implications. Home-based workers needed the protection of labor laws. "Marginal" workers who gathered "free" goods such as garbage sorters or gum collectors needed a minimum wage. Women who cared for the sick, the elderly, and infants needed social policies to support them while they did this work. National governments, researchers, and activists and UN specialized agencies and funds such as UNIFEM, the ILO, the UNDP, UNESCO, and the FAO worked on getting this recognition into the design of statistics systems and in work on the ground.

The new attention to this form of work brought visibility to women's economic and social roles. It also challenged traditional dichotomies such as private and public and home and workplace; the new data revealed that such dichotomies are collapsed among poorer households or in certain forms of production and trade. Earlier perceptions that the exploited home worker was located only in the South changed as research made it clear that there were many such workers in the North. In addition, the valuation of such work changed as flexible work and globally competitive wages became visible components of the restructured global economy.

Taming Development

Women brought new understandings of poverty and inequality and the new economic challenges of the decade to the Nairobi women's conference of 1985. The conference changed the worldwide women's movement and its understanding of and its intersection with development debates and practice in a number of significant ways. At Nairobi, the many opportunities to meet and build bridges matured and politicized the women's movement and exposed them more intimately to the politics of global governance. Whereas Copenhagen had been marked by divisions among women in developing and developed countries about what the priorities of the worldwide women's movement should be, at Nairobi, there was "widespread recognition that political issues are women's issues, and that the women's movement is a fundamentally political movement."[61] Margaret Papandreou, the official delegate from Greece, spoke eloquently and persuasively about this issue, asking why the issues of women's reproductive rights or equal pay for equal work were less political than apartheid or the right of a refugee woman to a homeland.[62]

The location of a UN world conference for women in a developing country gave many women from the North experiential knowledge about underdevelopment in general and the impact of structural adjustment in particular. As Margaret Snyder recalls:

> [B]y the time you got to Nairobi ... consensus was possible. For one thing, western women had experienced the economic downturn, so they knew it got in the way of advancement of women in their countries. They also had a chance, meeting in a developing country, to go out in the countryside and meet women who were carrying water, and using new technologies for water, and planting trees—building their nation tree by tree, so to speak. That changed their attitudes.[63]

Another change was the growth of knowledge that incorporated feminist values and focused on women. By 1985, regional networks of women academics and researchers had grown around the world. These included the Association of African Women for Research and Development, the Women and Development Unit of the University of the West Indies in Barbados, the Asian Women's Research and Action Network, the Pacific and Asian Women's Forum, the Indian Association Women's Studies, and so on.[64] The Nairobi conference provided a venue for these networks to share information and form joint platforms. Women's Studies International (WSI) held workshops at the NGO Forum on "Women's Studies as a Strategy for Educational Change," "Theoretical Perspectives in Women's Studies," and "Teaching Methods." Members of WSI saw women's studies as a way to change educational systems to take into account issues such as exploitation and inequality.[65] Other networks did the same, holding workshops and forging a solidarity based on analysis of shared knowledge.

The newly founded DAWN network made its debut at Nairobi and presented a number of panels at the NGO Forum that introduced its alternative development paradigm related to the three sections of their Nairobi document:

- "Gender and Class in Development Experience," about grassroots initiatives
- "Systemic Crises, Reproduction Failures," about the impact of regional macroeconomic issues
- "Alternative Visions, Strategies and Methods," about the way forward[66]

Peggy Antrobus has written of DAWN's contributions at the Nairobi conference:

> With the emergence of DAWN feminists at the NGO Forum at Nairobi in 1985, Third World women found a voice that was to challenge and change the discourse on women and development. By locating women's experience of development in the colonial and neo-colonial context and the macro-economic policies that

reflected this colonial relationship, we introduced an analytical framework that was to change the terms of the debate on women's issue worldwide.... It provided the global women's movement the tools for advancing a different perspective on all development issues, from environment to human rights, from population to poverty.[67]

Thus, the concerns and knowledge about poverty and its links with macroeconomics were exposed at Nairobi and it was established that an "only for women agenda" would not suffice. This was the kind of point that Vida Tomšič and the NAM had been making earlier.

Nairobi also provided a venue for proponents of two quite different models of women and development to enter into dialogue and learn of each other's work. One woman bureaucrat from the U.S. Agency for International Development who had worked to incorporate WID into that agency's development paradigm later recalled the painful experience of realizing that she and her colleagues needed reeducation after Nairobi. "We had to learn to listen to those whom we wanted to assist and to understand how they wanted us to work with them, not for them." She also recalled the powerful impact of DAWN's new paradigm: "[W]omen of the South truly took over the women in development enterprise at the Nairobi world conference on women in 1985."[68]

Thus, there was a sense of unison in not only recognizing the punishing nature of what was being offered as development but also an analysis and a way forward in the project of taming development, of making it friendly through that analysis and the solidarity built across divides at Nairobi.

The Peace Tent was more than a metaphor at the NGO forum in Nairobi. Women in the tent discussed, elaborated, and mobilized opinion about the links between absence of conflict and development. A corollary was also argued— that inequality is often perpetrated by inappropriate development ideas. The tent provided a space for dialogues between Soviet and American women, Palestinian and Israeli women, and women from Iran and Iraq. A large patchwork globe that was mounted outside the tent attracted signatures from women of all continents who agreed with its statement that "as a woman I have no country ... my country is the whole world." The globe was presented to Leticia Shahani, secretary-general of the UN conference, on the closing day of the forum.[69]

The Nairobi conference was a landmark in changing the definition of peace: "Peace includes not only the absence of war, violence and hostilities at the national and international levels but also enjoyment of economic and social justice, equality and the entire range of human rights and fundamental freedoms within society."[70] Eleven paragraphs of the Nairobi Forward-Looking Strategies for the Advancement of Women specifically addressed questions of women and peace.

Several efforts had been made since the 1980s to reveal the gender-differentiated experience of conflict. From the 1980s, the United Nations increasingly took
account of the impact of armed conflict on women as mothers and caregivers.

Women's peace movements brought the issues of women as refugees, women
as targets of the enmity and therefore as victims of rape to the attention of the
UN. They also emphasized the importance of changing the international conventions on war crimes and compensation for the injuries to accommodate this
difference. Some progress was made in responding to these findings by the UN
system.

In 1985, the UN High Commissioner for Refugees organized a Round Table
on Refugee Women, and the Executive Committee, for the first time, adopted a
conclusion highlighting the problems of refugee women.[71] This was the start of
the UNHCR's engagement with the issue of refugee women as a particular group
that needed special attention, which finally led in 1992 to the Guidelines on the
Protection of Refugee Women.[72]

Many other useful responses recognized the gendered experience of conflict.
For example, Security Council resolution 798 of 18 December 1992 referred to
the "massive, organized and systematic detention and rape of women, in particular Muslim women, in Bosnia and Herzegovina." The council established a
Commission of Experts (the Yugoslav Commission) to investigate violations of
international humanitarian law committed in the former Yugoslavia; in its interim report, it listed systematic sexual assault as one of the priority areas in its
ongoing investigations.

Thanks to the Women's Caucus for Gender Justice and the willingness of some
states, the International Criminal Court defines rape, sexual slavery, forced im-
pregnation, forced sterilization, and any other form of sexual violence as war
crimes and grave breaches of the Geneva Convention. The two ad hoc war crime
tribunals, the International Criminal Tribunal for the Former Yugoslavia (ICTY)
in 1992 and the International Criminal Tribunal for Rwanda (ICTR) in 1994,
prompted the international community to include these acts as crimes against
humanity.

In 1995, the UNHCR took note of the problem and issued a set of guidelines
on preventing and responding to sexual violence against refugees. "Much of the
impetus for these trends in international criminal law applicable in armed conflict
can be traced to the women's human rights movement," it wrote.[73] Two UN thematic rapporteurs were appointed with mandates directly concerning the issue
of sexual violence during armed conflict (special rapporteur on systematic rape,
sexual slavery, and slavery-like practices during periods of armed conflict and
special rapporteur on violence against women, its causes, and consequences).[74]

There is certainly a new consciousness about these issues now. Rape by soldiers, especially in occupied territories, was regarded in the past as normal or inevitable. What feminists have done is to make visible the invisible and to make unacceptable what was once considered part of war. By revealing the deeper social injuries of conflict and engaging in dialogue across distance within the peace tent, these efforts of members of the worldwide women's movement in their tent attempted the impossible. They argued that development had to be tamed if peace—and therefore less human cruelty—was to be landed or made a reality.

When the delegates at Nairobi sang, "Woman time a'come," they had no doubts about the strength they had built over the previous ten years. "Yaid better be prepared,"[75] they warned the world, and they lived up to the warning by the energies and exertions they brought to their communities and countries and the world in the next ten years.

Changing Conduits to Power

Conferences, Networks, and Caucuses

In the 1990s, the United Nations sponsored an unprecedented series of world conferences, starting with the World Summit for Children in New York in 1990 and continuing with the Earth Summit in Rio de Janeiro in 1992, the World Conference on Human Rights in Vienna in 1993, the International Conference on Population and Development in Cairo in 1994, the World Summit for Social Development in Copenhagen in 1995, and the Fourth World Conference on Women in Beijing 1995. At each of these conferences, women used new tools and skills to bring issues connected to women and development to the agenda.

While there are many critical assessment of what the conferences actually do in terms of concrete commitment, the documents—including NGO statements— that have emerged from each conference show that a remarkable degree of international agreement has been reached on the norms and values needed to construct a just, peaceful, and sustainable world civilization. The real utility of the conferences lay in the diffusion of knowledge and as "a marketplace for ideas."[76] The lead-up to conferences and the follow-up and post-conference assessments provided momentum for the mobilization of the women constituency and for dialogue, sometimes partnership, and often information-sharing between governments and civil society. These conferences facilitated the birth of new national, regional, and transnational networks over the decade that made conferences tools in women's hands, instruments they used to shape or engineer the agendas to provide platforms for their concerns.

The conferences also brought to light and made visible strong differences among women in terms of location, priorities, class, and race—all the conventional classifications of society, politics, and economics. Often these distances are also part of the overall North-South tensions and disparities. However, women have sustained what can be called strategic, fluid forms of identity, choosing to come together or fall away as required by a strategy on an issue or at a particular place or time to optimize the advantage of the conference spaces. This technique of using multiple identities and coming in as collectives according to the situation is a characteristic of the strategizing of excluded groups. The women's constituency perfected it during this decade through networks, caucuses, and coalitions.

Throughout the UN Decade for Women, women's organizations built networks within and across national boundaries, sharing information and supporting each other's activism. The cluster of conferences that followed "sparked an extraordinary mobilisation of women's groups across borders."[77] Private foundations supported the process with financial resources for the new movements, and the UN provided nodes or poles around which women could organize with its worldwide conferences.

Networks of women emerged during the 1970s and 1980s and into the 1990s. Sara Longwe, director of the African Women's Development and Communication Network (FEMNET) and founder of the Zambian Women's Association, says that it is the UN Women's Decade regional meeting held in Arusha, Tanzania, in October 1984 that helped form FEMNET.

Networking as a conscious form of organizing emerged for many reasons, both pragmatic and value-based. The pragmatic considerations were a recognition that global problems had to be countered on a global scale and that networking improves the effect, visibility, and efficiency of the people involved in advancing a cause.

The strength of these networks lay in their exceptional ability to enhance and deepen critical thinking and creativity through dialogue and exchange, to address global problems by joining forces to take global action, to transcend isolation and strengthen local action, to link local organizing efforts and structures to international ones, to facilitate participation, and to be flexible and respond

---

Box 4.2. Women's Regional Networks

African Women's Development and Communication Network (FEMNET) was set up in 1988 to share information, experiences, ideas, and strategies among African women's NGOs through communications, networking, training, and advocacy to advance women's development and equality and other human rights in Africa. It also aims to provide an infrastructure for and a channel through which these NGOs can reach one another and share information, experiences, and strategies.

Asian Women's Research and Action Network (AWRAN), founded in 1982, is a network of women from ten Asian countries whose goal is to integrate research and action to bring about vital change to women's lives, especially in the grassroots communities of Asia. The organization collects, collates, and disseminates information about research on women throughout Asia.

Association for Women's Rights in Development (AWID) is an international membership organization founded in 1982 that connects, informs, and mobilizes people and organizations committed to achieving gender equality. It works to shape policy on women and development by facilitating debates and by building capacity of those working in the field of women and development.

Association of African Women for Research and Development (AAWORD) was formed in 1977, the first regional institution with the goal of facilitating research by African women on questions of gender and development. Its mission is to build a strong African women's movement by linking women's human rights to the theory and practice of development and to highlight women's contributions to sustainable development. Its role as a space where connections could be made between women-centered research and political and intellectual trends in Africa helped establish women's studies and gender studies on the continent.

Development Alternatives with Women for a New Era (DAWN), founded in 1984, is a feminist network of women, researchers, and activists from the economic South that promotes alternative approaches to development and stimulates coalition-building and platforms for articulating the perspective of poor women. Its goal is to sustain models of development that are people-centered, holistic, and sustainable by serving as a catalyst for debate on key developmental issues.

International Women's Rights Action Watch (IWRAW) was established in 1986 after the Nairobi conference. It monitors implementation of CEDAW. From its early years it has organized seminars for women from UN member states to follow up the juridical process connected with implementation and monitoring of the convention. Today it is a global network of activists, researchers, and organizations that focuses on the advancement of women's human rights.

ISIS International was formed in Geneva in 1974 to serve as a channel for women's voices, strengthen feminist analysis, and support the feminist movement across the globe. It functions as an action-oriented women's resource center by creating solidarity networks and providing information that will help women from various regions of the world overcome gender inequalities.

Women and Development Unit (WAND) was launched in 1978 at the University of West Indies, Barbados, as a link between academics and activists. Over the years, it has worked with government planners, rural women's groups, and NGOs to ensure that development plans benefit women. WAND participants question development models and work to create a macroanalysis that explains political and structural barriers to women's full participation in development.

Women in Informal Employment: Globalizing and Organizing (WIEGO), formed in 1997, is a worldwide coalition of institutions and individuals concerned with improving the status of women in the economy's informal sector. Member organizations include SEWA, Harvard University, and UNIFEM. It strives to improve the status of the informal sector through compiling better statistics, conducting research, and developing programs and policies.

Women's Environment and Development Organization (WEDO) was formed in the early 1990s during the preparatory process for the UN Conference on the Environment and Development. It has developed an effective NGO lobbying strategy that it uses at UN world conferences and it has helped expand NGO activity at those conferences.

Sources: AAWORD Web site at http://www.afard.org/English/In_engl.htm; "About WIEGO: Origins and Mission," available at http://www.wiego.org/textonly/about.shtml; Antrobus, "A Caribbean Journey"; AWID Web site at http://www.awid.org; The Human Rights Databank; Timothy, "Walking on Eggshells at the UN"; FEMNET Web site at http://www.femnet.or.ke/programmes.asp; Pietilä, *Engendering the Global Agenda;* Jain, "The Dawn Movement," in *Routledge International Encyclopaedia of Women,* edited by Chris Kramarae and Dale Spender (New York: Routledge, 2000); Isis— Women's International Cross-Cultural Exchange Web site at http://www.isis.or.ug/about.htm; Pereira, "Between Knowing and Imagining"; Odejide, "Profile of Women's Research and Documentation Centre."

quickly to new and changing situations. Political scientist Peter Haas has analyzed the unique roles networks can play in a society: "Networks of knowledge-
based experts can through their command of knowledge and information play a
fundamental role in helping states identify their interests, framing issues for debate and proposing specific policies and international policy coordination."[78]

There are several examples of networks achieving goals and forwarding agendas at UN conferences. Members of WEDO, a network that formed in preparation for the UN Conference on Environment and Development in Rio in 1992,
used conference skills they had honed in Mexico City, Copenhagen, and Nairobi
to successfully bring women's concerns into the official conference document,
Agenda 21. Before the conference, it set up task forces to analyze the draft of the
original Agenda 21 and compare it with their own document, Women's Agenda
21. By the end of the process of the conference, women's issues were mentioned
hundreds of times in Agenda 21. WEDO used the new tool of the Women's Caucus in Rio, "a bridge between the official deliberations and the parallel NGO
deliberations."[79]

The Global Campaign for Human Rights, which gathered half a million signatures from all over the world for a petition proclaiming that "Women's Rights
Are Human Rights," was able to influence the outcome of the UN conference on
Human Rights held in Vienna in 1993. Charlotte Bunch and Niamh Reilly note
that "[t]he petition is a good illustration of how networking occurs in women's
organisations. At the time the petition was launched there was no women's human rights network, but there were international networks of women's movements that took it up."[80] The campaign was strengthened by regional networks
and various other groups and coalitions, and Bunch and Reilly write that "[t]his
is what networking is all about; utilizing the communications systems that exist
and moving an idea in a way that does not have to have ownership in one place."[81]
The UN conference on human rights provided the impetus for this campaign,
revealing the symbiosis between conferences and networking.

Women used the caucus once again as an effective tool at the prepcoms for
the International Conference on Population and Development in 1994. It provided a vehicle with which other NGOs and networks could ally. At the conference itself, the more experienced Women's Caucus, once again organized by
WEDO, built carefully and methodically on past UN documents to demonstrate
that human rights applied to population policies and programs. Through the
caucus, new groups such as the Women's Alliance were able to gain access to the
conference process. The joint efforts of women's networks and NGOs and the
Women's Caucus successfully created a broad consensus among conference delegates that "economic development and population decline is most effectively
fostered by promoting women's rights."[82]

The 1995 World Summit for Social Development in Copenhagen provided, perhaps for the first time, an opportunity for the convergence of the major people's movements for social and economic rights. Indigenous people, workers, women, the handicapped, minorities and migrant workers, and associations of the poor or their lobbyists made for a melting pot, each politicizing the other toward the larger goal of a right to equitable development. For the first time, the world's leaders and governments committed themselves to the goal of eradicating poverty "as an ethical, social, political and economic imperative. . . . At the highest political level, then, the Summit has assumed the commitment to achieve equality and equity between women and men and to promote a gender perspective in decision-making processes as inherent to more humane development for us all."[83] At the social summit, the women's movement received an education about the politics of development and its link to the politics of rights. The right to development was endorsed by the working classes and other excluded groups, who felt that it was central and superior to human rights as a concept. Issues of collective rights, a political platform of the oppressed, challenged the dominance of the human rights discourse.

Through networking, women learned to define common grounds and work within differences. For example, West European women worked with women of other regions to develop gender perspectives on population issues in a way that attempts "to account for the different interests and ideologies at stake."[84] They learned to go beyond pure opposition to negotiate, argue, and garner political support for their cause. They also made strategic choices about what changes to push for and what to ignore.

New Wings in the Architecture: The UN's Women-Only Spaces

UNIFEM is a small entity within the United Nations, yet it has successfully brokered its resources to emerge as a leader on a number of issues that are important to the worldwide women's movement and as a node around which organizations in the movement can gather to focus their energy. The women's movement is a significant component of its success; having an outside constituency that is fully mobilized and articulate has enabled UNIFEM to both draw on that resource and provide highly visible leadership on the issues it identifies as key.

UNIFEM is an autonomous structure associated with the UNDP, which gives it access to a strong base from which to cultivate donors. It also gives women in developing countries greater access to the fund; they can apply for assistance through any UNDP country office.[85] Although its budget is small compared to the resources of the UNDP, financing for the fund has been relatively solid and has grown over time; between 1978 and 1994, voluntary contributions increased from $4 million to $11 million.[86] UNIFEM used some of this money for projects that later were supported by other UN agencies; in the three-year period 1985–1988, the fund attracted nearly double its own investment to projects to benefit women in developing countries.[87] By 2000, UNIFEM's resources approached $30 million.

In its first fifteen years, UNIFEM operated effectively as a catalyst, funding women's projects that attract other sources of financial support or become self-supporting.[88] UNIFEM's location within the UNDP also gave it access to the network of the program's country offices, more bases from which to reach the women it wanted to collaborate with. During this initial period of its history, UNIFEM took the innovative step of making NGOs the executing agents of funded projects at a time when the larger system focused on its own organizations and on governments. It set up revolving credit funds that generated renewable resources for poor women and their families. It helped design projects of other organizations to benefit both men and women.[89] But more than anything else, it demonstrated women's understanding that poor women are their own agents for change rather than recipients of charity. UNIFEM officials visited women in their home countries to hear their ideas about what changes were needed. As former director Margaret Snyder notes, "We liked to sit under a tree and talk with women to find out their concerns." Building knowledge from the ground up in this way enabled UNIFEM to move from a project-by-project mode of operation into programming.[90]

Since the mid-1990s, UNIFEM has broadened its program. One of its strengths is its close relationship with regional organizations; examples include the South Asian Association for Regional Cooperation, the Economic Community of West African States, the Intergovernmental Authority on Development, and the South African Development Community. Relationships with these organizations are reciprocal: UNIFEM works with them to strengthen their capacity with regard to gender equality and women's rights, and issues that are developing on the ground often filter up to UNIFEM as key issues of focus for the future. Another way that ideas filter up to UNIFEM is through its subregional offices, which act as a network for the women's movement. One subregional office may pick up an idea or model from its region and share it with colleagues in other UNIFEM offices. A good example is UNIFEM's work on women's security issues. Its African Women in Crisis Programme, which supports internally displaced women, is an expansion of work that was begun in East Africa by Laketch Dirasse well before the UN had become engaged with peacebuilding operations of this nature. Her work gave UNIFEM the legitimacy to build a worldwide program on this issue.

UNIFEM also serves as a point of coalescence for the issue of violence against

Table 4.2. Income for UNIFEM, INSTRAW, and UNDP, 1985, 1990, 1995, and 2000 (in U.S. dollars)

	UNIFEM	INSTRAW	UNDP
1985	2.8M	.5M	873M
1990	9.3M[1]	2.3M	1,200M
1995	15.5M	1.3M	1,620M
2000	29.4M	.2M	634M

Note: 1. 1991 figure.

Sources: Yearbook of the United Nations 1985, 1990, 1995, 2000; "INSTRAW's Profile for the New Millennium" (Santo Domingo: INSTRAW, 1998).

women, which concerns the women's movement worldwide. It has built on work begun in networks around the world to bring the work of the movement into the UN's programming through such methods as regional UN interagency campaigns. Its Trust Fund in Support of Actions to Eliminate Violence Against Women, established in 1997, supports projects that work on this issue using funds it raises from governments and private donors. By 2004, the fund had disbursed over $8 million to 175 initiatives in ninety-six countries that work to educate the public about the nature and scope of violence against women and ways to end the behavior. In November 2004, UNIFEM linked the issues of development, peace, and violence against women when it awarded grants to twenty projects addressing gender-based violence in seventeen developing countries in post-conflict situations.

The fund has also responded to globalization by supporting women's networks working on macroeconomic issues and works to ensure that gender is taken into account in the formation of trade policies. For example, it supported the establishment of a new network of nongovernmental organizations called Red Mercosur to work on developing common strategies to advance gender issues and women's rights within the Mercosur trade treaty. The network successfully broadened existing women's NGO alliances to include other actors, such as trade unions and universities. UNIFEM also supports networks that seek greater political participation from women, including support for voter education and training women to be parliamentarians. UNIFEM's Global HIV/AIDS Framework lays the foundation for activities that address empowering women to prevent transmission and mitigate impact.[91]

A UNDP administrator has noted that UNIFEM "punches way above its weight." Although one might wish he had chosen other language, the viewpoint he expresses is accurate. UNIFEM is one of the smallest of the UN funds and programmes, yet it is expected to keep up with its larger counterparts in terms of its influence on UN processes and its delivery of results. UNIFEM's head is at the D-2 level rather than the assistant secretary-general (ASG) level of the UNDP's heads of regional bureaus. As such, she is blocked from attending some decision-making meetings that are open only to those at the ASG level or above. The success of the fund is due largely to the commitment of its staff, its network of subregional offices and connections with regional organizations, and the strong support it receives from the worldwide women's movement.

Like UNIFEM, INSTRAW was set up as an autonomous entity within the UN. However, it has struggled financially almost from the outset. In its first decade, INSTRAW was influential in supporting research on time use and other topics related to collection of data on women's work in the informal sector.[92] It also contributed sections to reports by UNIFEM and the world surveys on the status of women in development. But donors are much more interested in "product" for their investment, and it is difficult to persuade them that research that may change policies on the ground has as much value as concrete programs and projects.

In the mid-1990s, the Secretary-General initiated a program of reform that emphasized consolidation of programs and funds, and INSTRAW was targeted as a vulnerable fund that should be merged with UNIFEM. Neither fund wanted the merger, but financial considerations were the rule of the day. Donors, sensing difficulties, cut funding, and by the mid-1990s INSTRAW was in serious trouble. Its collaborative work with the UN Statistical Office, the ILO, and the ECA to further research on women's contributions in the informal economy became extremely difficult to carry out as it struggled with cuts in staff and lack of essential equipment such as computers.[93] INSTRAW entered what its Board of Trustees called a vicious cycle: "Inadequate levels of funding hindered the sustainability of the Institute's operations, resulting in low level of programme implementation, thereby affecting its ability to attract funds and sufficient human resources."[94]

In 1999, a study by the UN's Joint Inspection Unit recommended that INSTRAW remain a separate fund. Its decision was influenced by its understanding of the value of the research INSTRAW conducts and the support the fund received through the Beijing Platform for Action, which demonstrated "the enormous need for new methodologies in research and training if its strategic objectives are to be fulfilled," particularly in the area of feminization of poverty, which has yet to be accurately measured.[95] INSTRAW now receives minimal funding from the United Nations, but it still must raise the bulk of its funds.[96]

INSTRAW coped with dwindling financial resources during its crisis years by placing a greater emphasis on networking. It now implements a threefold strategy of networking with focal points, regional umbrella organizations of civil society, and ad hoc associations. The Internet has played a role in increasing the institute's outreach; it offers online training packages and courses on capacity-building in gender and development, peacekeeping, forestry, the environment, and promoting gender equality. INSTRAW also provides Web-based training sessions for women on issues such as gender and development, women's reproductive health, and gender and peacekeeping. It is also conducting research on the economic contributions of migrant women through remittances and financing for development.[97] INSTRAW's former director wrote in 1998 that "the need for focused policy research and training on gender relations is greater than ever before," particularly in the context of globalization's threats to the advancement of women.[98]

The diverging stories of these two women's spaces at the UN illustrate the importance of outside support if these small spaces are to succeed. UNIFEM's programming and projects appeal to its constituency of the women's movement because it draws ideas from that source. INSTRAW has worked to fulfill its mandate as well, but it has not enjoyed the strong support of movement organizations. This is partly explained by its location in Santo Domingo rather than New York; distance from the corridors of power has played a role. Its story also speaks to the difficulties of persuading donors and potential supporters of the value of research designed to assist women in developing countries. In the final analysis, though, these two stories illustrate the power of women's networks. One fund thrived because of its immersion in the networks of the worldwide women's movement; UNIFEM's creativity was nurtured and supported by the support of its constituency of women. In contrast, INSTRAW suffered from its lack of access to these networks. The Internet may help it overcome the obstacles to this key component of women's way of working at the UN, and its recent mode of operation points in this direction.

The Mother House: The CSW

During the decade 1985–1995 several changes took place in the ways in which the UN system, especially its international activities as reflected in the General Assembly, committees, and conferences, interacted with the women's constituency. National mechanisms and specially women-focused agencies such as UNIFEM and INSTRAW as well as gender focal points in the various UN agencies actively followed their mandates to bring women into development approaches and programs and the conferences. This enlargement of the official and international space of advocacy for women impinged on the role the CSW had played earlier as the unique official structure for drawing attention to women's concerns and leadership within the UN.

The worldwide women's movement acquired a politically powerful identity at this time not only by participating in the UN world conferences but also by virtue of its increasing skills in dealing with UN procedures and agendas. Movement representatives learned the skills necessary to engage with the UN at each stage of the planning of conferences. They participated at the prepcoms, designed strategy, held caucus meetings, networked about the various agenda items being negotiated in the different committees, and worked as informed lobbyists at the conferences themselves. To some extent, the new strategy of working through conferences seems to have shifted or provided another conduit for influencing ideas, legal initiatives, structures, and policies, at both the international and national levels.

Almost as a necessary outcome, the conduit that had been used in the first two decades, the CSW, began to decline in its role and capacity. The International Women's Decade had given it many new responsibilities without the funding necessary to fulfill them. And with the birth of INSTRAW and UNIFEM, the instruments within the UN for implementing the platforms that emerged from the conferences became more diffuse, especially with regard to women and development.

Several other factors converged to weaken the role of the CSW. As the national mechanisms became stronger within the governments, governments sent their directors or chairpersons to represent them at the world spaces. These persons were typically bureaucrats from within the hierarchies of government who often had little political influence at home or with their country representatives at the UN. They could not wield the influence the early foremothers, who came to the CSW from strong social and political movements, had brought both to the UN and their own governments. In addition, the women's movements had become so self-confident that even within countries there was no strong desire or effort, as there had been in the 1970s and 1980s, to integrate their agendas into the documents and reports that are prepared at the national level toward conferences and that are often conduits used at the conference or to influence national official delegations to the conferences. It was as if the one—the strength of the international women's movement—had to weaken the earlier procedures. Academics, activists, and members of the women's movement ceased to be the people who went to the CSW.

The CSW reached a low point in 1980, when it was suggested that the commission be abolished as part of a restructuring of ECOSOC. But a counterproposal gave the commission the central role in reviewing how well the Nairobi Plan of Action was implemented, and the Copenhagen conference recommended that the commission be strengthened.[99] This was the proposal that passed. But the controversy highlighted an important question: From what direction was change coming? From within the UN or from the external women's movement groups? One thing was clear: the ways that women accessed power within the UN was changing.

Amina Mama acknowledges that the UN has been a good vehicle for bringing feminist concerns to the international arena, but she worries that "UN feminism" has co-opted the more radical voices from the various women's movements. She calls this the "bureaucratized version of feminism spawned by the United Nations" and feels that individuals who represent this kind of feminism are responsible for the "burgeoning development industry" that Africa has been "subjected to."[100]

The institutional architecture for the advancement of women both at the UN and at the national official or governmental level is being reconsidered as the world moves out of 2005. The external or world-level landscape—political, economic, and social/cultural—has changed in the last ten years in particular, and certainly it has changed from the time the national and other focal points for women's advancement were mandated in 1975.

In 2004, an Expert Group Meeting on the Role of National Mechanisms in Promoting Gender Equality and the Empowerment of Women was convened by the Division for the Advancement of Women in preparation for CSW meetings of March 2005. The report from this meeting says:

> While there have been many important achievements over the past decade, many constraints and challenges persist. A large number of those identified in 1995 still remain. Many national machineries still have very unclear mandates and are uncertain about their functions. They are sometimes caught between awareness of the need to work more constructively with gender mainstreaming and influence policy and programme development at national level, and the more concrete demands of local constituencies of women who would like to see the national machinery play a more traditional role and implement projects. Many national machineries lack the support from political leadership which would ensure that their roles and work was taken seriously and that there was real potential for developing collaboration with other parts of the government. In some cases, the political leadership leaves everything relating to women and gender equality to the national machinery, which works against gender mainstreaming.[101]

In section five of their report they continue:

> Transformations in geopolitics and in global and national systems of production and governance, as well as in society and culture that were already underway prior to the 1995 Beijing conference have intensified in the past decade. These have had important implications for gender relations and for the role, issue focus, relevance,

and impact of national mechanisms for gender equality. These changes stem from market liberalization and governance reforms as well as other processes including the HIV/AIDS pandemic, urbanisation, new forms of conflict, increased migration, and new communication and other technologies.[102]

Following this analysis there was a call to restructure the roles and flexibility of these focal points.

These statements about national mechanisms could as well apply to the institutional architecture for women within the UN system. As the practice of having UN world conferences on women declines, and therefore the opportunities for global negotiations through the NGO conduits declines, it is the mother house, the CSW, that perhaps will be the space for the international negotiations once again. As there is an increase in the level and power of women's participation in formal politics—and this phenomena was noticed at the recent expert group meeting—it is likely that delegates to the CSW will once again come from the movements, not the bureaucracies. The ground is shifting under the structures, and what will emerge is still unclear. The next phase of this story further affirms this reopening of new spaces—a challenge for the UN, the worldwide women's movement, and development.

The decade under review revealed many of the dilemmas and disjunctions of women's history with the United Nations, including both the disjunction between the increasing strength of women's voice and the decline in the condition of women at the ground and the increasing spaces for women's advocacy at the world body and doubts about the value of those spaces. While the work that was done in this decade was instrumental in making the UN world conference at Beijing in 1995 a path-breaking event in many ways, the events of the period also foreshadowed the dramatic changes that were about to emerge, both in global governance and in people's responses to those changes.

5

Lessons from the UN's Sixth Decade, 1996–2005

> *"The main thing of the powerless is to have a dream,"*
> *[Aunt Habiba] often told me while I was watching the stairs,*
> *so that she could embroider a fabulous one-winged green bird*
> *on the clandestine mrema she kept hidden in the darkest corner*
> *of her room. "True, a dream alone, without the bargaining*
> *power to go with it, does not transform the world or make the*
> *walls vanish, but it does help you keep a hold of dignity."*
> —Fatema Mernissi[1]

- **Poverty and Inequality Strike the Globe**
- **Beijing**
- **Women within the UN**
- **Full Circle: From "Gender" to "Women"**
- **Thinking for the Future: The Way Forward?**

By the turn of the century, the harsh impact of structural adjustment policies had greatly increased inequality around the globe. The convergence of militarization, globalization, and conservatism has dealt a blow to the progress that was made at the UN on the social justice front and changed political configurations in ways that have hampered its ability to respond to the crisis. These changes revealed the fragility of the gains made in the arenas of women's rights and development policy and practice, especially in the period 1985–1995. The UN's responses to the growing crisis, such as its advocacy of microcredit for poor women and the Millennium Development Goals, have been unable to address the root causes of poverty and its attendant problems.

However, there has been progress in several areas. The gendering of various dimensions related to the theaters of war culminated in the now-famous Security Council resolution 1325 on women, peace, and security, which was a first for women.[2] There has also been a shift in the location of the energy of the women's movement from global to regional and national spaces. The momentum generated by the significant conferences and development of networks in the previous decade has continued at the national and even local levels.

The period also ushered in the beginnings of what can be called the political maturing of the women's movement. Because the worldwide women's movement had established its political identity over the previous decades through its effective participation in world arenas, it has become possible for that movement to engage with other social and political movements with a strong sense of self.

While the women's movement has gained in strength and confidence, women at UN headquarters in New York, its Secretariat, where policy is set, ideas are generated, and data is gathered and analyzed, remain largely excluded from the corridors of power, despite some modest progress. Perhaps in response to their small numbers, women have adopted mainstreaming as a strategy to access resources at the world body.

The way forward in the new political context is not clear. Yet this review of sixty years of history suggests some possible strategies and offers signs of hope from recent developments on the ground. Despite the challenges and disappointments of recent years, women's journey with the United Nations on development issues is by no means over.

Poverty and Inequality Strike the Globe

The reflections that emerged at the end of the millennium were accompanied by a number of studies and surveys by UN organizations and other sources. These studies continued the bad news of the previous decade: inequality was growing, poor people had even less access to economic markets, and gender parity was absent in governments. Traditional economics was unable to account for these changes.

The harsh and unequal impact of poverty on women and men is affirmed in many sources. UNIFEM's *Progress of the World's Women* report for 2000 noted that although many obstacles to women's employment had crumbled, women in Sub-Saharan Africa and Eastern Europe faced deteriorating economic conditions; many lived in nations facing increased indebtedness, which is often correlated with lower rates of schooling for girls, and household income inequality increased across a wide range of countries in both developed and developing nations. These trends suggest that "poor women have not enjoyed much of the fruits of any progress."[3]

The Department of Economic and Social Affair's *World's Women 2000* noted higher rates of unemployment for women than for men and a higher proportion of women than men in the informal economy. The report found that women spend more time doing unpaid work and less time earning money for their labor than men. It suggested that "assets controlled by women have a more positive and significant effect on expenditures for children, such as education and clothing, than those controlled by men."[4]

UNESCO's 2000 *World Culture Report* emphasized inequality of access to resources, political power, information, and the media. Such inequalities impact people's capacity to make choices, which is the true capability to exercise rights. The report underscores the fact that women often experience unequal access because of barriers linked to or attributed to cultural practices.[5]

An FAO review concluded that rural women are primary victims of hunger and poverty despite the fact that they are crucial partners in combating these problems and achieving global food security. It concluded that "the most disadvantaged population in the world today comprises rural women in developing countries, who have been the last to benefit—or [are] negatively affected by— prevailing economic growth and development processes. Gender bias and blindness persist; farmers are still generally perceived as 'male' by policy-makers, development planners and agricultural service deliverers."[6]

But perhaps the most important survey on the topic of women and development during this period was the Division for the Advancement of Women's 1999 *World Survey on the Role of Women in Development*. It focused on the most urgent issues of the day: globalization, gender, and work. In contrast to much of development policy of this time, the survey focused on the central issue of employment. This was a position women in developing countries supported. The survey focused on the changing nature of the labor markets and the feminization of labor, providing support to UN constituencies such as the ILO that were trying to understand ways to circumvent the harmful effects of globalization. Its strongest contribution, however, is the endorsement it gave to the findings of feminist economists around the world that macroeconomics is not gender neutral and has gender-asymmetric effects. Its recommendations advanced from a general concern for engendering macroeconomics to specific interventions in the design of international measures regarding trade policy and core labor standards. It recommends the stabilization of capital flows and coordination of global economic demand as measures to protect and enhance the value of women's labor.[7]

In 1993, the General Assembly passed a resolution on the "First United Nations Decade for the Eradication of Poverty" that recognized that "poverty is a complex and multi-dimensional problem with origins in both the national and international dimensions and that its eradication in all countries, in particular in developing countries, has become one of the priority development objectives for the 1990s in order to promote sustainable development." In 1996, the assembly resolved that 1997–2006 would be the First United Nations Decade for the Eradication of Poverty.

Soon after the proclamation, the Commission on Human Rights appointed A.-M. Lizin as an independent expert on the question of extreme poverty and human rights. She submitted two reports, the first in 1999 and the second in 2000.[8] Her reports make a strong case for linking rights to extreme poverty; they see extreme poverty as a violation of human rights:

> Poverty hits women especially hard and leads to serious violation of their rights. Extreme poverty is linked to prostitution and exploitation, both sexual and physical, of young girls and women. . . .
>
> Deep poverty can exclude people from society, placing them in an illegal situation in their own country. Such people perceive social service or police intervention as actions they cannot appeal, since justice is by and large out of their reach. Society should see the poor as people who are capable of thinking, reflecting and having something to say about poverty, the world and human rights. A better understanding of poverty and better policies to eradicate it can be developed only by understanding the poor themselves and therefore by working in partnership with them.[9]

Her analysis of extreme poverty and its gendered aspects was forward looking, resonating with Sen's analysis of capabilities and entitlements and the concept of human security, all ideas that have since taken center stage.[10]

The effects of extreme poverty on women were so severe that the WHO's *International Classification of Diseases* gave it its own disease code:

> The "world's most ruthless killer" is coded as Z59.5. It has meant widening gaps between rich and poor, between one population group and another, between age groups and *between the sexes*. It has caused more suffering to more people than anything else on earth. And it has got worse over the last ten years. Despite improvements in education and health, for hundreds of millions of women, Z59.5 has meant lives lived closer to the edge than before. Beneath the rhetoric of "post-feminism" and "equality between the sexes" lies another, more sinister, phenomenon.[11]

In the face of such a lethal enemy, women in poverty zones crafted strategies to enable them and their families to survive. Gradually, the central role of women in fighting poverty, not just experiencing it in cruel unequal ways, was recognized. In 2000, the International Fund for Agricultural Development emphasized in its Lending Policies and Criteria that "the group deserving more particular attention is poor rural women, who are the most significant suppliers of family labour and efficient managers of household food security."[12] Several

challenges to current analysis and initiatives appeared as a response to the interest in poverty and especially women in poverty. For the UN, other development
agencies, and member governments, microcredit and the informal economy took
center stage in the economic domain.[13] Combating violence against women became the common agenda in the social sector domain. In the political domain, it
could be suggested that women drew politics to themselves: empowerment, leadership, devolution of power in structures, and deepening democracy, became
the lead themes.

The UN's Response: Microcredit for Poor Women

From the early 1970s, women's movements in a number of countries identified
credit as a major constraint on women's ability to earn an income. Since women
did not own assets that could be used as collateral, banks were unwilling to provide credit to them. Collective savings or thrift societies have long been a part of
women's traditions worldwide across culture and class. Groups and agencies that
lobby for women and development began to take note of the Kautaha system in
Tonga in the Pacific,[14] the Peruvian Kitchens,[15] and the informal credit funds of
the market women of Ghana.[16] The culture of women became a resource that
provided a solution; women formed groups to access group collateral and bank
credit was provided. This economic tool took a great leap forward into visibility
in this era. By the 1980s, microfinance institutions had emerged such as the
Grameen Bank and Americans for Community Co-operation in Other Nations
(ACCION) that specifically target impoverished people. By the 1990s, the evidence clearly showed that women had a higher rate of repayment than almost
any other population. The growing influence of gender lobbies within donor
agencies and NGOs led these institutions to place a greater emphasis on targeting women in their microfinance programs.

Microcredit for women was enthusiastically welcomed by the UN and women's
groups. It seemed to be a solution that would give women the resources they
needed to build livelihoods. Yet studies soon demonstrated that even this solution was tainted by patriarchal relations within the household.[17]

Microcredit for women dovetailed nicely with the UN's new understanding
of the importance of the informal economy. Policymakers had come to realize
that both in terms of the total number of workers and in terms of the volume
and value of the goods and services workers provided, the informal economy,
where women predominated, was the core rather than the periphery of many
national economies.[18] Microcredit became the way to place poor women on the
"economic superhighway"—as if this one intervention could provide the good
life for women living in poverty. This intervention was often used instead of

projects designed to create jobs or interventions that put social-welfare grants or social security provisions in place for women. This was a definite shift in policy; before globalization and the reemergence of the outwork system, the goals of the main interventions on behalf of workers in the informal economy were to protect their legal rights and use moral arguments as the basis for minimum wage legislation.

Converting a traditional practice among women to a state- and bank-led program became high on the agenda of the UN agencies; health agendas or other human welfare elements were often added to these projects. This was a throwback to the 1980s approach to women and development that stressed income generation as the goal of development projects and added human development elements to that model. Microcredit as a poverty removal program fit neatly into the paradigm of financial self-sustainability that is currently dominant at most donor agencies and in the models of microfinance promoted in publications by the USAID, the World Bank, the UNDP, the World Bank's Consultative Group to Assist the Poor, and the international NGO Microcredit Summit Campaign.[19]

The approach also fits into the privatization and nongrant approach to poverty removal, which stresses linking the poor to capital markets. This model assumes that increasing women's access to microfinance services will in itself lead to individual economic empowerment, well-being, and social and political empowerment. However, research and evaluations reveal that such assumptions need to be challenged. Anne Marie Goetz and Rina Sen Gupta show that in South Asia, a high proportion of individual loans targeted toward women are co-opted by men. Even where women do gain greater access to resources, they may do so at the expense of increases in their burden of labor, leaving them exhausted.[20] Judith Bruce shows that men may reduce their levels of contribution to household expenditure as women's access to resources increases.[21] In other words, when women have access to and control over resources, they may not always be able to effectively mobilize these resources to support sustainable livelihoods. Women may feel compelled to invest resources, including their labor, in "family" businesses or in their children, identifying their own interests with those of other household members and leaving themselves vulnerable in the event that their family breaks down.

Despite these problems with the microcredit model, the momentum behind the idea, which was triggered by the realities of coping with the power of globalization, led to a Micro-Credit Summit in 1997 as a culmination of a global movement.

The very first of the UN's Millennium Development Goals is the eradication of extreme poverty. But challenging the disparities and inequalities at all lev-

Box 5.1. Microcredit as Salvation for Poor Women?

In the 1990s, major lending institutions launched a global movement to extend microcredit to 100 million of the world's poorest families, especially the women of those families, for self-employment and other financial and business services by the year 2005.

The World Bank had already launched a Consultative Group to Assist the Poor with a $200 million microfinance fund in 1995. The UN Development Program said it would expand its services with a $31 million program, "MicroStart," to be funded jointly with donor nations. The Inter-American Development Bank said it would invest $400 million in microfinance over five years. The U.S. Agency for International Development allocated $120 million a year for microcredit in 1996 and 1997. And Hillary Rodham Clinton, the honorary co-chair of the 1997 Micro-Credit Summit, said that the president's current budget would include $1 billion to be spent over five years on community development banking in the U.S.

From a banker's point of view, microcredit has been a success. Pioneered by SEWA and the Grameen Bank, the strategy of making small loans to self-employed women has grown from the first loan of $1.50 to an herb seller to loans to over 3 million borrowers; 90 percent of the loans are repaid in full. From a development point of view, the picture is less clear. As WEDO points out, microcredit by itself cannot undo the larger structures that put women in poverty, and it cannot overcome the overpowering force of globalization on national economies. Nor does it undo gender-based discrimination that has been practiced for centuries. WEDO's president, Bella Abzug, urged attendees at the summit to take further steps to empower women seeking microcredit: "I ask you to back the borrower-knows-best principle and resist the temptation to think you know best. . . . I ask you to support women as owners, entrepreneurs, shareholders, board members and decision-makers on all levels—not target women or treat them as mere 'beneficiaries.'"

Source: "Micro-Credit Summit Convened for Macro-Changes in Poor Communities," *WEDO News&Views,* June 1997, available online at http://www.wedo.org/news/June97/micro.htm.

els—global, national, and local—is not the central goal. The document took refuge behind the argument that the persistence of poverty, conflicts, and violence and the concomitant throwbacks to conservatism and violations of human rights were the reality on the ground and that governments and their "networks," namely the UN, were no longer at the helm of world affairs.

Despite so much knowledge and analysis of the damage being caused at all levels and in all spheres—political, economic, and social—by growth-led development with strong doses of liberalization, the ruling paradigm, the order, could not be dislodged. The connection between knowledge, analysis, and action was not made—perhaps could not be made. The UN's decision to choose poverty removal as a focus was like bandaging a wound after inflicting the injury, an approach that recalled the debates during the peak of the structural adjustment experience. At that time, in order to cope with the "strong medicine" administered to developing countries, safety nets were advised to pick up dislocated people, and "bad governance," including human rights violations, was named as the reason the patient could not recover. No matter what the academic critique of structural adjustment was, no matter how cogent the analysis within the UN of national struggles under structural adjustment programs and their havoc-causing consequences, it could not be undone.[22] The modernization project could not be budged.

Several analysts linked these trends to the neoliberal economic paradigm. Shahra Razavi, writing for the UN Research Institute for Social Development (UNRISD), suggests that "the consolidation of a market-led development model denies vast groups of women the opportunity to claim entitlements and achieve more secure livelihoods." Macroeconomic decision-making remains "particularly resistant to feminist incursions." One finding that emerged from the UNRISD research is "the tendency for women to be confined to the less lucrative segments of the non-farm sector, in the form of survivalist strategies, which do not offer good long-term prospects."[23] Economist Diane Elson pointed to the shrinking of public dialogue on macroeconomic policy. "Macro-economic policy is constructed in neoclassical economics as something beyond social dialogue and public debate." She adds, "Technocratic calculation has become independent of democratic deliberation."[24]

Beijing

Many Voices Speak

The Beijing World Conference on Women took place after fifteen years of structural adjustment had wreaked havoc in the lives of women around the world.

The trade liberalization policies of the Washington Consensus had taken their toll on the economies of many developing countries. The conference was an unusual combination of celebration of the success of the worldwide women's movement and a rising undertone of protest about the economic damage women in both the North and the South were forced to cope with.

After two decades of learning and growing, the women's movement had reached a political maturity evident at Beijing in its ability to accommodate difference, articulate clear goals and policies for national governments and the UN, and speak to the world about its agenda for change. With 6,000 delegates from member states, more than 4,000 representatives of accredited NGOs, and 30,000 participants at the NGO Forum, it was the largest UN conference to date.[25] The Beijing Declaration and Platform for Action consolidated and expanded concepts of women's human rights and "moved the global agenda for the advancement of women into the twenty-first century and beyond."[26] UNIFEM's director Noeleen Heyzer notes the professionalism and intense commitment of tens of thousands of women who participated in the preparatory committee meetings: "If you think about 50,000 who went to Beijing you could almost triple that number for the preparatory process. What was being generated was political will."[27]

Beijing is well known for its inclusion of women's NGOs, and the NGO Forum was the largest ever. At the NGO space there was a vivid demonstration of the movement's expertise, specialization, and capacity to disseminate and network that had become a feature of women's gatherings. Publications, campaigns, demonstrations (both against and for issues) from regions as well as special interests kept the "camp" throbbing. It was a feast of knowledge and power. Women's NGOs brought contributions that integrated macroeconomics, geopolitics, spiritual beliefs, and life experience.

Delegates to the NGO Forum, Deborah Stienstra notes, felt that "after much of the lobbying around governmental texts had been done, non-governmental representatives still felt that more needed to be said about what their alternative vision of the world was."[28] Anticipating that the formal conference document would not reflect their views, they had gathered a month before the conference to begin drafting their own declaration. They continued the process at the conference, and after three days of intensive consultation they delivered the NGO Beijing Declaration.

The NGO declaration noted that "the globalization of the world's so-called 'market economies' is a root cause of the increasing feminization of poverty everywhere. This violates human rights and dignity, the integrity of our ecosystems and the environment, and poses serious threats to our health." It called for cancellation of multilateral debt, sustainable and ecologically sound development, recognition and implementation of the agendas of people's movements, and expansion of the definition of intellectual property rights to make indigenous women the primary beneficiaries of the commercial use of their knowledge. It asked governments to keep their commitments to measure women's unwaged work and include it as a contribution to GDP in national accounts. It offered a South-based model of women and development:

> Dominant development models have been based upon the appropriation of resources from the South by the North and the transfer of ideas, technologies and methodologies from the North to the South. We must build upon alternative models that currently exist in both South and North, which are based on equality, mutual respect, true participation and accountability to all women. These models must be economically and socially equitable and environmentally sound. All development projects must take into account their effects on women, including the additional workload imposed on women by unsustainable and inappropriate technology.[29]

Many indigenous women contributed to this document, bringing a worldview that integrates spiritual belief and life practice. Melalini Trask, who was involved in the drafting of the NGO declaration, writes: "Women, all females, are a manifestation of Mother Earth in human form. . . . The new world order, which is engineered by those who have abused and raped Mother Earth, colonized, marginalized and discriminated against us, is being imposed on us viciously. This is re-colonization coming under the name of globalization and trade liberalization."[30] Indigenous women see violence against women in a much larger frame than the individual rights–based frame of the Beijing Platform for Action. Victoria Tauli Corpuz, a convener of the Asian Indigenous Network, notes that "a key lesson from Beijing is that the struggle for women's rights must be conducted in the context of fighting at the same time against the inequities between nations, classes and races."[31] The women in the NGO Forum offered a sophisticated and nuanced understanding of women's development while the larger conference was still in the stage of understanding and defining the problems.

Women used other means to express their views. From day two of the conference until the final day, a large group of NGOs led by Latin American women took over the central escalators in the conference center. They held placards that read "Justicia Economica Ya!" ["Economic Justice Now!"] and chanted "Jus-tice!" "Jus-tice!"[32] Virginia Vargas, the Latin American and Caribbean NGO coordinator for the NGO Forum, used most of the time allotted to her to stand before the governmental plenary in silence. The banner she unfurled spoke volumes: "Transparency—New Resources—Economic Justice."[33]

Such views were taken into account at the conference, but not at the deep analytical level its articulators had hoped. Charlotte Bunch, Mallika Dutt, and Susana Fried note that "the Beijing Platform does acknowledge the negative impact of structural adjustment policies and calls for recognition that women's unwaged work constitutes a large percentage of national economies. But no effort was made to address the causes of these problems and governments remain engaged in practices that perpetuate them."[34]

In many ways, the Beijing conference was the culmination of a journey begun in 1975. It brought all the elements of the diversity that was increasingly represented at the world venues, yet it represented the unity of women when they met the Other, namely the state and unjust regimes, including economic regimes. It also was the end of a process. It had developed an agenda that could stay with the nations and the movements for some time because it was so comprehensive. The momentum that was built up prior to the conference from countries and regions was so strong that it carried Beijing home. As with all celebrations of an apex, there can be no real repeat of that performance. Nor need there be, as the ways in which the worldwide women's movement now needs to mobilize itself and participate in challenging new empires needs to change and is changing even as this book is being written.

Changing Women's Relationship to Power

Throughout the preparatory process for Beijing, Gertrude Mongella, the secretary-general for the conference, spoke of the need to move from analysis to action. At the conference, a consensus was reached that enough is enough, that women had done enough speaking, enough offering of ideas on how to overcome the oppression of discrimination. There was an almost universal or palpable desire to be in power, to be in leadership, to change the terms of the relationship with the great globe; the mode of operation shifted from one of stating demands and needs to one of seeking control over the decision-making process. There was optimism about this strategy, a belief that women would bring new values to public decision-making. A 1991 UN expert group meeting on women and public life had concluded that women did in fact bring different values to the public arena, including a concern for justice and the ethical dimensions of politics, an awareness of the need for consensus, and a concern for future generations.[35]

Since 1995, the proportion of women in sixteen countries has reached that benchmark of 30 percent or more that the UN has set as the critical mass where women can have an impact on policymaking. This is not insignificant; Amina Mama points out that numbers are extremely important when it comes to political power:

> It has become clear that without further measures, the still modest increase in the number of women does not translate into qualitative changes in the institutions

themselves, or in the services they deliver. Nor is it proving enough to overcome the male domination of policy and decision-making. The numerical representation remains at the stipulated target level, and over time is easily subverted, especially in the absence of any definable women's constituency. In multi-party systems, women are divided across parties, and during elections, the vote is simply rigged to favour women who will uphold the interests of the competing parties, rather than pursuing gender interests.[36]

Women have just begun to enter the mainstream of formal decision-making; yet table 5.1 indicates that they are meeting with some success, albeit with regional differences. The proportion of women in legislatures and parliaments reached a high of 14.8 percent in 1988, only to drop to 11.7 percent in 1997, a figure the Division for the Advancement of Women noted was far too close to a situation in which "women are regarded at best as a 'special-interest group' rather than half of humankind."[37] Now, in 2004, the worldwide figure is 15.6 percent.[38] It would seem that women are slowly gaining ground in their quest for formal power. Yet only the Nordic region has reached the 30 percent considered to be the threshold that moves women from a special-interest group into a political force to be reckoned with.

Some governments have instituted affirmative action policies to bring women into formal politics as a response to Beijing. African nations are experimenting with gender quotas and minimum thresholds. In Uganda, for example, the pro-

Table 5.1. Regional Averages of Women in World Parliaments, 1994, 2000, 2004

	November 1994[1]	November 2000[2]	October 2004[3]
Nordic Countries	35.9	38.8	39.7
Americas	12.5	15.6	18.6
Europe[4]	11.5	13.8	16.4
Asia	13.2	14.9	15.1
Sub-Saharan Africa	10.8	12.5	14.4
Pacific	12.7	13.6	12.5
Arab States	3.6	3.6	6.9

Notes: 1. 10 November.
2. 15 November.
3. 30 October.
4. Organisation for Security and Co-Operation in Europe member countries, excluding Nordic countries.

Source: Inter-Parliamentary Union, "Women in International Parliaments," available at
http://www.ipu.org/wmn-e/world.htm.

Box 5.2. The Critical Mass of 30 Percent

The introduction of the concept of critical mass and the setting of the target level was a result of work by the Division for the Advancement of Women of the UN Secretariat. A number of scholars had begun to speak of the need to reach a "critical mass" of women in decision-making groups. . . .

In the mid-1970s, an American feminist scholar did a study of the incidence of women in business, looking for sex-based differences. She reviewed studies of the behavior of minorities in task-oriented groups to find out what level of participation was necessary for the minority members to function effectively as a group to press their interests. The scholar estimated that when the proportion of minority members reached about 30 percent, they were able to influence decision-making by pressing their own interests. At levels lower than that, if the minority members were to be effective, they had to act more like those of the majority. If they were not successful using this approach, they were reduced to the status of ineffective dissenters.

The argument was that the critical mass phenomenon could apply to politics as well. The concept of critical mass, however, circulated only in feminist scholarly circles. It was not part of the debate at either national or international levels in terms of public policy. It fell to the UN Secretariat's DAW to bring the information into the policy debate. In the UN's statistical publications on advancement of women, the norm of 30 percent was used as an indicator of progress, including in *The World's Women: Trends and Statistics* and its 1995 update.

Source: John Mathiason, "UN Secretariat: The Gatekeepers of Ideas," in *Beijing! UN Fourth World Conference on Women,* 196–198.

---

portion of women members of parliament has increased from 18 percent in 1993 to 25 percent in 2003 and women are taking up leadership roles at the national and regional levels.[39] The experience of Central and Eastern European countries after transition to market systems suggest that affirmative action may be a crucial component of women's access to political power. Before transition, these countries had quotas for many categories of representation, including gender. The quotas did not survive the transition, and women's participation in legislatures dropped from 22 percent in 1987 to 6.5 percent in 1993.[40]

In a number of countries, there is a trend to devolve government into locally elected agencies, creating new opportunities for women to enter formal political spaces. For example, a study of India's decentralization of development administration, ushered in with the 73rd and 74th amendments to the Constitution in 1993, found that political restructuring led to deepening of representation.[41] Positive discrimination, or affirmative action, resulted in 3 million men and women coming into elected local governance overnight, of whom one million were women and another half a million were members of social categories who have been historically subjected to caste and other forms of domination. The proximity of elected government gave a strong handle to excluded groups to participate and hold the state accountable. It also brought them into formal avenues of power. The value of local councils was flagged much earlier in various countries where localization of government had begun prior to 1995: China (1949), the Philippines (1991), and Bangladesh (1959).[42]

At Beijing, the link was made between mainstream politics and the content of economic policy. Participants recognized that if economics has gone wrong and fitted itself in favor of the rich, it was because of too little, rather than too much, politics. The long journey of the women's movement and analysis of past strategies led to a goal that women must occupy at least one-third of formal political spaces. It could be argued that carrying forward this idea was both an example of bringing national experience to international agendas and a furthering of ideas that had long been nurtured and put forward by the women's movement.[43] The Inter-Parliamentary Union, which emphasizes the importance of accountability, a feature of elected governments and democratic processes, was a strong presence at the conference. It emphasized the need to reconsider the power of technocratic decision-making, as different from political decision-making.

Women within the UN

A Chilly Climate

While women on the outside were transitioning into the quest for formal power, women within the UN struggled to move into decision-making roles within the world body. The issue of gender equity in the UN's promotion practices has been a topic on the agenda for decades. In 1974, the General Assembly set the goal of achieving an "equitable balance" of men and women within the UN by 1980. In 1985, the Nairobi Forward-Looking Strategies set 2000 as the year when there would be "participation of women on equal terms" at the UN.[44] Reform seems always just around the corner. Yet in 1993, legal scholar Hilary Charlesworth wrote about the "almost perfect absence of women from senior

> ### Box 5.3. The Inter-Parliamentary Union Promotes
> ### Women's Political Power
>
> A key international organization that is working to bring more women into political power is the Inter-Parliamentary Union (IPU), which houses the Meeting of Women MPs. Nineteen percent of its members are women parliamentarians. The IPU has adopted the strategy of mainstreaming women's issues; thus women members enjoy both their own separate space and the institutionalization of women's issues. The union's Programme for Partnership Between Men and Women provides assistance to new democracies to ensure that women play a role in creating the political institutions of their countries.
>
> In 1995, the IPU drafted a "Plan of Action to Correct Present Imbalances in the Participation of Men and Women in Political Life" as its contribution to the Beijing conference. The Plan of Action talks about two interwoven concepts: parity—the idea that persons of one or the other sex are different but equal, and partnership—the idea that a "creative synergy" can be crafted between men and women to tackle community problems.
>
> The IPU conducts studies for the UN on the proportion of women in politics worldwide, and it holds seminars and symposiums to discuss ways of changing the imbalance of women in political positions. Women participate in the IPU at all levels, and the organization feels that if they were absent, it would undermine its credibility and legitimacy. However, the IPU recognizes that a great deal needs to be done to bring women into political power. In 1945, women were 3 percent of parliamentarians worldwide; in 2000, that number had grown to 13 percent. Change is happening, but much more needs to be done.
>
> *Source:* Inter-Parliamentary Union, "Women's Movement at the IPU: 1945–2000," available from the IPU, Geneva, Switzerland.

levels of decision-making within the United Nations." Efforts to change this situation have proceeded over the decades, but the rate of progress has been glacial, as Charlesworth puts it. Women did not advance to the level of under-secretary-general until the late 1980s, and the percentage of women at that level has not increased in over a decade. Although the percentage of women in middle management positions has slowly increased over the years, the number is still far from the 50 percent that would represent gender equity (see table 5.2).[45]

Table 5.2. Women in the Secretariat of the United Nations, 1950, 1976, 1985, 1995, and 2004 (by number and percent total grade)

	1950		1976		1985		1995		2004	
	n	%	n	%	n	%	n	%	n	%
USG	—	—	—	—	—	—	2	10.0	6	26.0
ASG	9	50.0	1	5.0	4	13.3	2	14.3	8	38.0
D-2	1	6.6	2	2.5	3	3.3	14	19.4	22	30.0[1]
D-1	0	0.0	9	4.5	22	8.5	39	17.2	89	41.0
P-5	10	3.9	47	9.7	43	7.5	136	28.3	161	34.0
P-4	85	14.7	130	14.4	166	20.1	234	33.7	298	41.0
P-3	226	42.9	248	24.7	260	32.1	250	39.7	319	49.0
P-2	NA	NA	213	34.5	199	43.9	180	47.6	184	51.0
P-1	NA	NA	49	48.0	14	54.3	0	0.0	—	—

Notes: P-1 and P-2 are entry-level grades; P-3 and P-4 are journeyman grades; P-5 and D-1 correspond to middle management; D-2 corresponds to senior management. ASG is assistant secretary-general; USG is under-secretary-general.

1. In recent years, the Secretariat has experienced what some call "grade creep," such that D-1 professionals now function largely in the same decision-making roles as ASGs.

Sources: Report of the Secretary-General to the CSW on the Participation of Women in the Work of the United Nations, ECOSOC document E/CN.6/132, 16 March 1950, in *The United Nations and the Advancement of Women,* 137; Szalai and Croke, "Women on the Professional Staff and at Decision-Making Levels of the United Nations System: 1971-1976," 2:29; *Report of the Secretary-General on Improvement of the Status of Women in the Secretariat,* GA document A/C.5/40/30, 8 November 1985; *Report of the Secretary-General to the General Assembly on Improvement of the Status of Women in the Secretariat,* GA document A/50/691, 27 October 1995, in *The United Nations and the Advancement of Women,* 736; *Improvement of the Status of Women in the United Nations System: A Verbal Report in Response to General Assembly Resolution 59/164 of 20 December 2004,* Item 3(A) of the Provisional Agenda, CSW, Forty-Ninth Session, 28 February–11 March 2005.

The slow pace of change may be explained by three aspects of the UN bureaucracy. First, member states nominate candidates for secretariat posts. Informal networks of support from which women are often excluded operate to nominate men; in 1993, forty-nine states failed to nominate women to posts. This may be due in part to the small numbers of women in levels of government that would prepare them for such positions, but regional differences may play a part as well. Member states in Africa, the Middle East, and Eastern Europe were far less likely to appoint women than states from other regions.[46]

Second, the principle of equitable geographical distribution—the idea that secretariat posts should be filled with representatives from member states based on the size of overall membership at the UN, assessed contributions of member states, and population of member states—sometimes works against women candidates. A highly qualified woman from a member state that is oversubscribed according to the UN's complex calculus for geographical distribution will probably lose out to a male candidate from a member state that is undersubscribed.[47] In 1992, Suzan Habachy, focal point for women in the Secretariat, noted that some member states preferred to forgo filling a post if it was attached to the requirement that they nominate a woman: "If there must be a woman, a country risks not having *anyone in the Secretariat.*"[48]

Finally, UN reform agendas sometimes work against advancement of women. The Nairobi Forward-Looking Strategies recommended that governments appoint more women as diplomats and to decision-making posts within the United Nations system; 159 governments agreed to these goals. Yet one year later, the UN initiated a reform package designed to cut costs in the face of pressure to downsize its overall budget from the United States. Hiring freezes in upper-level positions ensued, and women's opportunities for advancement decreased. Margaret Galey points out that the goals of these two reform efforts were in some sense incompatible: the UN reform effort was motivated by efficiency and cost-cutting, while the goals of the Forward-Looking Strategies were shaped by a desire for equity and justice.[49]

Yet these structural factors do not fully explain the chilly climate for women at the UN. Over the decades, women have shared stories of discrimination and patronization that sound remarkably consistent. Claire de Hedervary, who worked in the Secretariat in the 1960s and 1970s, remarked in the early 1980s that "the ingenuity of men [at the UN] in finding excuses for not recruiting and promoting women is truly impressive and is not unlike that of a child who can give a hundred reasons for not eating spinach."[50] Margaret Snyder, director of UNIFEM in the 1980s and early 1990s, recalls a meeting with a UNDP official in which she explained to him the conceptual framework UNIFEM had arrived at to help it make decisions about which projects to fund. The official responded, "But Ms. Snyder, you're not supposed to conceptualize."[51] After her retirement, a former under-secretary-general revealed how hostile he had been toward the establishment of UNIFEM as a permanent fund.[52] And Kristen Timothy writes about the sexual harassment women at the UN have been subjected to. There was no institutional mechanism for filing a sexual harassment grievance at the UN until 1992.[53]

Mainstreaming

The consensus at Beijing that women must claim formal power to directly shape public policy led to a new strategy and idea called mainstreaming gender. ECOSOC offered a definition of mainstreaming in 1997, describing it as

the process of assessing the implication for women and men of any planned action, including legislation, policies or programs, in any area and at all levels. It is a strategy for making the concerns and experiences of women as well as of men an integral part of the design, implementation, monitoring and evaluation of policies and programs in all political, economic and societal spheres, so that women and men benefit equally, and inequality is not perpetuated.[54]

Mainstreaming has many meanings, but all revolve around the idea that women's contributions, ideas, and knowledge should enter into decision-making and policymaking. It can mean embedding gender concerns in a program or making women's concerns visible in public debates. It is seen as a method of linking women to the bigger, better-resourced, and more powerful arenas of thought and action.

The mainstreaming project became the new idea at the UN. It has been taken on board by the UNDP, UNIFEM, the FAO, the Division for the Advancement of Women, and many other UN entities. This is in part a measure of the political capital women have built up over the decades through the international conferences; when the consensus at Beijing was that mainstreaming was the necessary departure, the UN listened.[55]

Yet even in the earliest days of mainstreaming some warning flags were raised. Shahra Razavi and Carol Miller at UNRISD noted in 1995 that mainstreaming was much more than a new rhetoric; it required substantial commitments of human resources from staff with expertise on gender issues and much time for training—changing the mindset of the individuals that comprise an entire institution requires more than one training seminar. As one donor agency noted, "A few days of training is barely a beginning for an officer who wishes to become competent in gender analysis."[56] But after an extensive study of three UN bodies—the ILO, the UNDP, and the World Bank—Razavi and Miller concluded that very little work on women in development was taking place "beyond the small circle of staff directly responsible for WID/gender work." They asked how far limited WID resources should be spread across an organization—"Where should the balance lie between diffusing responsibility and strengthening existing WID capacity?"—noting that mainstreaming had increased staff awareness of gender issues at the expense of strengthening in-house WID/gender expertise.[57]

Another question that might be asked is what tangible resources the mainstreaming strategy is able to claim. Since mainstreaming has taken hold of almost every UN agency, program, or fund, it has been extremely difficult to follow the money designated for women. Funds are folded into every project and budget—they are mainstreamed—such that no one at the UN really knows how much money is being dedicated to women's work at the world body. A recent study by outside experts is tracing funds through the UN's byzantine accounting system to yield answers to such questions.[58]

At the turn of the century, at the special session of the UN General Assembly also called Beijing +5, the debate seemed to suggest both disappointment that the mainstream structures still needed pressure to take notice of women and their concerns and some fatigue as well as anger at having to maintain a separate identity after so much energy had been expended, collective lobbying had been done, knowledge had been uncovered to show the value of understanding women's "difference."

Given the small proportion of women at the UN in posts that carry the status and weight of expertise necessary to influence policy or even gain respect from colleagues in training sessions, it is unlikely that the UN's strategy of using women as experts in gender analysis will yield the transformation of consciousness at the world body necessary to ensure that all policy—development or otherwise—is scrutinized to ensure that differential impacts on women are understood and accounted for.

Encountering the Wall

Despite the valuable intellectual contributions women brought to development thought at the UN and strong efforts by the Division for the Advancement of Women and the Office of the Special Advisor on Gender Issues to promote gender equality, women remain a largely marginalized group within the world body—a ghetto. A 2000 report of the UN's Inter-Agency Committee on Women and Gender Equality (IACWGE) concluded that little attention is paid to gender equality concerns in the program budget process at the world body, although the ILO is seen as an example of good practice.[59] After studying twenty-seven UN entities, the report pointed to a failure to integrate gender fully into all mechanisms, a lack of data disaggregated by sex, and a lack of willingness to see the relevance of gender dimensions to poverty. It also noted that while many UN agencies had included planning and budgets for gender mainstreaming, such efforts had not been successful, largely due to a lack of understanding of what terms such as "gender mainstreaming" and "gender equity" mean in practice.[60]

The main conclusion of a Division for the Advancement of Women assessment of the system-wide medium-term plan for the period 1996–2001 was that while considerable progress had been made (particularly in the twelve critical areas of the Beijing Platform for Action) and policy commitments had been achieved, obstacles to progress remain, including the absence of strategic planning and channels of communication, lack of consistent commitment and compliance with the gender mainstreaming strategy, uneven understanding of gender as a concept and of the implications of gender factors, and lack of willingness to see relevance of gender dimensions to issues such as poverty and AIDS.[61]

Policymaking Success

Despite their struggles in other areas of encounter with the UN, women have enjoyed remarkable success in the areas of peace and treatment of women in wartime. During this decade a number of issues relating to women in wartime emerged as areas of concern: rape of women as a weapon, the woman's body as a site of war, and the special needs of women refugees, many of whom care for children. The value of this "gendering" of war zones becomes clear when it is placed against the fact that wars, armed conflicts, the production and sale of small arms and other weapons, and military expenditures boomed in this period.

Women achieved some notable victories in the war zone. For example, after the conflict in Rwanda and Burundi, the UN set up the International Criminal Tribunal for Rwanda in Arusha, Tanzania, to try the war crimes in 1994. This tribunal broke many barriers and boundaries in the legal framework for dealing with war crimes; it took into account and responded to the gendered aspects of conflict such as rape and set the standard for offering judicial services to those afflicted and the knowledge base about what was happening and why to women in conflict zones.[62] In a related development, the advocacy groups established for the International Criminal Court at its birth in 1998 included more women and more-advanced concepts of justice.[63]

The ad hoc International Criminal Tribunal for the former Yugoslavia, established in 1992, is another example of operational success in mainstreaming women's rights. But the tribunals continued to compile a mixed record on investigations and prosecutions of crimes of sexual violence that occurred in the period to which they relate. It was only in February 2001 that the ICTY issued a landmark verdict for rape, torture, and sexual enslavement, holding that rape and enslavement rose to the level of crimes against humanity in the Bosnian town of Foca.

The landmark Akayesu verdict of 1998 was the first and only case as yet in which rape was held to be an act of genocide. The ICTR has pronounced several more indictments for rape. In some cases, however, the rape count was added only belatedly, typically when witnesses alluded to rape and sexual violence while testifying in court, raising serious questions about the competence of those in charge of investigations and their capacity to draft indictments.[64]

But the landmark achievement of the decade for women peace workers, resolution 1325, came about through the efforts of UNIFEM. It could be suggested that this resolution set things right. For the first time, gender was included in the deliberations of the Security Council. The resolution legally requires member states to take up a large number of initiatives to increase participation of women at all levels and stages of the peacemaking process. With this resolution, the Security Council moved from a "gender-neutral" body to one that is committed to work for women's involvement at all levels of conflict prevention and peacekeeping. These include involving women's NGOs and women in official roles in negotiations to make peace and the implementation of peacebuilding, a recognition of the fact that women clearly have the capacity to participate in and direct these activities.[65]

As always, the victory is not fully satisfactory—for example, the resolution does not set any quotas for the number of women and there are no fixed time schedules. Some areas are rather ambiguous; it is not clearly spelled out how "gender perspectives" will actually be incorporated into field operations. However, it notes that effective monitoring and evaluation (by NGOs, UN agencies, and governments) is critical for the implementation of its recommendations— a recognition of women's work in creating a coalition of NGOs, headed by International Alert, that has launched an international campaign to promote women's participation in peacebuilding.

Gender Peace Audits have been launched as a way to bridge this gap between policy and practice and to ensure that resolution 1325 can be used as a tool to support the peacebuilding activities of women. Local organizations will play an important role to see if "the peacebuilding and security programmes are gender-sensitive and responsive to women's needs." Georgia (South Caucasus), Nigeria (West Africa), and Nepal (South Asia) were chosen for the first phase of the Gender Peace Audit.[66]

Resolution 1325 also specified that a study be carried out on the impact of armed conflict on women and girls, the role of women in peacebuilding, and the gender dimensions of the peace processes and conflict resolution. This study was under way in March 2002. To complement this process, UNIFEM appointed two independent experts, Ellen Johnson Sirleaf and Elisabeth Rehn, in August 2002 to do a field-based assessment on the impact of armed conflict on women and women's role in peacebuilding. Their principal findings and recommendations echo concerns that in areas of prevention, formal negotiations, peace operations, and disarmament, demobilization, and reintegration (DDR), women are still excluded and that "a gender perspective is not sufficiently incorporated."[67] It is also disturbing to note that codes of conduct were at times violated by peacekeepers and other humanitarian personnel. While progress is being made, it is necessary to broaden the focus and reexamine the issue of security. UN veteran Margaret Anstee says that because of the close relationship between development and security, the latter "is much more than a military or purely physical concept. Security embraces the whole question of the basic welfare of human beings. Nobody can be considered to have security if they don't have enough to eat, or they don't have access to basic needs."[68] The Canadian International Development Agency notes that it is necessary for women to move from analysis and creating methodological tools to political leadership: "investments in advocacy and resources are required to act on what has been learned and to use the tools that are increasingly available."[69]

In the midst of this highly conflict- and war-ridden landscape, violence against women (VAW) emerged as an all-too-vivid phenomena that cut across all nations, classes, and cultures and thus offered a focus around which women could mobilize across differences and multiple identities. Information was pouring in that from theaters of war to the home, women were experiencing physical and psychological injury in rapidly growing numbers.

Initially the discussions about violence against women, even at the CSW, were framed in terms of domestic violence and violence involving specific categories of women, such as women detainees and refugee women. It was viewed as a private matter between individuals that the state or international effort could do little about. The concerted efforts of the women's movement and the Nairobi Forward-Looking Strategies changed this perception; they pointed out that violence against women "exists in various forms in everyday life in all societies" and urged governments to take measures against such violence.[70] Women broadened the definition of violence against women to include the sale of girls, trafficking in women, and sex-selective abortion to eliminate the female fetus. VAW became a unifying platform for women's advocacy and action around the world.

The regions held conferences on VAW in preparation for Beijing +5. For example, the Southern African Development Community had a regional conference on VAW in 1998 attended by the chief justices of countries of the region and researchers, activists, and officials. One of the conclusions was that the only agencies that were really dealing with victims of violence were women's organizations, yet they received very little support from the state.[71] A widespread commitment emerged to address and overpower this specific violation; participants included UNIFEM, the CSW, the South Asian Association for Regional Cooperation, and domestic and international research agencies (for example, the International Centre for Research on Women).[72] This was one of the best examples of women's mobilization around a UN issue since the first UN conference on women in 1975, which provided a framework for advancement of this concern.[73]

Thus, whether it was in the economic domain, as in poverty, or in the social domain, as in trafficking in women or violence against women, the link with human rights, the understanding that all these were violations of basic human rights was understood and adopted as a priority on the women's agenda, both outside and inside the UN system. These linkages have entered mainstream thought at the UN; in its Millennium Report, it says "the cycle of violence begins with cultures that glorify violence and warrior virtues, and may be manifest in domestic violence."[74] Conflict has been linked to economics, both in terms of control over scarce or crucial resources and in terms of disparities in access to economic benefits of development. Although the issue of violence against women does not directly confront economic inequality at local and international levels, it is an issue on which some consensus can emerge when it is placed in a broader frame; women have always bonded across all divisions for the cause of peace.

Full Circle: From "Gender" to "Women"

Many movements within countries and the worldwide women's movement started with the use of the term "women" as the form of identity for its political endeavors, moving to "gender" as a necessary analytical tool for understanding inequality, discrimination, and subordination.

By the Beijing conference, a unified political will and greater fragmentation had simultaneously emerged within the movement. Multiple identities, diversity, and questions of difference had overwritten the earlier simplistic identity of "woman" or "the feminine."[75] The concept of gender, which played a valuable role in showing that the analysis of female subordination within various realms of the development experience was complex, was distracting or muting the political identity of "woman." Feminist thought had not produced an alternative definition; by the 1990s many feminisms had developed. The feminist ethic of emphasizing participation and democracy, inclusion, and multiple identities offered a space for such flowering but the setback of the emergence of a strong right-wing presence at the Beijing +5 conferences added to concern about the loss of a political identity.[76]

Some argued that gender as a term and an analytical tool had played a significant role, but the time had come to revert to the identity "woman" and reclaim its politics. While affirmation of diversity was the trend, there was also concern that a unifying thread needs to be used to keep the momentum of a global actor. Many UN agencies were eliciting suggestions for pegs on which some form of solidarity in the international women's movement could be hung.

Vanessa Griffen, coordinator of the gender program at the UN Asia Pacific Development Centre, warned that gender as a category of analysis could lead to strategies that were too conciliatory to males in power:

> The shift from tackling women's oppression under patriarchy (i.e. feminism) to a focus on gender equality as a development issue (i.e. gender mainstreaming and gender sensitivity) has been a cause of concern for some feminists because it has de-politicized the struggle for women's rights. Others argue that gender main-

streaming now in fact merely returns to the WID approach of "add women and stir." The question is whether "gender" is diverting the feminist agenda, which essentially is to resist women's subordination and patriarchal institutions. By focusing on gender concepts of equality, some perceive a move away from women's resistance to patriarchy and away from feminist concepts of transformation of social institutions to ensure women's rights and empowerment.[77]

Now the movement seems to be considering returning to "woman" or "feminine." In 1997, Sally Baden and Anne Marie Goetz wrote

> It is hard to find space in contemporary feminist theory for the genuine sense of connection *as women* of which so many women spoke in Huairou and Beijing, yet it seems dishonest not to bear testimony to the palpable sense of commonality in spite of great differences. . . . If we still find meaning in shared biology only because the world continues to behave and treat women as though this is their primary defining characteristic, this does not erase its meaningfulness as a point of connection among women.[78]

An expression of this full circle is the fact that the most unified visible theme on the international agenda agreed between international agencies and national agencies—be it the UN, the World Bank, the Commonwealth, or the national and regional women's networks—is violence against women.

It could be suggested that this became the focus both of UN events and agencies, a universally unifying issue, because it crosses all barriers of class, location, race, and other dividing characteristics. But it calls attention again to women's bodies, which ultimately become the core substance of identity. Therefore, in one sense, the choice of this pole represents the cycle of a shift from showing difference between men and women to showing difference and diversity among women to embracing gender—a social construct—now moving forward to the woman identity, the old word "woman" with which the movement started.

Thinking for the Future: The Way Forward?

By the turn of the new century, ground had shifted for each of the three groups in this book—the worldwide women's movement, the UN, and development thinkers and policymakers. The women's movement had gone from its first intoxicating coalescence in the mid-1970s through a period of learning to appreciate and value difference in the 1980s to an explosion of new identities—as workers, as women, as thinkers, as activists—by the 1990s. The growing pains of the movement had yielded valuable new insights about the valuation of women and their work and ways to use this knowledge to craft new models of development. The locus of creativity and new thought about development had shifted from North to South. The UN had often been a willing partner in the new intellectual explorations, incorporating women's knowledge and expertise into its survey methodology, its measurement tools, and its policymaking. Yet as deeply as some UN structures absorbed these new ideas, they did not permeate the consciousness of the world body. Despite great leaps forward in intellection about development that moved women from the periphery to the center, that began to see them as the holders of solutions to global problems, the poverty of the world's women increased and intensified. It seems the time has come to take a step back and ask some larger questions about why this is so.

Two clear lines of women's ideation have emerged or revealed themselves. One is the provisioning of knowledge, both in content and in source. This contribution included new methods of knowledge creation, a resistance to boxing or ironcladding ideas into unbudgeable theories. This knowledge emerges from lived experience and learning and building from the ground—local thinking. The other thread is method, which in some ways is also part of the creation of knowledge, namely women's strategizing, uniting across traditional differences in order to assert their collective political will, using their own spaces or the place of one's own to develop the strength of unity, even if temporarily, as well as expanding and transforming the spaces that were set up by the UN or development discourse. Women have managed these two pathways, balancing on stilts, an art they are still practicing after sixty years.

Another revelation is that over the past sixty years, two trajectories relative to women and development indicating oppositional trends have emerged. The first trajectory is the emergence of a strong political presence in the global scene of the worldwide women's movement. There is now a widespread consciousness of the necessity of engaging in gendered analysis that recognizes both difference and inequality and its implications for development design. The other trajectory reveals that the situation on the ground for many women, especially those living in poverty and in conflict-ridden situations, seems to have worsened, despite the fact that it has been addressed specifically by both the UN and development thought.

The question that arises then is why does this disjunction exist after sixty years of what appears to be a vibrant and ostensibly effective partnership between the UN and the women's movement? How much of the oppositional trajectories can be attributed to the external atmospherics of global power politics and its attendant economics? How much can be attributed to other factors, such as the style of functioning and priorities of the worldwide women's movement or its experience of the gendered institutional architecture in both the UNs, the UN as secretariat and the UN as states? What are the spaces, the ideas, and the issues that can mobilize these agencies? What can bring into reality the old/new mandates of the UN and of development to remove poverty, inequality, and injustice?

The very beginning of women's quest was for equality or for overpowering, if not effacing, inequality. The strategy of leveling the playing fields by bringing in laws, introducing the power of rights, and finding ways to move women out of what looked like disadvantaged positions seemed all right for several decades. But it was clearly not enough. There was deep, widespread, unimaginable, and invisible discrimination. The women's movement responded to this by making inequality visible and by crafting the most comprehensive and brilliant convention to move society and the state to weed it out. But that did not take care of the ignorance and invisibility of women's value as citizens, workers, providers who are equal if not even richer in value than men. So the movement generated new knowledge to show the role of women in development—again with the expectation that revealing truth would lead to women's equality with men. But that strategy still disabled them because they had no voice in the determination of their lives and its road map. Thus, the notion of equal participation, of equal power, of leadership was worked into the notions of ways to redress inequality. So the unpeeling of the layers of inequality goes on, and it is a blot on the humanscape that inequality is now on the increase across all divides.

The United Nations

The United Nations is widely seen as the institution that embodies the collective conscience of the world. It remains the only forum in which a global women's movement might engage governments in relation to agendas in which they are heavily invested.[79] Yet the United Nations and its agencies and programs are facing a threat that is not only financial but political. The power landscape is changing drastically in many parts of the world, and many countries are struggling to safeguard their borders and their sovereignty. Implementation of development programs, even though their content may have been designed carefully and sensitively within a human rights framework, is likely to face many difficulties.

Arms of the UN such as UNIFEM with the unique ability to access both governments and civil society have facilitated women's organizing and voice and strategizing, and they have provided intellectual leadership. UN conferences have produced outcomes that women can take home as a mandate for change. But there is widespread recognition of the limitations and dangers of giving priority to another UN conference. Bisi Adeleye-Fayemi, executive director of the African Women's Development Fund, notes that the movement cannot rely on a "UN space that [has] benefited us every now and then." She notes the need to find mechanisms that will enable women "to push agendas which would take us along for the next 20 to 30 years."[80]

Yet the entire world of nations and peoples, especially the excluded and those suffering under various types of injustice, need the United Nations, the inter-governmental body of equals. There are many suggestions for how to redesign the institutional architecture of the UN to enable it to perform its mandated role. In this revisiting and rethinking process, there is a need to introduce the experience of gendered architecture as it has been conceived and has operated in the last sixty years. This review points to the fact that women's special agencies that were set up both as international agencies and as national machineries have suffered from marginalization, ghettoization, and the demeaning gaze that ex-cluded peoples and women have experienced at all societal levels worldwide. Even in such difficult circumstances, these agencies have also been torchbearers within the systems.

The Worldwide Women's Movement

In the years 2000 to 2005, there have been many collective reflections by var-ied configurations of the worldwide women's movement about what went wrong. These include meetings hosted by AWID and DAWN and the regional confer-ences of AAWORD. Reflections emerged at the Conference of NGOs at Beijing +5 at the UN in New York. The conference noted the stark contrast between eventful and "successful" UN conferences on women, on the one hand, and the grim picture of the situation of women and children in many parts of the world, on the other. The conversations that took place at this conference led to other gatherings dedicated to this issue.

One such reflection took place in Kampala in 2002 on the sidelines of the World Women's Congress, a biennial activity of women scholars of the women studies networks.[81] At this meeting, participants from diverse regions identified the situation and what needs to be done. For example, Bisi Adeleye-Fayemi said, "The critical difference is that there are now more human agencies. Two decades ago, there were women feeling helpless and hopeless. Now there are women in every community who are prepared to take the agendas forward." Adeleye-Fayemi feels that the next step is for "women at all levels within Africa and outside of Africa [to] critically engage with the state." Eudine Barriteau, head of the Center for Gender and Development Studies at the University of the West Indies, Bar-bados, brings another view of the state, suggesting that "the states have become so powerless that they really cannot refuse the IMF, the World Bank, and so on. There is a real encroachment on their sovereignty."

The state as a site of contestation has been one of the problematiques in the intellectual journey of feminist analysis. The difficulty is related to women's ex-perience with power as it has been conceived and exercised historically.[82] Power has been related to force and oppression, and formal politics has often been seen

as derived from that notion of power. However, by the time women's long journey across world conferences and conventions brought them to Beijing in 1995,
there seemed to be a universally accepted view that the time for putting forward
agendas for consideration was over. There was an affirmation of the importance
of entering politics, an arena formerly conceived of as the polluted stream to
which the response invariably was *nethi nethi*. This was a shift in the thinking;
earlier the question had been "Who wants to sit at that table?" Now the thinking
was "Let us sit at the table but change its structure, its meaning, and its method."
Women in the Inter-Parliamentary Union have already done significant groundwork for this new focus and have knowledge to share.

Debates and considerations are taking place about how to reinvent the "table."[83]
Simultaneously there is a concern that language that had seemed to enable
women's quest for justice and dignity, namely empowerment and mainstreaming,
has "turned hostile," to use the language of the courts, where if a witness turns
hostile the intended outcome gets reversed. Mainstreaming as an idea has had a
contested journey and diverse outcomes. Its operational values have depended
on specific circumstances of method. It has often been trivialized, co-opted to
the exclusion of those special women's spaces, those powerhouses. Empowerment is often stripped of the realpolitik of power. The language, like gendering,
has become a mask, and thus the noise that women have arrived or that now
gender is central in UN policymaking (as claimed in the UN's *1999 World Survey*) clouds the reality. This masking of ground-level realities by the sense of
achievement suggested by adoption of feminist language could be part of the
explanation for the downswing in women's condition.

Independently, the women's movement is questioning itself to understand
the phenomena of losing ground both at the UN conferences and in the reality
on the ground. Some of the analysis suggests that the fragmentation of society, a
larger social phenomena that has emerged paradoxically alongside globalization, has also injured the capacity to form a united collective political will from
the identity "women."[84]

But the one task that seems crucial to reclaiming the power of identity that
was inscribed in the early years of the UN is the forging of a unity over the
fragmented identities—to accommodate women's commitment to diversity and
pluralism and democracy within a collective political will and intellectual argument with the world.

Development

Development has perhaps suffered the most of the three areas of focus in this
book. Its earlier avatar as an enabling hand, an alternative to economistic nar-

rowness, something associated with support for the less privileged or less endowed, has been co-opted into the neoliberal paradigm. The UN's arrangements with the corporate sector, euphemistically called "partnerships" in the Global Compact; its accommodation of privatization of public goods, even the basic amenities; and the quest for financing for nonprofit activities has changed the face of what was once a benign idea. The earlier incarnation of development is now not identifiable except in the Human Development Reports, which keep reminding the world of its need to make human well-being central to all effort. The march of globalization as well as the overarching power of the rich countries in forums such as the World Trade Organization and the inability of the idea of development as it is constructed within economic theory to deal with these forces suggests that as an idea it can be abandoned.

What seems to emerge out of this narration of informed energetic—and often ineffective—struggles is that many aspects of the existing approaches to understanding poverty, inequality, and development must be rethought, reconceptualized, and restated if they are to provide due recognition of the roles and expectations of women. Given the recent affirmation that the number of poor are increasing and the proportion of women within that group is increasing, it seems clear that the engines of economic growth in operation today are inappropriate for achieving the kind of growth that reflects the spirit of the UN Charter. It is time to reconsider the underpinnings of the theories of growth and the goals of the trade regimes.

The first need is to reconsider the paradigm of development itself, the identification of the engines of growth. Instead of seeing the poor as a target group who need special ladders within a framework of economic development, enabling them to become economic and political agents could itself become the engine of growth. Thus, from a "trickle down," or social safety net approach, it would be useful to look at what can be called the "bubbling up" theory of growth. This alternative theory argues that putting incomes and political power in the hands of the poor could generate the demand and the voice that would direct development. The purchasing power and the choices of the poor could direct the economy to a pro-poor or poverty-reducing economy. The review of the past seems to suggest some dramatic reversal of the current theories of where the engine of growth lies if the interest is in poverty eradication.[85]

Mahatma Gandhi in fact had designed such a theory and a proposal for its practice. To some extent it could even be said that such a theory is close to, though not the same as, Keynes's theory of stimulating an economy by generating effective demand. Here the further detailing is: Whose effective demand? Whose purchasing power? Gandhi's talisman, his test for action, was this: "Whenever you are in doubt, or when the self becomes too much with you, apply the following test: Recall the face of the poorest and the weakest man/woman whom you may have seen and ask yourself if the step you contemplate is going to be of any use to him."[86]

If the Millennium Development Goals are to achieve their object of poverty removal, even in 2020 if not 2015, then trade ideas need to have economic models that optimize employment or freedom from hunger as their goals. In other words, economic growth patterns and their operations need to be crafted afresh rather than by tinkering with development models.

In the current global context of increasing disparities, dreadful pandemics such as AIDS and the widespread recognition of the scourges of persistent hunger and unemployment all seem to converge in women's location in poverty. It seems crucial to make a quantum leap in ideation to fulfill women's aspirations and struggles for justice. Thus, the argument of this book is to suggest that new insights into how to redress this unacceptable situation have to come from women. The revelatory aspect of this story can be summarized in the importance of space for the excluded to claim their rights and the need to upturn hierarchies of local and global, of the intellect and action. Those on the ground know what ideas will help; peoples' movements around the globe suggest that it is time to invert the power hierarchy suggested in the axiom "Think globally, act locally." It is time to act globally in solidarity with local brilliance—to think locally and act globally.

Nethi nethi has been a useful tool in women's hands. We know what we do not want, what does not work. We must continue to use it until we reach the goal of removing the poverty that hurts women and children so much.

What Does the Future Hold?

This attempt to capture the engagement of a lively and continuously moving struggle for emancipation with a deeply structured and layered global agency dedicated to equality and justice reveals that the dialogue between the UN and the constituency it sought to serve has been inconclusive. The history contained in this volume is one of many views of the same history, many stories within old stories.

A major fault line that runs through narrations of history and their knowledge base—whether it is political, economic, or social history, and thus not only this one related to the UN—is the failure to take note of, to understand and respect and absorb, women's ideational and intellectual skills and outputs in the area of theoretical and analytical knowledge. While some of the values emerging from the understanding of poverty, inequality, discrimination, conflict resolution, deepening participation, method, and politics that this interaction or partnership generated have been applied or followed on belatedly, recognition of the intellectual and leadership powers of women has remained in the ghettos. The *minds of men* have not changed.

Men's rejection of women's intellect reflects hierarchies more dramatically than all the other hierarchies that have been mentioned in previous chapters. The turning away from giving recognition to women, their understanding of phenomena, their challenging of the basis of knowledge and their claim to be recognized, hinges on how women are valued, and hierarchies of value are embedded everywhere in the knowledge base. Unless that valuation of woman is budged, knocked down, the web of inequality in which women are caught may not quite tear.

The worldwide women's movement has not been able to become that political presence that can command attention to its ideas. This broad-based, globally mobilized, revolutionary collectivity that could heal and rebuild a scarred planet has not been able to play its role, become that political presence that could encash its intellectual achievements in the name of justice. The sky sometimes looks like it is falling down over women, and other times it looks as if, like poor Sisyphus, women keep pushing up the large stone, exclusively and endlessly, without breaking the spell.

The wall, the unchanged minds of men, is not a sufficient explanation in itself for this harmful and frustrating situation. Part of the reason for the failure of the extraordinary momentum of the 1980s and 1990s to reach that next stage of development is the restlessness of the women's movement.[87] For instance, any valorization of the identity "woman" is labeled essentialism or is placed in a political context as the "white feminist agenda," the Other who sets one agenda when there are many agendas because of the diverse conditions and stratifications of the constituency. Such namings and placings almost immediately put away such aspirations of unity as untenable and unwanted. Other differences—of location, race, class, sexuality, religion—have at times been emphasized at the expense of the commonalities within the movement that can build strength to move forward.

This knocking away of every attempt to build unity has been one of the most difficult bridges to cross. It has blocked the capability of the constituency of women to strike back at the empire—not just the empire as notified in the recent coalitions at the World Social Forums but the multifaceted empire that includes the other dominations within the metadomination of economic models and forces.[88]

Reports of the experience of women and their intersections with other global resistance coalitions from the World Social Forum meeting in Mumbai in January 2004 provide a close-up of the wall, the impenetrable power domains held by men and conventional political ideas.[89] It also reveals that there is work to be done to break out of this impasse. There are hopeful signs. New coalitions of people's movements, which first began at the World Summit for Social Development in 1995, have taken off, and coalitions to show power, to voice collective protest have in some sense replaced or superseded NGOs in terms of visibility and mobilization. And women's movements are allying themselves, albeit with difficulties, with these broad-based protests.

Yet even as they move into new and unfamiliar alliances in the mainstream, women have insisted on their own tent, the women's tent, already a traditional element of world gatherings, including the World Social Forum spaces. This is an overt acknowledgment that women need their own space—*as women*—to share experiences, work through conflict, build new strategies for change, create a solidarity based on their common experiences of being the excluded. And the experience of exclusion can quickly be turned into a celebration of difference, an enjoyment of the richness of culture that women create for and with each other—a feast. How women choose to use the space of their tent is the determining factor—Can they use it to expand their territory? Or will it become an isolated ghetto? These are not idle questions. The women's tent is much more than an architectural structure, however temporary and movable. It is a symbol of the dilemma women have always faced—To be or not to be? Enter the mainstream or remain apart? The location of the women's tent in the social space of newly emerging world spaces is a good sign. Women at those gatherings have the choice of entering the mainstream from a women-only space from which they can draw strength and voice. The peace tent of the worldwide women's conferences has gone on the road.

This is an encouraging sign. The women's movement needs to find new ways of moving forward, of gathering its capital of knowledge and experience and history and reshaping it into a new political force. It needs to build on its successful introduction of feminism as common currency—today feminist analysis is a term that is used just like political or economic analysis. It has a legitimacy and a subject depth that is understood. This is one contemporary element that was unknown in the 1940s, a new force in the current scenario. Women's increased visibility—an outcome of the spaces and opportunities for building opinion that UN conferences offered—has made it possible to insert women-oriented concerns and agendas into international discourse and practice. Many of the final documents of the various UN conferences during the period 1995 to 2000 have separate sections devoted to women, however inadequate and subject to critique they may be.

However, for every suggestion of a gain, there is the critique not only of the inadequacy of that gain but also of its politics. Declarations do not challenge the form of knowledge from which they emerge. While conference outcome documents might acknowledge that women may not have the same concerns and interests as men, this is not a real victory because the masculine worldview contained in the rest of the document goes unchallenged. Since the focus is often on the right to participate, it does not question the world that is already constituted by men. While "feminist practices" might define NGO forums, "the masculine organizational forms of governments and the United Nations [circumscribe] the official conferences."[90]

Perhaps a way women can stimulate new thought and create space in which to strategize is to combine the peace tent with the women's tent as a way to encroach upon and occupy the entire global governance landscape. Peace is still the most unifying theme of the worldwide women's movement. It is still the moral high ground almost uniquely occupied by women. And they have brought powerful reasoning into the debates. Recall Alva Myrdal then and millions of women now. Yet in the international arena, including that which the UN drives, women are not taken into front line positions in war and peace negotiations or in prevention of conflict. Another wall. But by battering at that wall with their arguments, knowledge, and historical experience, perhaps the next generation can become a roaring mass that breaks it down.

That next generation of feminists will imagine and usher in a future, a new way of walking this long journey to equality. Scholar and feminist Lourdes Arizpe has a message for them:

> We need meaning. I see a great challenge today in finding new meanings because so many conflicts that we see, so many desperate acts come from the fact that people are no longer finding new meaning. And they are not finding any meaning, because the constitutive aspects of culture have been completely left out of development models and completely left out of contemporary politics.[91]

Indian political scientist Rajeev Bhargava sees this meaning in his definition of culture "as a complex but specific ideational configuration, cluster of thoughts, and pictures that transforms human biological organisms into agents who lead and experience meaningful lives. It is a web of embedded understandings and representations about the self and its relation to other selves and to the natural world, and includes conceptions of good and bad, right and wrong, virtues and vices, and so on."[92]

Another, a Magsaysay Award–winning priest who works in South Korea for peace, also sees culture's value for self-worth:

> Culture means the way in which a group of people live, think, feel, organize themselves, celebrate and share life. In every culture, there are underlying systems of values, meanings and views of the world, which are expressed, visibly, in languages, gestures, symbols, rituals and styles.[93]

There is an idea that culture, civilization, can revitalize a dominated, fragmented, poverty- and conflict-ridden South. However, some of the cultural traditions in the world, if not all of them, have embargoes on many aspects of women's freedom. It is here that culture conflicts with women's access to the universality of human rights; often traditions and religious practices hurt and discriminate. This problem, the women's question, keeps coming up again and again in discussions on celebrating culture, safeguarding culture and tradition in order to give political identity and self-confidence and strength to nations, especially those emerging from the subordination of culture that takes place during colonization.[94]

However, such cooptation or positioning or interpretations of culture can be resisted; culture needs to be overpowered by the other interpretation of it as sophisticated, open-ended, fluid understandings of self—a notable quality of women's use of identities. As the Buddhist priest says, culture provides an extraordinarily enabling environment for building self-confidence and peaceful, not warring, attitudes. It provides a mode of resistance to domination, but it also provides a space for an enhanced experience of life, as Bhargava says. Kum-Kum Bhavnani and others are now suggesting that the new concept of women's engagement with development should be called WCD: women, culture, and development.[95] Another road map.

The shape of the future of the women's movement with the UN is not yet clear. The world body has much work to do before women assume their proper place there—sixty years is a long time to wait. True reform will not happen until the political will is created and activated to fully bring women into the mainstream with equal privileges, access to resources, and decision-making roles, until women's intellectual contributions are received as the luminous ideas for which the world body was once well known. The experience of the past six decades has shown that much can be accomplished when the synergy flows between the UN and the women's movement.

Notes

Series Editors' Foreword

1. Thomas G. Weiss, Tatiana Carayannis, Louis Emmerij, and Richard Jolly, *UN Voices: The Struggle for Development and Social Justice* (Bloomington: Indiana University Press, 2005).

2. Louis Emmerij, Richard Jolly, and Thomas G. Weiss, *Ahead of the Curve? UN Ideas and Global Challenges* (Bloomington: Indiana University Press, 2001), xi.

Introduction

1. Linda Gordon, "What's New in Women's History," in *A Reader in Feminist Knowledge*, edited by Sneja Gunew (London: Routledge, 1991), 73.

2. Gordon, "What's New in Women's History," 75.

3. Weiss and Carayannis, "Whither United Nations Economic and Social Ideas?" http://www.sagepub.co.uk/journals/details/issue/sample/a016326.pdf.

4. Bangasser, "The ILO and the Informal Sector."

5. *Report of the World Conference of the International Women's Year*, 208.

6. *Report of the World Conference of the United Nations Decade for Women: Equality, Development and Peace, Held in Copenhagen*, 258–259.

7. *Report of the Fourth World Conference on Women*, 649.

1. Setting the Stage for Equality, 1945–1965

1. Tickner, *Gender in International Relations*.

2. UN Division for the Advancement of Women, *1999 World Survey on the Role of Women in Development: Globalization, Gender and Work*, vii.

3. Pietilä, *Engendering the Global Agenda*, 9.

4. Miller, "'Geneva—the Key to Equality,'" 231.

5. The 1948 convention is available at http://www.oas.org/CIM/english/Convention%20Civil%20Rights.htm; the 1952 convention is in *The United Nations and the Advancement of Women*, 164. See also "The United Nations and the Status of Women," *UN Review*, March 1961, col. 8.

6. Ana Figueroa, "Three Stages of the Convention on Political Rights of Women," *United Nations Bulletin* 13, no. 1 (1 July 1952), 37.

7. "Women Delegates at the UN Charter Conference," in *Women Go Global*.

8. Anderson, *Joyous Greetings.*

9. For example, the Convention Relating to the Settlement of the Conflict of the Laws concerning Marriage (12 June 1902) and the Convention Relating to the Settlement of the Conflict of Laws and Jurisdictions as Regards to Divorce and Separation and the Convention Relating to the Settlement of Guardianship of Minors (12 June 1902).

10. The Declaration of Philadelphia made the following statements:

Labour is not a commodity.

Freedom of expression and of association are essential to sustained progress.

Poverty anywhere constitutes a danger to prosperity everywhere.

All human beings, irrespective of race, creed or sex, have the right to pursue both their material well-being and their spiritual development in conditions of freedom and dignity, of economic security and equal opportunity.

For more about the declaration, see http://www.ilo.org/public/english/bureau/inf/download/brochure/pdf/page5.pdf.

11. Miller, "'Geneva—the Key to Equality.'"

12. The subcommission was appointed on 16 February 1946 by a resolution of ECOSOC. It held its first meeting, which lasted a fortnight, in April 1946 at Hunter College. "Economic and Social Council (ECOSOC) Resolution Establishing the Commission on Human Rights and the Subcommission on the Status of Women," E/RES/5(I), 16 February 1946, in *The United Nations and the Advancement of Women,* 109–110.

13. Miller, "'Geneva—the Key to Equality,'" 239.

14. Ibid., 228, 230–231, 235.

15. Figueroa, "Three Stages of the Convention on Political Rights of Women," 37.

16. For the historical origins of this debate, see Miller, "'Geneva—the Key to Equality,'" 222, 233, 236, 238. For the debate within the early CSW, see "1945–1962, CSW Focuses on Women's Rights, Customs and Traditions Harmful to Women," in *Women Go Global.*

17. Quoted in Miller, "Geneva—The Key to Equality," 233.

18. Galey, "Women Find a Place," 14.

19. "Virginia Gildersleeve," in *Women Go Global.*

20. "Statement Made by the Chair of the Subcommission on the Status of Women to ECOSOC Recommending That the Status of the Subcommission be Raised to Full Commission (extract)," in *The United Nations and the Advancement of Women,* 112.

21. Pietilä and Vickers, *Making Women Matter,* 115; Pietilä, *Engendering the Global Agenda,* 14. For more about the genesis of the CSW, see "Status of Women: Great Scope of Commission's Work," *United Nations Bulletin* 1, no. 7 (16 September 1946): 11–13.

22. Mathiason, "The Commission on the Status of Women," in *The Long March to Beijing.*

23. Mathiason, "United Nations Office of Women's Affairs?" in *The Long March to Beijing.*

24. Begtrup, "Statement Made by the Chair of the Subcommission on the Status of Women to ECOSOC Recommending That the Status of the Subcommission be Raised to Full Commission," in *The United Nations and the Advancement of Women,* 112, emphasis added.

25. Glendon, *A World Made New,* 71, 111–112.

26. Human Rights Commission, Third Session, E/CN.4/SR.50, p. 9, quoted in Glendon, *A World Made New,* 112; Eckert, "Universality by Consensus." For Eleanor Roosevelt's objections

to a separate commission, see Mathiason, "Mrs. Roosevelt's Letter," in *The Long Road to Beijing;* and Galey, "Women Find a Place," 13–14.

27. For a brief description of the activities of Equal Rights International, the women's group that emerged from the League of Nations and women's organizations to focus on the issue, see the description of its archival collection at the Women's Library in Great Britain: http://www.aim25.ac.uk/cgi-bin/frames/fulldesc?inst_id=65&coll_id=6848.

28. For an excellent discussion of this debate in the international women's movement, see Miller, "'Geneva—the Key to Equality.'"

29. Ibid., 223.

30. Marie-Helen Lefaucheux, "Work for Women's Equality of Status," *United Nations Bulletin* 4, no. 8 (15 April 1948): 343.

31. Boutros-Ghali, "Introduction," in *The United Nations and the Advancement of Women,* 8. For more on women's suffrage worldwide, see Hannam, Auchterlonie, and Holden, *International Encyclopedia of Women's Suffrage.*

32. Begtrup, "Statement Made by the Chair of the Subcommission on the Status of Women," 111.

33. *Report of the Secretary-General to the CSW on Discrimination Against Women in the Field of Political Rights,* 15 March 1950, E/CN.6/131, in *The United Nations and the Advancement of Women,* 124.

34. Begtrup, "Statement Made by the Chair of the Subcommission on the Status of Women," 111.

35. *Convention on the Political Rights of Women, adopted by the General Assembly on 20 December 1952,* in *The United Nations and the Advancement of Women,* 164.

36. *Summary of the Statement made by Secretary-General Dag Hammarskjöld to the Eighth Session of the CSW on, among Other Things, the Participation of Women in the Work of the United Nations,* E/CE.6/SR.149, 8 April 1954, in *The United Nations and the Advancement of Women,* 166.

37. "List of Member States," UN Press Release ORG/1317, 26 September 2000. Available at http://www.un.org/Overview/unmember.html.

38. For women's contributions to liberation movements in Africa, see Snyder, "Bibliographic Essay: Women and African Development."

39. Boutros-Ghali, "Introduction," 27.

40. *Yearbook of the United Nations,* 1955 onward.

41. Chowdhry, "Engendering Development? Women in Development (WID) in International Development Regimes."

42. "The Status of Women," *Yearbook of the United Nations 1956* (New York: Columbia University Press, 1957), 236.

43. "Session on Status of Women Is Reviewed by Members," *United Nations Bulletin* (15 June 1950): 547.

44. ECOSOC resolution 445C, 28 May 1952.

45. "The Status of Women," *Yearbook of the United Nations 1958* (New York: Columbia University Press, 1959), 219.

46. Galey, "Women Find a Place," 19.

47. Only four African countries achieved independence before 1960: Egypt in 1952 and Morocco, Tunisia, and Sudan in 1956.

48. Arjun Sengupta defines negative rights as those freedoms that the state is expected to protect—the right to life, free speech, liberty, and so forth; those laws that are already in place that prohibit others from killing, silencing, or unjustly imprisoning individuals. Positive rights are those social rights associated with freedoms that the state needs to secure through positive action. Sengupta, "Right to Development as a Human Right."

49. "The Status of Women," *Yearbook of the United Nations 1956* (New York: Columbia University Press, 1957), 235.

50. Ibid.

51. "Political Rights of Women: Resolution Unanimously Approved," *United Nations Bulletin* 1, no. 17 (25 November 1946): 22–23.

52. "The Political Rights of Women," *Yearbook of the United Nations 1946–1947* (Lake Success, N.Y.: UN Department of Public Information, 1947), 178–179.

53. See Miller, "'Geneva—the Key to Equality,'" 235–238.

54. "Political Rights of Women: Resolution Unanimously Approved," *United Nations Bulletin* 1, no. 17 (25 November 1946), 22.

55. Begtrup, "Statement made by the Chair of the Subcommission on the Status of Women," 111.

56. Boutros-Ghali, "Introduction," 17; "ECOSOC Resolution Defining the Function of the CSW and Requesting Member States to Provide the Commission with Data on the Legal Status and Treatment of Women in Their Countries," E/RES/48 (IV), 29 March 1947, in *The United Nations and the Advancement of Women*, 120–122. For more on the UN's use of surveys, see Ward, *Quantifying the World*.

57. *Report of the Secretary-General to the CSW on the United Nations Educational, Scientific and Cultural Organization (UNESCO) Study of Educational Opportunities for Women*, E/CN.6/146, 9 May 1950, in *The United Nations and the Advancement of Women*, 152.

58. *Report of Secretary-General to the CSW on Discrimination Against Women in the Field of Political Rights*, E/CN.6/131, 15 March 1950, in *The United Nations and the Advancement of Women*, 134–135.

59. The results were published as *Report to the Governments of Ceylon, India, Indonesia, Japan, Pakistan, the Philippines and Thailand on Conditions of Women's Work in Seven Asian Countries*. See Gaudier, "The Development of the Women's Question at the ILO," chapter 4, "The Years 1950–1974."

60. Kristiansen, "Review of UNESCO's Past and Present Work on Gender and Women."

61. The text of the UNESCO convention is available at http://www.unesco.org/shs/human_rights/wcb.htm.

62. UNESCO published the results of the survey findings in the 1950s: Maurice Duverger, *The Political Role of Women* (Paris: UNESCO, 1955); and A. Appadorai, *The Status of Women in South Asia* (Calcutta: Orient Longmans Ltd., 1954).

63. Convention on the Political Rights of Women (1952), Convention for the Suppression of the Traffic in Persons (1949), Convention on Equal Remuneration (1951), Convention on the Nationality of Married Women (1957), Convention on Consent to Marriage, Minimum

Age for Marriage and Registration of Marriages (1962). For more on these conventions, see *The United Nations and the Advancement of Women*, 20–22, 77–78.

64. *Report of the Secretary-General to the CSW on Discrimination Against Women in the Field of Political Rights*, E/CN.6/131, 15 March 1950, in *The United Nations and the Advancement of Women*, 134–136.

65. Glendon, *A World Made New*, 29. Roosevelt's response to the fact that there were only sixteen women present at the early UN meetings was to invite them to tea at her hotel, where they worked on ways to increase women's influence in the new organization.

66. "Session on Status of Women Is Reviewed by Members," *United Nations Bulletin* 8, no. 12 (15 June 1950): 546.

67. The General Assembly has six committees: the First Committee (Political and Security), the Second Committee (Economic and Financial), the Third Committee (Social, Humanitarian and Cultural), the Fourth Committee (Trusteeship), the Fifth Committee (Administrative and Budgetary), and the Sixth Committee (Legal). Governments appoint members of their delegations to the Third Committee and nominate members of the CSW. These are often civil servants from the ministries, and sometimes they are members of parliament and public figures. Margaret Bruce noted that the Third Committee was disparagingly called "the ladies' committee" in the 1970s. She wrote, "It is as if men would have no concern with 'women's issues,' and women nothing to contribute to 'world issues.'" "Women and Policy-Making at the United Nations," 63.

68. Tinker, "The Making of the Field," 34. For more about the UN's development decades, see Jolly, Emmerij, Ghai, and Lapeyre, *UN Contributions to Development Thinking and Practice*.

69. Tinker, *The Percy Amendment Promoting Women in Development*.

70. Boutros-Ghali, "Introduction," 27.

71. Ibid.; Snyder and Tadesse, "The African Context," 76.

72. Winslow, "Specialized Agencies and the World Bank," 156.

73. Speech delivered by Dr. Gro Harlem Brundtland to the CSW; available at http://www.who.int/director-general/speeches/1999/english/19990303_un_commission_women.html.

74. Marchand and Parpart, "Exploding the Canon: An Introduction/Conclusion," 11.

75. Berry, "Lakshmi and the Scientific Housewife."

76. Ibid.

77. See Babbitt, "The Productive Farm Woman and the Extension Home Economist in New York State."

78. Çagatay, "Engendering Macro-Economics."

79. Ibid.

80. Benería, "The Enduring Debate over Unpaid Labor."

81. Waring, *If Women Counted*. For more about the UNSNA, see Ward, *Quantifying the World*.

82. Aslaksen and Koren, "Unpaid Household Work and the Distribution of Extended Income," 65.

83. UNIFEM East and South East Asia, "Valuation of Unpaid Work," Gender Issue Fact Sheet 1, available at http://www.unifem-eseasia.org/resources/factsheets/Gendis1.htm.

84. Jain, "House Work."

85. Available at http://www.unhchr.ch/html/menu3/b/p_genoci.htm.

86. "Article 1, The 1951 Convention Relating to the Status of Refugees," available at http://www.unhcr.org.uk/info/briefings/basic_facts/definitions.html.

87. Quoted in Baines, "Gender Construction and the Protection Mandate of the UNHCR: Responses from Guatemalan Women," 247–248.

88. Ibid.

89. *United Nations Bulletin* (November 15, 1952): 454.

90. Ibid.

91. For more about Women Strike for Peace, see Amy Swerdlow, *Women Strike for Peace: Traditional Motherhood and Radical Politics in the 1960s* (Chicago: University of Chicago Press, 1993).

92. Women for Peace Web site: http://www.womenforpeace.org.

93. Press release, "WSP Calls for Nuclear Weapons Abolition after CTBT," Washington, D.C., 24 September 1996. Available at http://prop1.org/2000/ctbtwsp.htm.

94. Ibid.

95. Cora Weiss, president of The Hague Appeal for Peace, "It's an Honor to Honor Elise Boulding," 30 March 2001, http://www.Haguepeace.Org/Index.Php/Speech9. Accessed 12 June 2002.

96. Emma Rothschild, "An Infinity of Girls: The Political Rights of Children in Historical Perspective," Centre for History and Economics, 2000.

97. Maj-Britt Theorin, "Alva Myrdal and the Peace Movement," 2. Available at http://www.pcr.uu.se/conferenses/myrdal/pdf/maj_britt_theorin.pdf.

2. Inscribing Development into Rights, 1966–1975

1. Quote in "Minerva Bernardino," in *Women Go Global.*

2. Snyder, "The Politics of Women and Development," 96.

3. "International Development Strategy for the Second United Nations Decade," GA resolution 2626 (XXV), 24 October 1970.

4. Personal communication, Margaret Snyder, 10 October 2004. For Gloria Scott's reminiscences about working as one of the few women at the Secretariat in the 1960s, see "Breaking New Ground at the UN and the World Bank."

5. In 1960, there were six members from developing countries on the CSW; by 1969, that number had grown to nineteen. Oral history interview of Margaret Snyder, 28 March 2002, 45, in the Oral History Collection of the United Nations Intellectual History Project, The Graduate Center, The City University of New York.

6. See "Status of Women" in *Yearbook of the United Nations* for 1950 (p. 561), 1952 (p. 490), and 1961 (p. 813) (New York: Columbia University Press, 1951, 1953, 1963).

7. Boutros-Ghali, "Introduction," 19.

8. Ibid., 27.

9. Ibid., 28–29.

10. "Programme of Concerted International Action for the Advancement of Women," GA document A/RES/2716 (XXV), 15 December 1970, in *The United Nations and the Advancement of Women*, 179.

11. "Convention on the Political Rights of Women," GA resolution 640 (VII), 20 December 1952, available at http://www.unhchr.ch/html/menu3/b/22.htm.

12. See Fraser, "The Convention on the Elimination of All Forms of Discrimination Against Women."

13. For more on the evolving role of NGOs vis-à-vis the UN during this period, see Otto, "Nongovernmental Organizations in the United Nations System"; Willitts, "The Pattern of Conferences."

14. Hussein, "Crossroads for Women at the UN," 10.

15. "General Assembly Resolution Adopting the Declaration on the Elimination of Discrimination Against Women," GA document A/RES/2263 (XXII), 7 November 1967, in *The United Nations and the Advancement of Women*, 175.

16. Sen, *Development as Freedom*.

17. Boutros-Ghali, "Introduction," 31.

18. Mathiason, "On to Mexico City, 1968–1975," in *The Long March to Beijing*.

19. Galey, "Women Find a Place," 20.

20. "Resolution IX Adopted by the International Conference on Human Rights in Teheran on Measures to Promote Women's Rights in the Modern World and Endorsing the Secretary-General's Proposal for a Unified Long-Term United Nations Program for the Advancement of Women," GA document A/CONF.32/41, 12 May 1968, in *The United Nations and the Advancement of Women*, 177–179.

21. Galey, "Women Find a Place."

22. General Assembly resolution IX endorsed the unified long-term program for the advancement of women. See "Resolution IX Adopted by the International Conference on Human Rights," in *The United Nations and the Advancement of Women*, 177–179.

23. "General Assembly Resolution Outlining a Program of Concerted International Action for the Advancement of Women," GA document A/RES/2716 (XXV), 15 December 1970, in *The United Nations and the Advancement of Women*, 179–181.

24. Galey, "Women Find a Place," 20.

25. Emmerij, Jolly, and Weiss, *Ahead of the Curve? UN Ideas and Global Challenges*, 62.

26. ILO, "Convention (No. 142) Concerning Vocational Guidance and Vocational Training in the Development of Human Resources," available at http://www.austlii.edu.au/au/other/dfat/treaties/1986/2.html.

27. ILO, "Recommendation Concerning the Employment of Women with Family Responsibilities," 22 June 1965, available at http://www.ilo.org/public/english/employment/skills/recomm/instr/r_123.htm.

28. "Unesco's Contribution towards Improving the Status of Women," in *UNESCO, Records of the General Conference, Twentieth Session Paris, 24 October to 28 November 1978*, vol. 1, *Resolutions*, 137. Available at http://unesdoc.unesco.org/images/0006/000670/067023E.pdf.

29. Boserup, *Women's Role in Economic Development*.

30. Snyder, "The Politics of Women in Development," 97.

31. Boserup, *Women's Role in Economic Development*, 53, quoted in Jaquette, "Gender and Justice in Economic Development," 61–62.

32. Razavi and Miller, "From WID to GAD."

33. Suellen Huntington, "Issues in Woman's Role in Economic Development: Critique and Alternatives," *Journal of Marriage and the Family* 37, no. 4 (1975): 1001–1012 as quoted in Jaquette, "Gender and Justice in Economic Development," 64. For critiques of Boserup, see Benería and Sen, "Accumulation, Reproduction and Women's Role in Economic Development: Boserup Revisited." Benería and Sen's essay first appeared in 1981 in *Signs* VIII, no. 2.

34. Boserup joined the ECE's Research Division in 1947. She later headed the Industrial Analysis Section, where she conducted agricultural research in cooperation with the FAO. She was at the ECE for ten years. Boserup, *My Professional Life and Publications 1929–1998*, 15.

35. Razavi and Miller, "From WID to GAD."

36. Snyder, "The Politics of Women and Development," 97. Margaret Snyder, who was at the ECA at the time, brought the plan she and Daria Tesha had completed the previous year, called "The Five-Year Programme for Pre-Vocational and Vocational Training of Girls and Women Towards Their Full Participation in Development (1972–1976)." It was attached to the meeting papers as an addendum. Oral History of Margaret Snyder, 34.

37. UN, *Integration of Women in Development: Report of the SG*, ECOSOC document E/CN.5/481, 14 November 1972. Quoted in Snyder, "The Politics of Women and Development," 97.

38. "The Status of Women," in *Yearbook of the United Nations* (New York: UN Office of Public Information, 1976), 555.

39. Tinker, "The Making of a Field," 29.

40. Boutros-Ghali, "Introduction," in *The United Nations and the Advancement of Women*, 32.

41. Snyder and Tadesse, *African Women and Development*, 28, 32.

42. Tinker, "Challenging Wisdom, Changing Policies," 72; Boutros-Ghali, "Introduction," 32; Pietilä, *Making Women Matter*, 82–83.

43. The quote is from the text of the resolution the CSW drafted for ECOSOC; "Integration at All Development Levels," ECOSOC resolution E/5109, 24 May 1972. Quoted in "The Status of Women," *Yearbook of the United Nations 1972* (New York: UN Office of Public Information, 1975), 449, 457.

44. Snyder, "The Politics of Women and Development," 98. *Women Go Global* elaborates on the OECD's engagement with women and development: "The Development Assistance Committee (DAC) of the Organization for Economic Cooperation and Development held its first meeting on the integration of women in development in 1975 in conjunction with the conference on women in Mexico City. A number of informal meetings were then held among DAC members between 1977 and 1981 when a DAC Correspondent's Group on Women in Development was created. In 1981 the Group attained advisory status to the DAC and became the Expert Group on Women and Development. In 1995, the Group was renamed the Working Party on Gender Equality." "Women's Year Theme: Equality, Development, and Peace," in *Women Go Global*.

45. Tinker, "Challenging Wisdom, Changing Policies," 72.

46. Kardam, "The Tripartite System of the United Nations Development Programme," 24.

47. Ibid., 25.

48. Bhavnani, Foran, and Kurian, "An Introduction to Women, Culture and Development," 4.

49. Connelly, Li, MacDonald, and Parpart, "Feminism and Development: Theoretical Perspectives."

50. Razavi and Miller, "Gender Mainstreaming," 14.

51. Szalai and Croke, "Women on the Professional Staff and at Decision-Making Levels of the United Nations System: 1971–1976," 30.

52. Ibid., 72.

53. Ward, *Quantifying the World,* 188.

54. "The Population Commission," *Yearbook of the United Nations 1969* (New York: UN Office of Public Information, 1972), 421; "The Population Commission," *Yearbook of the United Nations 1967* (New York: Office of Public Information, 1969), 440.

55. Jolly, Emmerij, Ghai, and Lapeyre, *UN Contributions to Development Thinking and Practice,* 189.

56. Black, *The Children and the Nations,* 246; Seltzer, *The Origins and Evolution of Family Planning Programs in Developing Countries,* chapter 2.

57. See Jolly, Emmerij, Ghai, and Lapeyre, *UN Contributions to Development Thinking and Practice,* 189.

58. "Status of Women," *Yearbook of the United Nations 1965* (New York: Columbia University Press, 1967), 471.

59. "General Assembly Resolution Reiterating That Organizations in the United Nations System Take Measures to Ensure Equal Opportunities for the Employment of Qualified Women at the Senior and Professional Levels and in Policy-Making Positions," GA document A/RES/ 3009 (XXVII), 18 December 1972, in *The United Nations and the Advancement of Women,* 182. See Mathiason, "A Step towards a United Nations Office for Women," in *The Long March to Beijing* for the story of how Sipilä got her appointment and for an affectionate description of her very "un-UN" management style.

60. Sipilä had studied the relationship between family planning and the status of women during her ten years as a member of the CSW. The Secretary-General appointed her as special rapporteur on the issue of the connections between the status of women and family planning. Her *Study on the Interrelationship of the Status of Women and Family Planning* was published on 27 November 1973 as ECOSOC document E/CN.6/575, Add. 1, 2, and 3. Pietilä and Vickers, *Making Women Matter: The Role of Women in the United Nations,* 74, 82, 119, 125.

61. Helvi Sipilä, *Status of Women and Family Planning: Report of the Special Rapporteur Appointed by the Economic and Social Council Under Resolution 1326 (XLIV),* ECOSOC document E/CN.6/575/Rev.1, 1975, 4.

62. Ibid., 5.

63. Ibid., iii.

64. Pietilä, *Engendering the Global Agenda,* 21.

65. Galey, "Women Find a Place," 21; Snyder, "The Politics of Women and Development," 98.

66. These projects were financed by UNESCO, the UNDP, and UNICEF.

67. Kristiansen, "Review of UNESCO's Past and Present Work on Gender and Women," 20.

68. *Director-General's Report to the General Conference on UNESCO's Contribution to the Improvement of the Status of Women,* 19 C/14, 30 September 1976, quoted in Kristiansen, "Review of UNESCO's Past and Present Work on Gender and Women," 20.

69. Ibid.

70. Ibid.

71. UNESCO 97 EX/ 2 add., Annexe I and 97 EX/ Decision 3.1.1.

72. They are the Seminar on the Participation of Women in Public Life (Ulan Bator, Mongolia, 1965), Seminar on Measures Required for the Advancement of Women with Special Reference to the Establishment of a Long-term Programme (Manila, 1966), two Seminars on the Civic and Political Education of Women (Helsinki, 1967, and Ghana, 1968), Seminar on the Effects of Scientific and Technological Developments on the Status of Women (Iasi, Romania, 1969), two Seminars on the Participation of Women in the Economic Life of Their Countries (with reference to the implementation of article 10 of the Declaration on the Elimination of Discrimination Against Women) (Moscow, 1970, and Libreville, Gabon, 1971), Interregional Meeting of Experts on the Integration of Women in Development (New York, 1972), International Forum on the Role of Women in Development (New York, 1974), Regional Consultation for Asia and the Far East on the Integration of Women in Development with Special Reference to Population Factors (Bangkok, 1974), Regional Seminar for Africa on the Integration of Women in Development with Special Reference to Population Factors (Addis Ababa, 1974), Regional Seminar for Latin America on the Integration of Women in Development with Special Reference to Population Factors (Caracas, 1974), and United Nations Interregional Seminar on Women, the Media and the Arts (Sydney, 1975). See *United Nations and the Advancement of Women,* 85–90, for a complete listing of UN regional meetings on women's issues.

73. Van Rooy, "The Frontiers of Influence." For more about the World Food Conference, see Thomas G. Weiss and Robert S. Jordan, *The World Food Conference and Global Problem-Solving* (New York: Praeger, 1976).

74. Mathiason, "On to Mexico City, 1968–1975," in *The Long March to Beijing.*

75. "Resolution IX Adopted by the International Conference on Human Rights in Teheran on Measures to Promote Women's Rights in the Modern World and Endorsing the Secretary-General's Proposal for a Unified Long-Term United Nations Programme for the Advancement of Women," GA document A/CONF.32/41, 12 May 1968, in *The United Nations and the Advancement of Women,* 177–178.

76. "Proclamation of Teheran, Final Act of the International Conference on Human Rights, Teheran, 22 April to 13 May 1968," GA document A/CONF. 32/41 at 3 (1968).

77. The Women's International Democratic Federation was founded in 1946 "to mobilize women to secure their economic, political, and civil rights, and for peace, disarmament, national independence, social progress, and a new international economic order." The federation's policies were closely linked to women in socialist states and their allies. Sally Shreir, ed., *Women's Movements of the World: An International Directory and Reference Guide* (London: Longmans, 1988), 377.

78. Pietilä, *Engendering the Global Agenda,* 30–32; Pietilä, *Making Women Matter,* 75–76.

79. Gutierrez, *Macro-Economics.*

80. "The Status of Women," *Yearbook of the United Nations* (New York: UN Office of Public Information, 1975), 446.

81. Scott, "Breaking New Ground at the UN and the World Bank," 20–21.

82. Pietilä, *Engendering the Global Agenda,* 35.

83. Oral history interview of Leticia Shahani, 27 November and 11 December 1999, 18, in the Oral History Collection of the United Nations Intellectual History Project, The Graduate Center, The City University of New York.

84. *Report of the World Conference of the International Women's Year,* in *The United Nations and the Advancement of Women,* 210.

85. Snyder, "Walking My Own Road," 42.

86. Gachukia, "Education, Women, and Politics in Kenya," 330.

87. "Introduction: NGO Tribune Held in Mexico City," in *Women Go Global.*

88. Lamas, Martínez, Tarrés, and Tuñon, "Building Bridges."

89. Ibid.

90. Women's Feature Service Web site, available at http://www.wfsnews.org/aboutus.html.

91. The Convention on the Prevention and Punishment of the Crime of Genocide (1948) and The Convention Relating to the Status of Refugees (1951).

92. "Women's Participation in the Strengthening of International Peace and Security," GA resolution 3519 (XXX), 15 December 1975.

93. "Declaration on the Protection of Women and Children in Emergency and Armed Conflict," GA resolution 3318 (XXIX), 14 December 1974.

94. Oral history of Leticia Shahani, 15.

95. *Report of the World Conference of the International Women's Year,* in *The United Nations and the Advancement of Women,* 210.

3. Questioning Development Paradigms, 1976–1985

1. Quoted in Karin Kapadia, "Introduction: The Politics of Identity, Social Inequalities and Economic Growth," in *The Violence of Development: The Politics of Identity, Gender & Social Inequalities in India,* ed. Karin Kapadia (London: Zed, 2002), 1.

2. Louis Emmerij, paper prepared for the North-South Round Table on Imperatives of Tolerance and Justice in a Globalised World, 26–27 November 2002, Cairo.

3. Kristiansen, "Review of UNESCO's Past and Present Work on Gender and Women," 78.

4. Ibid., 16n59.

5. Angola (liberated 1975, joined 1976), Cape Verde (liberated and joined in 1975), Comoros (liberated and joined in 1975), Djibouti (liberated and joined in 1977), Guinea-Bisseau (liberated and joined in 1974), Mozambique (liberated and joined in 1975), São Tomé and Principe (liberated and joined in 1975), Zimbabwe (liberated and joined in 1980).

6. For the UN's response to this work, see Ward, *Quantifying the World,* 173–187, 277–279.

7. Goldschmidt-Clermont, *Unpaid Work in the Household.*

8. Ibid.

9. Geneva: ILO, 1983.

10. Jain and Mukherjee, "Women and Their Households" (portions of this study were also published in Jain and Banerjee, eds., *Tyranny of the Household*); and Jain, "Valuing Work: Time as a Measure."

11. Jain, "Indian Women; Today and Tomorrow."

12. Jain and Chand, "Report on a Time Allocation Study."

13. Jain, "Importance of Age and Sex Specific Data Collection in Household Surveys."

14. Jain, "House Work."

15. Interview with Ms. Madhubala Nath, former head of UNIFEM India, 2002.

16. Chang Pilwha, "Women's Studies in Korea," in *Beijing and Beyond: Toward the Twenty-First Century of Women,* special issue of *Women's Studies Quarterly* XXXIV, nos. 1 and 2 (Spring/Summer 1996): 317–326. At Ewha Woman's University, an exciting project was launched where more than a dozen male and female academics worked on an interdisciplinary research project in women's studies that examined literary traditions, religious views, and intellectual history. These pioneers used this research to publish the first textbook on Korean women's studies. Quote on page 323.

17. Masini, "The Household, Gender, and Age Project."

18. All-China Women's Federation, *The Impact of Economic Development on Rural Women in China* (Tokyo: United Nations University, 1993).

19. Ibid.

20. In December 1975, the General Assembly passed two resolutions: "General Assembly Resolution Calling for the Integration of Women in the Development Process," A/RES/3505, and "General Assembly Resolution Calling for Increased United Nations Assistance for the Integration of Women in Development," A/RES/3524.

21. Tinker, "The Making of a Field," 45.

22. Jaquette, "Losing the Battle/Winning the War."

23. Mazumdar, "The Non-Aligned Movement and the International Women's Decade," 1.

24. Gerry Helleiner, "Reflections on Global Economic Governance," available at http://www.robarts.yorku.ca/pdf/doha_helleiner2.pdf.

25. Ibid.

26. INSTRAW, "The Concept of Self-Reliance and the Integration of Women into Development," 211.

27. Declaration on the Establishment of a New International Economic Order, quoted in Tomšič, "Policy of Non-Alignment," 3.

28. Tomšič, "Policy of Non-Alignment," 10.

29. Ibid., 14.

30. "Final Document," Conference of Non-Aligned and Other Developing Countries on the Role of Women in Development, Baghdad, 6–13 May 1979, GA document A/34/321, page 6.

31. Ibid., 7.

32. Jain, "Role of Women in Development."

33. Statement at North-South Roundtable, 26–27 November 2002, Cairo.

34. Tomšič, "Policy of Non-Alignment."

35. Mazumdar, "The Non-Aligned Movement and the International Women's Decade."

36. Ibid.

37. *Report of the World Conference of the United Nations Decade for Women: Equality, Development and Peace,* GA document A/CONF.94/35, in *The United Nations and the Advancement of Women,* 253.

38. One of the NGO resolutions by Third World women spoke of their concern about "the role of multinational corporations in the so-called developing nations, a role based on the

exploitation of cheap labor in those countries and aimed at meeting the needs of the industrialized countries, not those of the so-called developing ones. We draw attention . . . to the unacceptable work conditions in their factories." Another resolution noted that multinationals "frequently relocated from one tax-free, free-trade zone to another." They referred to this early expression of globalization as "economic neo-imperialism." "NGO Resolutions," *Forum 80*, 25 July 1980. *Forum 80* excerpts are available in *Women Go Global*.

39. "WIDF Calls for Action Now," *Forum 80*, 29 July 1980.

40. "NGO Resolutions."

41. "Forum within Forum," *Forum 80*, 18 July 1980.

42. "Regional Approach to Development," *Forum 80*, 24 July 1980; Eve Hall, "Women Are the 'Slaves of Slaves,'" *Forum 80*, 16 July 1980.

43. For more about the Copenhagen conference, see Bunch, "U.N. World Conference in Nairobi: A View from the West"; and Çagatay, Grown, and Santiago, "The Nairobi Women's Conference."

44. "The Wrong Kind of Politics," *Forum 80*, 28 July 1980.

45. Jaquette, "Crossing the Line," 197.

46. "Convention on the Elimination of All Forms of Discrimination Against Women," GA resolution A/RES/34/180, 18 December 1979.

47. "Declaration on the Participation of Women in Promoting International Peace and Cooperation," GA resolution A/RES/37/63, 3 December 1982.

48. Fraser, "The Convention on the Elimination of All Forms of Discrimination Against Women," 77.

49. See ibid., 84–88.

50. Ibid., 84–85.

51. Otto, "Gender Comment," 18–19.

52. Steady, "African Women at the End of the Decade."

53. Rebecca Cook, quoted in Nüket Kardam, "Engendering International Relations' Discourses," paper presented at the workshop Reshaping of International Relations, Marmara University, Istanbul, 18–19 May 2001, 13.

54. "Fact Sheet No. 22, Discrimination against Women: The Convention and the Committee," available at http://www.unhchr.ch/html/menu6/2/fs22.htm.

55. The resolution calling for the drafting of DEDAW was introduced to the General Assembly by twenty-two developing and Eastern European nations. See Fraser, "The Convention on the Elimination of All Forms of Discrimination Against Women," 78–79.

56. CEDAW, "Consideration of Reports Submitted by States Parties under Article 18 of the Convention on the Elimination of all Forms of Discrimination Against Women," Article 4, "Acceleration of Equality Between Men and Women," CEDAW/C/ISR/1-2, 8 April 1997, available at http://www.un.org/esa/gopher-data/ga/cedaw/17/country/israel/C-ISR-P1.EN.

57. Kristiansen, "Review of UNESCO's Past and Present Work on Gender and Women."

58. Ibid.

59. In 2000, Margaret Anstee, who was with the UN for four decades, said it was "only 15 years ago that I was being told that a woman cannot hold the job of High Commissioner for Refugees. There were prejudices about all sorts of things. But now all these jobs—UNHCR

[UN High Commissioner for Refugees], WFP [World Food Program], UNICEF, UNFPA—are being filled by women, as they should be. But that is at the top. I think there is a problem at the middle levels. I think it is difficult within the structure. In the case of very high-profile political appointments there is a feeling now that it has to be a woman here or there, and that is done." Oral history of Dame Margaret Joan Anstee, 119, 14 December 2000, in the Oral History Collection of the United Nations Intellectual History Project, The Graduate Center, The City University of New York. The sexism at the UN was so great in the late 1970s that many women from developing countries chose not to work at UN headquarters even though they were qualified: "What is less often heard is that some potential women candidates have indicated that they are not attracted to the United Nations and feel that they are better off in their own countries. Some see the United Nations as male dominated, not only in its administrative practices, but also in the programmes it supports, especially in the area of development. They consider that they can be more effective at home in helping those most in need." Bruce, "Women and Policy-Making at the United Nations," 77.

60. CEDAW, "Consideration of Reports Submitted by States Parties under Article 18," Article 11, "Employment."

61. CEDAW, "Consideration of Reports Submitted by States Parties under Article 18," Article 11 (3), "Pregnancy and Maternity Leave."

62. Otto, "Gender Comment," 13.

63. UN Division for the Advancement of Women, "History of an Optional Protocol," available at http://www.un.org/womenwatch/daw/cedaw/protocol/history.htm.

64. "Declaration on Equality of Opportunity and Treatment for Women Workers," adopted by the 60th Session of the International Labour Conference, ILO Geneva, 1975, available at http://www.wiram.de/gendersourcebook/instruments/instrumentsconventions.html.

65. Ibid.

66. Ibid.

67. Asia Pacific training manual on the CEDAW Convention, "Why and How We Should Use the CEDAW Convention: An Overview: The Significance of the CEDAW Convention," International Women's Rights Action Watch, Kuala Lumpur, 2002.

68. Tomšič, "Policy of Non-Alignment," 3–29.

69. Snyder, *Transforming Development*, 26.

70. *Report of the World Conference of the International Women's Year*, in *The United Nations and the Advancement of Women*, 203.

71. Snyder, *Transforming Development*, 26.

72. Ibid., 45.

73. Ibid., 64.

74. Snyder, *Transforming Development*, 45, 64, 69–71; see GA resolution A/RES/39/125, 14 December 1984, in *The United Nations and the Advancement of Women*, 303.

75. "INSTRAW's Profile for the New Millennium," 9. For more of INSTRAW's history before 1980, see Scott, "Breaking New Ground at the UN and the World Bank," 21.

76. Tinker, "Challenging Wisdom, Changing Policies," 74.

77. Bouayad-Agha and Hernández, *An Evaluation of the United Nations International Research and Training Institute for the Advancement of Women*, 4.

78. "General Assembly Resolution . . . Establishing an International Research and Training Institute for the Advancement of Women (INSTRAW)," in *The United Nations and the Advancement of Women*, 215.

79. "General Assembly Resolution Establishing the Voluntary Fund for the United Nations Decade for Women," in *The United Nations and the Advancement of Women*, 303.

80. *Integrating Women into a State Five-Year Plan* (India: Institute of Social Studies Trust, 1978).

81. Jain, "Development as if Women Mattered," 11.

82. A/CONF.116/5 and Add.1–14.

83. Sen and Grown, *Development, Crises, and Alternative Visions*, 35, 83–84. Quote on page 80.

84. Ibid., 87.

85. NAM Conference Declaration, 1985.

86. Snyder and Tadesse, "The African Context," 15.

87. Ibid.; Snyder, "Women Determine Development," 620.

88. Quoted in Snyder and Tadesse, *African Women and Development*, 31. Ester Boserup used *The Status and Role of Women in East Africa* to support the arguments in her book *Women's Role in Economic Development* (p. 34).

89. Snyder and Tadesse, *African Women and Development*, 41.

90. Ibid., 84.

91. Ibid., 101.

92. Oral history interview of Adebayo Adedeji, 6–7 March 2001, 41, in the Oral History Collection of the United Nations Intellectual History Project, The Graduate Center, The City University of New York.

93. Quoted in Snyder and Tadesse, *African Women and Development*, 163. See also Sadig Rasheed and Makha D. N. Sarr, "From the Lagos Plan of Action to the Thirteenth Special Session of the United Nations General Assembly," in *The Challenge of African Economic Recovery and Development*, edited by Adebayo Adedeji, Owodunni Teriba, and Patrick Bugembe (London: Frank Cass, 1991), 13–36.

94. Lagos Plan of Action, chapter 12, available at http://www.uneca.org/adfiii/riefforts/ref/other2.htm.

95. Ibid.

96. Quoted in Snyder and Tadesse, *African Women and Development*, 38.

97. Oral history of Adebayo Adedeji, 57.

4. Development as if Women Mattered, 1986–1995

1. Neither institution is governed democratically. Whereas in the United Nations General Assembly, each country has one vote and small as well as wealthy countries are represented on many UN committees, at the World Bank and the International Monetary Fund, power is roughly proportional to the wealth of each country. Thus, the more a nation-state is likely to need the financial help of the two institutions in the form of aid or loans, the less of a say it has in their policies.

2. Easterly, "The Lost Decades."

3. Easterly, "The Lost Decades." See Figure 1a: Predicted vs Actual per Capita Growth for Developing Countries (Assuming Constant Intercept across Decades), 30.

4. Paul Krugman, quoted in Easterly, "The Lost Decades," 3.

5. Mingst and Karns, *The United Nations in the Post–Cold War Era.*

6. Chinua Achebe, *Things Fall Apart* (Oxford: Heinemann Educational Publishers, 1958).

7. *The World's Women 1970–1990;* UNDP, *Human Development Report 1995; Adjustment, Globalization, and Social Development: Report of the UNRISD/UNDP International Seminar on Economic Restructuring and Social Policy (New York, 11–13 January 1995)* (Geneva: UNRISD, [1995]). The ECA provided a comprehensive and credible alternative to structural adjustment programs in 1989. The African Alternative Framework called for "adjustment with transformation," which called for a reduction in the continent's reliance on external trade and financing, promotion of food self-sufficiency, and greater popular participation in economic planning and decision-making. The "African Alternative Framework to Structural Adjustment for Socio-Economic Recovery and Transformation (AAF-SAP)" is available online at http://www.uneca.org/eca_resources/Publications/ESPD/old/aaf_sap.pdf.

8. South Commission, *The Challenge to the South,* 56.

9. Okin, "Poverty, Well-Being, and Gender: What Counts, Who's Heard?" 281. Okin notes that the poverty line is still referred to as the "$1/day line," a value that was set in 1985, even though the line had risen to $1.08 per day in 1993 due to inflation. She drew her analysis from Chen and Ravallion, "How Did the World's Poorest Fare in the 1990s?" and Yusuf and Stiglitz, "Development Issues: Settled and Open," 228 and 232.

10. Easterly, "The Lost Decades," 7.

11. Okin, "Poverty, Well-Being, and Gender: What Counts, Who's Heard?"

12. Kanbur and Squire, "The Evolution of Thinking about Poverty: Exploring the Interactions," 193.

13. Gaudier, "The Development of the Women's Question at the ILO."

14. UN Division for the Advancement of Women, "International Standards of Equality," 436.

15. Ibid., 435.

16. *World's Women 1970–1990,* 95.

17. Gertrude Mongella, "Preface," in *Women in a Changing Global Economy,* iii.

18. Moghadam, "The Feminization of Poverty? Notes on a Concept and Trends."

19. Çagatay, "Gender and Poverty."

20. Buvinić, "Projects for Women in the Third World: Explaining their Misbehaviour."

21. Jain and Mukherjee, "Women and Their Households."

22. Baden, "Gender, Governance and the 'Feminisation of Poverty.'"

23. Jackson, "Rescuing Gender from the Poverty Trap," 501.

24. Baden, "Gender, Governance and the 'Feminisation of Poverty.'"

25. Valerie Kozel and Barbara Parker, "A Profile and Diagnostic of the Poverty in Uttar Pradesh," World Bank, 2001.

26. Ibid., emphasis added.

27. *World Survey on the Role of Women in Development,* xvii.

28. UN Department of International Economic and Social Affairs, *World Survey on the Role of Women in Development* (1986), 19.

29. Ibid., 23.

30. Ibid., 53–54.

31. Ibid., 82.

32. *Executive Summary of the 1994 World Survey on the Role of Women in Development (extract)*, UN document ST/ESA/241, 1995, in *The United Nations and the Advancement of Women*, 490.

33. Morris David Morris, "Light in the Tunnel: The Changing Condition of the World's Poor," The Brown University Op-Ed Service, August 1996.

34. Manfred Max-Neef, *Barefoot Economy;* Manfred Max-Neef, *From the Outside Looking In: Experiences in Barefoot Economics* (Sweden: Dag Hammarskjöld Foundation, 1981).

35. See the web site at http://www.toes-usa.org.

36. Hazel Henderson, *Paradigms in Progress: Life Beyond Economics* (Indianapolis: Knowledge Systems, Inc., 1991).

37. Amartya Sen, "Foreword," in *Readings in Human Development: Concepts, Measures, and Policies for a Development Paradigm,* ed. Sakiko Fukuda-Parr and A. K. Shiva Kumar (New York: Oxford University Press, 2003), vii–viii.

38. Fukuda-Parr, "The Human Development Paradigm: Operationalizing Sen's Ideas on Capabilities."

39. Sudhir Anand and Amartya Sen, "Gender Inequality in Human Development: Theories and Measurement" in *Background Papers: Human Development Report 1995* (New York: Oxford University Press, 1996); *Human Development Report 1995;* Fukuda-Parr, "The Human Development Paradigm: Operationalizing Sen's Ideas on Capabilities."

40. UNDP, "The Revolution for Gender Equality," *Human Development Report 1995,* 4. Page numbers for the 1995 HDR are to the online version of the report.

41. Aasha Kapur Mehta, "Recasting Indices for Developing Countries, a Gender Empowerment Measure," *Economic and Political Weekly* XXXI, no. 43 (26 October 1996).

42. UNDP, "Towards Equality," *Human Development Report 1995,* 5–6.

43. UNDP, "Valuing Women's Work," *Human Development Report 1995,* 1.

44. UNDP, "Towards Equality," *Human Development Report 1995,* 5.

45. Ward, *Quantifying the World,* 115. See also pages 116–117, 177–178, and 275–277.

46. Carr and Chen, "Globalization and the Informal Economy."

47. International Labour Organization, *Women in the Informal Sector: Emerging Gender Issues in the Asia Pacific Region,* Unit 2: "Gender Issues in the World of Work," available at http://www-ilo-mirror.cornell.edu/public/english/region/asro/mdtmanila/training/unit2/asiainfm.htm.

48. Vishwanath, "Informal Economy: Safety Valve or Growth Opportunity?"

49. Carr and Chen, "Globalisation and the Informal Economy"; Chen, Jhabvala, and Lund, "Supporting Workers in the Informal Economy: A Policy Framework"; Charmes et al., "Women and Men in the Informal Economy: A Statistical Picture"; Standing, *Beyond the New Paternalism.*

50. Chen, "Women and the Informal Sector: Realities, Statistics and Policies," paper pre-

sented at the Economic Policy Forum, International Center for Research on Women, Washington, D.C., 15 March 1996, as quoted in "Rural Producers: Trends, Issues and Challenges for Socio-Economic Development," in Statistics Division, Economic and Social Department and the Women and Population Division, Sustainable Development Department, FAO, *Filling the Data Gap: Gender-Sensitive Statistics for Agricultural Development* (Rome: FAO, 1999), available online at http://www.fao.org/docrep/X2785e/X2785e00.htm; Mehra and Gammage, "Trends, Countertrends, and Gaps in Women's Employment."

51. Bangasser, "The ILO and the Informal Sector."

52. *World Labour Report 1992;* see also ILO, "Employment, Incomes and Equity."

53. Okine, *The Impact of the Informal Sector on the Economy;* Institut el Amouri, *Le Secteur informel: quelle place pour les femmes? (Cas de la Tunisie)* (Tunisia: Institut el Amouri, 1989); Marie-Dominique de Suremain, *Women's Involvement in the Informal Urban Economy: Colombia* (Geneva: UNESCO, 1989). A bibliography of UNESCO's publications on women and labor is available online at http://www.unesco.org/shs/shsdc/women/women/listdoc.htm.

54. Jhabvala, "SEWA and Home-Based Workers in India."

55. In the 1980s the idea to set an international labor standard for home-based workers was suggested by the ILO. An interdepartmental task force was formed in 1984 to study the feasibility and advisability of such a standard. This team suggested that further study was necessary. Around this time the ILO also brought out the World Employment Report on home-based work, which made the condition of the home-based worker more visible in the world. A later report that addresses this sector is *World Employment Report 1998–99: Employability in the Global Economy: How Training Matters* (Geneva: ILO, 1998).

56. Jhabvala, "SEWA and Home-Based Workers in India."

57. See UNIFEM's *Progress of the World's Women 2000,* 46, for a discussion of the Home Work Convention and women's roles in its passage. The convention is available on the ILO's Web site at http://www.ilo.org/ilolex/cgi-lex/convde.pl?C177.

58. Prügl, "What Is a Worker?" 203.

59. At the time, the Home-Based Workers' Convention was considered a victory for those working with poor women in the developing countries, where the majority of women were home-based workers with no protection by labor laws, but there has also been some resistance to its adoption; only four countries have ratified the convention over the last eight years.

60. In some ways, the Basic Income Grant was a reprise of India's 1950s Minimum Needs Programme.

61. Çagatay, Grown, and Santiago, "The Nairobi Women's Conference," 404.

62. "All Issues Political," *Forum 85,* 18 July 1985.

63. Oral history interview of Margaret Snyder, 28 March 2002, 55, in the Oral History Collection of the United Nations Intellectual History Project, The Graduate Center, The City University of New York.

64. Ibid., 407.

65. "To Change Everyone's Thinking," *Forum 85,* 17 July 1985.

66. Sen and Grown, *Development, Crises, and Alternative Visions,* 7.

67. Antrobus, "A Caribbean Journey," 144.

68. Chaney, "Full Circle," 208.

69. *Women Go Global.*

70. Paragraphs 13 and 303, *Report of the World Conference to Review and Appraise the Achievements of the United Nations Decade for Women.*

71. Executive Committee Conclusion, "Refugee Women and International Protection," No. 39 (XXXVI)—1985.

72. Available online at http://www.forcedmigration.org/sphere/pdf/shelter/unhcr/protection-women.pdf.

73. UNHCR, *Sexual Violence Against Refugees: Guidelines on Prevention and Response* (Geneva: UNHCR, 1995).

74. *General Exchange of Views on the Second Review and Appraisal of the Implementation of the Nairobi Forward-Looking Strategies for the Advancement of Women to the Year 2000,* GA document A/CONF.177/9, 21 August 1995, available at http://www.un.org/esa/gopher-data/conf/fwcw/off/a—9.en.

75. SISTREN Theatre collective, Caribbean song popularized at Nairobi, 1985.

76. Asit Bhattacharjee, talk given at a luncheon at UN headquarters hosted by Ambassador Kamalesh Sharma on 16 June 2001.

77. Higer, "International Women's Activism and the 1994 Cairo Population Conference"; Jain, "Networks, People's Movements and Alliances"; Karl, Anand, Blankenberg, van den Ham, and Saldanha, eds., *Measuring the Immeasurable.*

78. Peter M. Haas, "Introduction," *Epistemic Communities: International Policy Coordination International Organization* 46 (1992).

79. Chen, "Engendering World Conferences," 143–144, quote on 144.

80. Bunch and Reilly, *Demanding Accountability.*

81. Karl, Anand, Blankenberg, van den Ham, and Saldanha, eds., *Measuring the Immeasurable.*

82. Higer, "International Women's Activism and the Cairo Conference," 135–138.

83. Heyzer, Kapoor, and Sandler, eds., *A Commitment to the World's Women,* 180–181.

84. Karl, Anand, Blankenberg, van den Ham, and Saldanha, eds., *Measuring the Immeasurable.*

85. Snyder, *Transforming Development,* 47, 42. GA resolution 39/125 of 1984 is a legal document that "to this day is considered exceptionally precise and effective" (47).

86. Ibid., 78.

87. Ibid., 38.

88. Ibid., 36–37.

89. Ibid., 80.

90. Margaret Snyder, personal communication, 19 November 2004.

91. UNIFEM Web site.

92. UNSO/ECA/INSTRAW, *Handbook on Compilation of Statistics on Women in the Informal Sector in Industry, Trade and Services in Africa* (New York: United Nations, 1991); UNSO/ECA/INSTRAW, *Synthesis of Pilot Studies on Compilation of Statistics on Women in the Informal Sector in Industry, Trade, and Services in African Countries* (New York: United Nations, 1991); INSTRAW, *Methods of Collecting and Analysing Statistics on Women in the Informal Sector and Their Contributions to National Product: Results of Regional Workshop,* INSTRAW/BT/CRP/1 (Santo Domingo: INSTRAW, 1991).

93. Margaret Shields, "At INSTRAW: Survey of Activities and Accomplishments," *WIN*

News 19, no. 2 (Spring 1993): 6; "Interview with Martha Duenas-Loza, Acting Director of INSTRAW," *WIN News* 21, no. 4 (Autumn 1995): 25.

94. *Report of the President of the Board of Trustees of the International Research and Training Institute for the Advancement of Women: Note by the Secretary-General,* E/1999/105, 8 July 1999, 3.

95. Bouayad-Agha and Hernández, *An Evaluation of the United Nations International Research and Training Institute for the Advancement of Women,* 28.

96. Personal communication, Jeannie Ash de Pou, INSTRAW, 29 November 1994.

97. INSTRAW web site, www.un-instraw.org.

98. Yakin Ertürk, "Foreword" in *INSTRAW's Profile for the New Millennium,* 3–4.

99. Reanda, "The Commission on the Status of Women," 293–295.

100. Mama, "Postscript: Moving from Analysis to Practice?" 415.

101. United Nations Division for the Advancement of Women, "EGM/Overall Report/V 1.4" for the High-Level Meeting The Role of National Mechanisms in Promoting Gender Equality and the Empowerment of Women: Achievements, Gaps and Challenges, Rome, 29 November 2004–2 December 2004.

102. Ibid.

5. Lessons from the UN's Sixth Decade, 1996–2005

1. Fatema Mernissi, *Dreams of Trespass: Tales of a Harem Girlhood* (Reading, Mass.: Addison-Wesley, 1994), excerpts available online at http://www.bdancer.com/med-guide/culture/mernissi.html.

2. "Women, Peace and Security," UN Security Council resolution 1325, 31 October 2000, available online at http://ods-dds-ny.un.org/doc/UNDOC/GEN/N00/720/18/PDF/N0072018.pdf?OpenElement.

3. UNIFEM, *Progress of the World's Women 2000,* 11.

4. UN Department of Economic and Social Affairs, *World's Women 2000,* 118, 122, 125.

5. UNESCO Culture Sector, *World Culture Report: Cultural Diversity, Conflict, and Pluralism* (Paris: UNESCO Publishing, 2000).

6. "FAO Plan of Action for Women in Development," available online at http://www.fao.org/waicent/faoinfo/sustdev/WPdirect/WPre0001.htm#topofpage. This plan was a product of the twenty-eighth FAO conference in the fall of 1995.

7. *World Survey on the Role of Women in Development,* 29–30.

8. *Human Rights and Extreme Poverty: Report Submitted by Ms. A.-M. Lizin, Independent Expert, Pursuant to Commission Resolution 1998/25,* ECOSOC document E/CN.4/1999/48, 29 January 1999; *Human Rights and Extreme Poverty: Report Submitted by Ms. A.-M. Lizin, Independent Expert, Pursuant to Commission Resolution 1999/26,* ECOSOC document E/CN.4/2000/52, 25 February 2000.

9. *Human Rights and Extreme Poverty: Report Submitted by Ms. A.-M. Lizin, Independent Expert, Pursuant to Commission Resolution 1998/25,* paragraphs 111, 115, 118.

10. Amartya Sen, "Democracy as a Universal Value," 3–17; Commission on Human Security, *Human Security Now* (New York: Commission on Human Security, 2003). The Commis-

sion on Human Security was chaired by Sen and former UN High Commissioner for Refugees Sadako Ogata.

11. van der Gaag, "Women: Still Something to Shout About."

12. Båge, "The Well Fed Have Many Problems, the Hungry Only One."

13. Renana Jhabvala, "Bringing Informal Workers Centrestage," in *Informal Economy Centrestage: New Structures of Employment* (New Delhi: Sage Publications, 2003).

14. Devaki Jain, as Member of the Governing Council of APCWD, Report of a visit to Tonga Advisory Committee Meeting, Fiji 1976.

15. Women-run and -initiated community kitchens to feed the poor in Lima's low-income neighborhoods who were affected by structural adjustment. UNIFEM funded some of the Peruvian Kitchens.

16. Amoah, "Women, Witches and Social Change in Ghana," in *Speaking of Faith,* eds., Eck and Jau.

17. Farhan Haq, "Microcredit Reaches More Poor Women," *Third World Network,* available online at http:\\www.twnside.org.sg\title\micro-cn.htm.

18. For example, a recent ILO study found that informal employment accounts for one-half to three-quarters of nonagricultural employment in developing countries. Charmes et al., *Women and Men in the Informal Economy.*

19. See more about the Consultative Group to Assist the Poor at http://www.cgap.org/ and the Microcredit Summit Campaign at http://www.microcreditsummit.org/.

20. Goetz and Sen Gupta, "Who Takes the Credit? Gender Power and Control over Loan Use in Rural Credit Programs in Bangladesh."

21. Bruce, "Homes Divided."

22. Makandiwe, "Adjustment Political Conditionality and Democratisation in Africa" and "The Political Economy of Privatisation in Africa."

23. Razavi, ed., *Shifting Burdens.*

24. Elson, "Male Bias in Macro-Economics"; and Elson, "For an Emancipatory Socio-Economics," draft paper prepared for the discussion at the UNRISD meeting on "The Need to Rethink Development Economics," 7–8 September 2001, Cape Town, South Africa.

25. Timothy, "Walking on Eggshells at the UN," 59–60. Melalini Trask, vice chair of the General Assembly of Nations of the Unrepresented Nations and Peoples Organizations, notes that 20,000 women who wanted to attend the conference were denied visas by the Chinese government. *Feminist Family Values Forum* (Austin, Tex.: Plain View Press, 1996), 13.

26. Boutros-Ghali, "Introduction," 63.

27. Heyzer, "Seizing the Opportunity," 248. For more about Beijing's prepcoms, see "Five Regional PrepComs," in *Beijing! UN Fourth World Conference on Women,* ed. Anita Anand (New Delhi: Women's Feature Service, 1998), 92–93.

28. Stienstra, "Dancing Resistance from Rio to Beijing," 221.

29. NGO Beijing Declaration, available at http://www.vrouwen.net/vweb/wcw/ngodec.html.

30. Quoted in *Feminist Family Values Forum,* 14.

31. Corpuz, "Depoliticising Gender in Beijing."

32. Ibid.; Hochstetler, Friedman, and Clark, "Latin American NGOs and Governments."

33. Hochstetler, Friedman, and Clark, "Latin American NGOs and Governments."

34. Bunch, Dutt, and Fried, "Woman's Human Rights: A Global Referendum," 189.

35. *Report of the United Nations Expert Group Meeting on Women and Public Life,* Vienna, EGM/RWOL.1991.Rep. 1, 12–24 May 1991, quoted in DAW, "Women and Decision-Making," *Women2000* (October 1997): 4.

36. Mama, "Gains and Challenges: Linking Theory and Practice."

37. DAW, "Women and Decision-Making," 6.

38. Inter-Parliamentary Union, "Women in International Parliaments: Situation as of 30 October 2004," available at http://www.ipu.org/wmn-e/world.htm.

39. DAW, "Women and Decision-Making," 10.

40. Ibid., 11, quoting statistics from the Inter-Parliamentary Union.

41. Jain, "Panchayat Raj."

42. Jain, *For Women to Lead.* This study was sponsored by the Management and Governance Division of the UNDP.

43. Devaki Jain, "Women's Political Presence and Political Rights in India," paper presented at The New Face of Development International Development Conference, Washington, D.C., 13–15 January 1997.

44. Charlesworth, "Transforming the United Men's Club," 430–431.

45. Ibid., 422, 433.

46. Ibid., 435.

47. INSTRAW, "Women in the Secretariat," 18.

48. Ibid., italics in original.

49. Galey, "Gender Roles and UN Reform," 818–819.

50. Herdervary, "The United Nations," 693.

51. Margaret Snyder, personal communication, 19 November 2004.

52. Oral History of Margaret Snyder, 28 March 2002, United Nations Intellectual History Project, 81, in the Oral History Collection of the United Nations Intellectual History Project, The Graduate Center, The City University of New York; Snyder, *Transforming Development,* 67.

53. Timothy, "Walking on Eggshells," 55; see also Charlesworth, "Transforming the United Men's Club," 436.

54. "Report of the Inter-Agency Committee on Women and Gender Equality, third session, New York, 25–27 February 1998," as quoted in "Mainstreaming Gender in ITU-D Programmes," resolution 44, World Telecommunication Development Conference, Istanbul, 2002, at http://www.itu.int/ITU-D/isap/WTDC-02FinalReport/Section4/Resolutions/Reso44.pdf.

55. Razavi and Miller, "Gender Mainstreaming," 85.

56. Ibid., 83.

57. Ibid., 67.

58. An Inter-Agency Taskforce on Gender Mainstreaming in Programme Budget Processes is studying this issue. See "Introduction to the Work of the Taskforce on Gender Mainstreaming in Programme Budget Processes," available at http://www.un.org/womenwatch/ianwge/activities/CH-Statement-NY-workshop.pdf.

59. IACWGE, "Accounts and Accountability: A Synthesis Report of Phase 3 of the IACWGE

Project on Gender Mainstreaming in the UN Programme Budget Process, UN Task Force on Mainstreaming Gender Perspectives in Budget Process, June 2000." The IACWGE reports directly to the UN's Chief Executives Board for Coordination (formerly the Administrative Committee on Coordination).

60. Reeves, "Gender Evaluation within the UN System," 4.

61. *Assessment of the Implementation of the System-Wide Medium-Term Plan for the Advancement of Women 1996–2001: Report of the Secretary-General,* ECOSOC document E/CN.6/ 2000/3.

62. The International Criminal Tribunal for Rwanda, based in Arusha (Tanzania), was established in November 1994 by Security Council Resolution 955.

63. The International Criminal Court (ICC) was established by the Rome Statute of the International Criminal Court on 17 July 1998, when 120 states participating in the United Nations Diplomatic Conference of Plenipotentiaries on the Establishment of an International Criminal Court adopted the statute. The statute entered into force on 1 July 2002.

64. Human Rights Watch, *World Report 2002: Women's Human Rights,* available at http:// www.hrw.org/wr2k2/women.html.

65. For more on Resolution 1325, see Gréta Gunnarsdóttir, "Resolution 1325 in Light of the Status of Gender Issues at the UN," available at http://www2.hi.is/page/RIKK-resolution1325.

66. See Women Building Peace, "Gender Peace Audits," at http://www.international-alert.org/women/news.html.

67. *UNIFEM Currents,* August 2002.

68. Oral History of Margaret Anstee, 14 December 2000, 147–148, in the Oral History Collection of the United Nations Intellectual History Project, The Graduate Center, The City University of New York.

69. Canadian International Development Agency, "Gender Equality and Peacebuilding: An Operational Framework," available at http://www.acdi-cida.gc.ca/peace.

70. "The Nairobi Forward-Looking Strategies for the Advancement of Women," in *The United Nations and the Advancement of Women,* 345.

71. Devaki Jain, "Need of the Hour: Political Response to Violence against Women."

72. See the ICRW's web site at http://www.icrw.org.

73. Pietilä, *Engendering the Global Agenda,* 85.

74. "United Nations Reform Measures and Proposals: The Millennium Assembly of the United Nations," Fifty-fourth session, Agenda item 49 (b), GA document A/54/959, 8 August 2000, available at http://www.un.org/millennium/declaration.htm.

75. Coomaraswamy, "Identity Within."

76. Devaki Jain, "Feminism and Feminist Expression: A Dialogue" in *Women's Studies—A Crucial Key to Feminist Purpose,* ed. Kamala Ganesh (forthcoming).

77. Griffen, "Globalization and Re-inventing the Politics of a Women's Movement."

78. Baden and Goetz, "Who Needs [Sex] When You Can Have [Gender]?" 20.

79. Antrobus, *The Global Women's Movement,* 105.

80. "Revitalising the International Feminist Movement: A Report of the Consultations Held at Kampala, Uganda, July 22–25, 2002." Available at www.choike/documentos/ kampala%202002.pdf.

81. This paragraph draws on "Revitalising the International Feminist Movement."

82. For example, see *The Gender of Power,* edited by Kathy Davis, Monique Leijenaar, and Jantine Oldersma (London: Sage, 1991).

83. See Gita Sen and Sonia Correa with the DAWN Steering Committee, *Remaking the Social Contract* (London: Zed Books, forthcoming 2005).

84. Louis Emmerij, paper prepared for the North-South Round Table on Imperatives of Tolerance and Justice in a Globalised World, 26–27 November 2002, Cairo.

85. Devaki Jain, "Enabling Reduction of Poverty and Inequality in South Asia," in *Population and Poverty: Achieving Equity, Equality and Sustainability* (New York: UNFPA, 2003), 99–100.

86. Devaki Jain, *Minds, Bodies and Exemplars: Reflections at Beijing and Beyond* (New Delhi: British Council, 1996), 8.

87. Jain, "Capitalising on Restlessness."

88. Devaki Jain, "The Empire Strikes Back," *Economic and Political Weekly,* 11 January 2003; Arundhati Roy, "Confronting Empire," and Ezequiel Adamovsky and Susan George, "What Is the Point of Porto Alegre?" both in *World Social Forum: Challenging Empires,* edited by Jai Sen, Anita Anand, Arturo Escobar, Peter Waterman (New Delhi: The Viveka Foundation, 2004).

89. See DAWN Web site, www.dawn.org.fj, and the Web site of the Women's International Coalition for Economic Justice, www.wicej.org.

90. West, "The United Nations Women's Conferences and Feminist Politics," 178.

91. Dawn Lorentson Hemispheric Institute 3rd Annual Encuentro Lima, Peru, 2002, Seminar Course Project Interview with Lourdes Arizpe, available at http://hemi.nyu.edu/eng/seminar/peru/call/studentprojects/dlorenston.shtml.

92. Rajeev Bhargava, "Are There Alternative Modernities?" in *Culture, Democracy and Development in South Asia,* edited by N. N. Vohra (New Delhi: Shipra Publications, 2001), 9.

93. Quoted in Jain, "The Many New Faces of Economic Development and Some Questions on How to Land Justice."

94. Jain, "Democratising Culture."

95. Kum-Kum Bhavnani, John Foran, and Priya Kurian, ed., *Feminist Futures: Re-Imagining Women, Culture and Development* (London: Zed Books Ltd., 2003).

Bibliography

Adedeji, Adebayo, Mary McCowan, and Devaki Jain. *Impact Evaluation of the United Nations Development Assistance Framework (UNDAF)*. United Nations Development Programme, 2001.

Afshar, Haleh, and Carolyne Dennis. *Women and Adjustment Policies in the Third World*. Houndmills, Basingstoke, Hampshire: Macmillan Academic and Professional, 1992.

Allan, Virginia R., Margaret E. Galey, and Mildred E. Persinger. "World Conference of International Women's Year." In *Women, Politics, and the United Nations*, edited by Anne Winslow. Westport, Conn.: Greenwood Press, 1995.

Anderson, Bonnie S. *Joyous Greetings: The First International Women's Movement, 1830–1860*. New York: Oxford University Press, 2000.

Anker, Richard. "Female Labour-Force Participation: An ILO Research on Conceptual and Measurement Issues." *International Labour Review* 122 (Nov.–Dec. 1983): 709–723.

Antrobus, Peggy. "A Caribbean Journey: Defending Feminist Politics." In *Developing Power*, edited by Arvonne S. Fraser and Irene Tinker. New York: Feminist Press, 2004.

———. *The Global Women's Movement: Origins, Issues and Strategies*. London: Zed Books, 2004.

Aslaksen, Iulie, and Charlotte Koren. "Unpaid Household Work and the Distribution of Extended Income: The Norwegian Experience." *Feminist Economics* 2, no. 3 (1996): 65–80.

Babbitt, Kate. "The Productive Farm Woman and the Extension Home Economist in New York State, 1920–1940." *Agricultural History* 67, no. 2 (1993): 83–101.

Baden, Sally. "Gender, Governance and the 'Feminisation of Poverty.'" Paper presented at the Meeting on Women and Political Participation: 21st Century Challenges, UNDP, March 24–26, 1999, New Delhi, India. Available at http://mirror.undp.org/magnet/events/gender/india/Badefeb2.htm.

Baden, Sally, and Anne Marie Goetz. "Who Needs [Sex] When You Can Have [Gender]? Conflicting Discourses on Gender at Beijing." *Feminist Review* 56 (Summer 1997): 3–25.

Baden, Sally, with Kirsty Milward. *Gender Inequality and Poverty: Trends, Linkages, Analysis and Policy Implications*. Report prepared for the Gender Equality Unit, Swedish International Development Cooperation Agency (SIDA), Sussex, October 1997. Available at http://www.ids.ac.uk/bridge/reports/re30.pdf.

Båge, Lennart. "The Well Fed Have Many Problems, the Hungry Only One." *UN Chronicle* Number 3 (2001). Available at http://www.globalpolicy.org/socecon/develop/2001/1130food.htm.

Baines, Erin K. "Gender Construction and the Protection Mandate of the UNHCR: Responses from Guatemalan Women." In *Gender Politics in Global Governance,* edited by Elisabeth Prügl and Mary K. Meyer. Lanham, Md.: Rowman and Littlefield, 1999.

Bangasser, Paul E. "The ILO and the Informal Sector: An Institutional History." ILO Employment Paper 2000/9. Available at http://www.ilo.org/public/english/employment/strat/publ/epoo-9.htm#N_12_.

Barrow, Nita. "The Decade NGO Forum." *Africa Report* (March–April 1985): 9–11.

Bartkowski, Maciej. "Comparative Study of Women's Activities in the Inter-War Intergovernmental Organizations: The League of Nations, the International Labour Organization and the Pan American Union." *Rubikon* (May 2002). Available online at http://venus.ci.uw.edu.pl/~rubikon/forum/women.htm.

Basu, Amrita. *The Challenge of Local Feminisms: Women's Movements in Global Perspective.* Boulder, Colo.: Westview Press, 1995.

———. "Globalization of the Local/Localization of the Global: Mapping Transnational Women's Movements." *Meridians: Feminism, Race, Transnationalism* 1, no. 1 (2000): 68–84.

Basu, Kaushi. "On the Goals of Development." In *Frontiers of Development Economics: The Future in Perspective,* edited by Gerald M. Meier and Joseph E. Stiglitz. Oxford: Oxford University Press, 2001.

Battacharya, Debapriya, and Mustafizur Rahman. "Female Employment under Export-Propelled Industrialization: Prospects for Internalizing Global Opportunities in the Apparel Sector in Bangladesh." Occasional Paper No. 10, UNRISD, July 1999.

Bell, Emma. *Emerging Issues in Gender and Development: An Overview.* Bridge Report No. 58. Brighton, U.K.: Institute of Development Studies, November 2000.

Bell, Emma, Bridget Byrne, Julie Koch Laier, Sally Baden, and Rachel Marcus. *National Machineries for Women in Development: Experiences, Lessons and Strategies.* Report prepared for the Ministry of Foreign Affairs, Denmark, February 2002.

Benería, Lourdes. "Accounting for Women's Work: The Progress of Two Decades." *World Development* 20, no. 11 (1992): 1547–1560.

———. "The Enduring Debate Over Unpaid Labor." *International Labour Review* 138, no. 3 (August 1999): 287–309.

Benería, Lourdes, and Amy Lind. "Engendering International Trade: Concepts, Policy, and Action." In *A Commitment to the World's Women: Perspectives on Development for Beijing and Beyond,* edited by Noeleen Heyzer with Sushma Kapoor and Joanne Sandler. New York: UNIFEM, 1995.

Benería, Lourdes, and Gita Sen. "Accumulation, Reproduction and Women's Role in Economic Development: Boserup Revisited." In *The Women, Gender and Development Reader,* edited by Nalini Visvanathan, Lynn Duggan, Laurie Nisonoff, and Nan Wiegersma. London: Zed Books, 1997.

Berry, Kim. "Lakshmi and the Scientific Housewife: A Transnational Account of Indian Women's Development and Production of an Indian Modernity." *Economic and Political Weekly* (Special Article) (15 March 2003).

Bhavnani, Kum-Kum, John Foran, and Priya Kurian. "An Introduction to Women, Culture and Development." In *Feminist Futures: Re-Imagining Women, Culture and Development,* edited by Kum-Kum Bhavnani, John Foran, and Priya Kurian. London, New York: Zed Books Ltd., 2003.

Bienefeld, Manfred. "Global Markets: Threats to Sustainable Development." In *A Commitment to the World's Women: Perspectives on Development for Beijing and Beyond,* edited by Noeleen Heyzer with Sushma Kapoor and Joanne Sandler. New York: UNIFEM, 1995.

Black, Maggie. *The Children and the Nations: Growing Up Together in the Postwar World.* New York: UNICEF, 1987.

———. *Children First: The Story of UNICEF, Past and Present.* Oxford: Oxford University Press, 1996.

Boserup, Ester. *My Professional Life and Publications 1929–1998.* Copenhagen: Museum Tusculanum Press, 1999.

Bouayad-Agha, Fatih, and Homero L. Hernández. *An Evaluation of the United Nations International Research and Training Institute for the Advancement of Women (INSTRAW).* Geneva: Joint Inspection Unit, 1999.

Boulding, Elise. "Integration into What? Reflections on Development Planning for Women." In *Women and Technological Change in Developing Countries,* edited by Roslyn Dauber and Melinda L. Cain. Boulder, Colo.: Westview Press, 1981.

———. "Measures of Women's Work in the Third World: Problems and Suggestions." In *Women and Poverty in the Third World,* edited by Mayra Buvinić, Margaret A. Lycette, and William Paul McGreevey. Baltimore, Md.: Johns Hopkins University Press, 1983.

Braig, Marianne. "Women's Interests in Development Theory and Policy: From Women in Development to Mainstreaming Gender." In *Neue Ansätze zur Entwicklungstheorie* [*New Approaches to Development Theory*], edited by R. E. Thiel. Bonn: Deutsche Stiftung für Internationale Entwicklung, 1999.

Brenner, Johanna. "NGOs, Popular Feminism, and the Problems of Cross-Class Alliances." *New Politics* 19, no. 2 (Winter 2003).

Bruce, Judith. "Homes Divided." *World Development* 17, no. 7 (1989): 979–991.

Bruce, Margaret. "Women and Policy-Making at the United Nations." In *The United Nations & Decision-Making: The Role of Women,* edited by Davidson Nicol and Margaret Croke. New York: UNITAR, 1978.

Bunch, Charlotte. "Women's Human Rights and Development: A Global Agenda for the 21st Century." In *A Commitment to the World's Women: Perspectives on Development for Beijing and Beyond,* edited by Noeleen Heyzer with Sushma Kapoor and Joanne Sandler. New York: UNIFEM, 1995.

Bunch, Charlotte, and Roxanna Carrillo. "Feminist Perspectives on Women in Development." In *Persistent Inequalities: Women and World Development,* edited by Irene Tinker. New York: Oxford University Press, 1990.

Bunch, Charlotte, Mallika Dutt, and Susana Fried. "Women's Human Rights: A Global Referendum." In *Beijing! UN Fourth World Conference on Women,* edited by Anita Anand with Gouri Salvi. New Delhi: Women's Feature Service, 1998.

Bunch, Charlotte, and Niamh Reilly. *Demanding Accountability: The Global Campaign and Vienna Tribunal for Women's Human Rights.* New York: UNIFEM, 1994.

Buvinić, Mayra. "Projects for Women in the Third World: Explaining Their Misbehavior." *World Development* 14, no. 5 (1986): 653–664.

Buvinić, Mayra, and Geeta Rao Gupta. "Female-Headed Households and Female-Maintained Families: Are They Worth Targeting to Reduce Poverty in Developing Countries?" *Economic Development and Cultural Change* 45, no. 2 (January 1997): 259–280.

Çagatay, Nilüfer. "Engendering Macro-Economics." In *Macro-Economics: Making Gender Matter,* edited by Martha Gutierrez. London and New York: Zed Books, 2003. Available at http://www.undp.org/poverty/publications/wkpaper/wp6/wp6-nilufer.doc.

———. "Gender and Poverty." Social Development and Poverty Elimination Division, Working Paper Series, no. 5. (May 1998). Available at http://www.undp.org/poverty/publications/wkpaper/wp5/wp5-nilufer.PDF.

Çagatay, Nilüfer, Caren Grown, and Aida Santiago. "The Nairobi Women's Conference: Toward a Global Feminism?" *Feminist Studies* 12, no. 2 (Summer 1986): 401–412.

Caillods, Françoise, Maria Adélaïde Rocha, Maria Manuel Fonseca, Maria Graciette Claudino, Maria do Carmo Nunes, and Salma Zouari Bouattour. *Education et emploi des femmes au Portugal: une évolution constrastée.* Paris: UNESCO and IIEP, 1988.

Carr, Marilyn, and Martha Alter Chen. "Globalization and the Informal Economy: How Global Trade and Investment Impact on the Working Poor." Working Paper on the Informal Economy. Geneva: International Labour Office Employment Sector, 2002. Available at http://www.eldis.org/static/DOC12430.htm.

Centre for Women and Development Studies. *The Non Aligned Movement and the International Women's Decade.* New Delhi: Centre for Women and Development Studies, n.d.

Chachhi, Amrita, and Renee Pittin. "Multiple Identities, Multiple Strategies: Confronting State, Capital and Patriarchy." Available at http://www.antenna.nl/~waterman/pittin.html.

Chambers, Robert. "Poverty and Livelihood: Whose Reality Counts?" *Environment and Urbanization* 7, no. 1 (April 1995): 173–204.

Chand, M., D. Jain, R. Kalyandsundaram, and H. Singh. *Income-Generating Activities for Women: Some Case Studies.* New Delhi: Indian Co-operative Union, 1978.

Chaney, Elsa M. "Full Circle: From Academia to Government and Back." In *Developing Power,* edited by Arvonne S. Fraser and Irene Tinker. New York: Feminist Press, 2004.

Chant, S. "Women Headed Households: Poorest of the Poor? Perspectives from Mexico, Costa Rica and the Philippines." *IDS Bulletin* 28, no. 3 (1997): 26–48.

Charlesworth, Hilary. "Transforming the United Men's Club: Feminist Futures for the United Nations." *Transnational Law & Contemporary Problems* 4, no. 2 (Fall 1994): 422–454.

———. "Women as Sherpas: Are Global Summits Useful for Women?" *Feminist Studies* 22 (Fall 1996): 537–547.

Charmes, Jacques, Joann Vanek, Martha Chen, Marguerita Guerrero, Francoise Carré, Rodrigo Negrete, Jeemol Unni, Debbie Budlender, and others. "Women and Men in the Informal Economy: A Statistical Picture." Geneva: ILO Employment Sector, 2002. Available at http://www.wiego.org/papers/ilo_gender.pdf.

Chen, Martha Alter. "Engendering World Conferences: The International Women's Movement and the UN." In *NGOs, the UN, and Global Governance,* edited by Thomas G. Weiss and Leon Gordenker. Boulder, Colo.: Lynne Rienner, 1996.

———. "The Feminization of Poverty." In *A Commitment to the World's Women: Perspectives on Development for Beijing and Beyond,* edited by Noeleen Heyzer with Sushma Kapoor and Joanne Sandler. New York: UNIFEM, 1995.

Chen, Martha Alter, Renana Jhabvala, and Frances Lund. "Supporting Workers in the Informal Economy: A Policy Framework." Paper prepared for the ILO Task Force on the Informal Economy. Geneva: International Labour Office, November 2001. Available at http://www.eldis.org/static/DOC12433.htm.

Chen, Shaohua, and Martin Ravallion. "How Did the World's Poorest Fare in the 1990s?" *The Review of Income and Wealth* 47, no. 3 (September 2001): 283–300.

Chowdhry, Geeta. "Engendering Development? Women in Development (WID) in International Development Regimes." In *Feminism/Postmodernism/Development,* edited by Marianne H. Marchand and Jane L. Parpart. London and New York: Routledge, 1995.

Cloud, Kathleen. "Hard Minds and Soft Hearts: A University Memoir." In *Developing Power,* edited by Arvonne S. Fraser and Irene Tinker. New York: Feminist Press, 2004.

Cohen, Susan A. "The Road from Rio to Cairo: Toward a Common Agenda." *International Family Planning Perspectives* 19, no. 2 (June 1993): 61–66.

Connelly, M. Patricia, Tania Murray Li, Martha MacDonald, and Jane L. Parpart. "Feminism and Development: Theoretical Perspectives." In *Theoretical Perspectives on Gender and Development,* edited by Jane L. Parpart, M. Patricia Connelly, and V. Eudine Barriteau. Ottawa: International Development Research Centre, 2000.

Cook, Rebecca. "Women." In *The United Nations and International Law,* edited by Christopher Joyner. Cambridge: Cambridge University Press, 1997.

Coomaraswamy, Radhika. "Identity Within: Cultural Relativism, Minority Rights and the Empowerment of Women." *George Washington International Law Review* 34 (July 2001): 483–513.

Corner, Lorraine. "From Margins to Mainstream: From Gender Statistics to Engendering Statistical Systems." Available at http://www.undp.org/povertycentre/publications/gender/Margins2Mainstream_GenderStatistics-Corner-UNIFEM-Mar03.pdf.

———. *Women, Men and Economics: Gender Differentiated Impact of Macroeconomics* (New York: UNIFEM, 1996). Available at http://www.unifem-ecogov-apas.org/ecogov-apas/EEGKnowledgeBase/WomenMenEconomics/womenmeneconomics.html.

Corpuz, Victoria Tauli. "Depoliticising Gender in Beijing." *Third World Resurgence,* 61/61 (September/October 1995). Available at http://www.twnside.org.sg/title/gen-ch.htm.

Corral, Thais. "Can Women Make a Difference? Experiences at the UN Conferences." *Political Environments* 3 (March 31, 1996): 17.

DAC Source Book on Concepts and Approaches Linked to Gender Equality. Paris: OECD, 1998.

Daes, Erica-Irene. *The Advancement of Women through and in the Programmes of the United Nations System: What Happens After the Fourth World Conference of Women?* Geneva: Joint Inspection Unit, 1995.

D'Amico, Francine D. "Women Workers in the United Nations: From Margin to Mainstream?" In *Gender Politics in Global Governance,* edited by Mary K. Meyer and Elisabeth Prügl. Lanham, Md.: Rowman and Littlefield, 1999.

"DAWN Says No to Negotiations for Beijing+10 and Cairo+10." *DAWN Informs* (April 2003). Available at http://www.dawn.org.fj/publications/DAWNInforms/DIApri103.pdf.

Derryck, Vivian Lowery. "Searching for Equality: WID Needed at Home and Abroad." In *De-*

veloping Power, edited by Arvonne S. Fraser and Irene Tinker. New York: Feminist Press, 2004.

Desai, Manisha. "From Vienna to Beijing: Women's Human Rights Activism and the Human Rights Community." *New Political Science* 35 (Spring 1996): 107–119.

———. "Transnational Solidarity: Women's Agency, Structural Adjustment, and Globalization." In *Women's Activism and Globalization: Linking Local Struggles and Transnational Politics,* edited by Nancy A. Naples and Manisha Desai. New York: Routledge, 2002.

Development Assistance Committee, OECD. *DAC Guidelines for Gender Equality and Women's Empowerment in Development Co-Operation.* Paris: OECD, 1999.

Easterly, William. "The Lost Decades: Developing Countries' Stagnation in Spite of Policy Reform 1980–1998." World Bank, February 2001. Available at http://www.worldbank.org/research/growth/pdfiles/lost%20decades_joeg.pdf.

Eck, Diana L., and Devaki Jain, eds. *Speaking of Faith: Cross-Cultural Perspectives on Women, Religion and Social Change.* New Delhi: Kali for Women, 1986.

Eckert, Amy. "Universality by Consensus: The Evolution of the Universality in the Drafting of the UDHR." *Human Rights and Human Welfare* 1, no. 2 (April 2001).

Elias, Misrak. "Mainstreaming Gender in Development from UNICEF's Perspective." In *Seeds 2: Supporting Women's Work around the World,* edited by Ann Leonard. New York: Feminist Press, 1995.

Elson, Diane. "For an Emancipatory Socio-Economics." Draft paper prepared for the discussion at the UNRISD meeting on The Need to Rethink Development Economics, Cape Town, South Africa, 7–8 September 2001.

———. "Gender Aware Analysis and Development Economics." *Journal of International Development* 5, no. 2 (1993): 237–247.

———. "Gender Justice, Human Rights, and Neo-Liberal Economic Policies." In *Gender Justice, Development, and Rights,* edited by Maxine Molyneux and Shahra Razavi. New York: Oxford University Press, 2002.

———. "The Impact of Structural Adjustment on Women: Concepts and Issues." In *The IMF, the World Bank and the African Debt.* Vol. 2. *Social and Political Impact,* edited by Bade Onimode. London: Zed Books, 1989.

———. *Male Bias in the Development Process.* Manchester and New York: Manchester University Press, 1991.

———. "Male Bias in Macro-Economics: The Case of Structural Adjustment." In *Male Bias in the Development Process,* edited by Diane Elson. Manchester: Manchester University Press, 1991.

———. "Male Bias in Structural Adjustment." In *Women and Adjustment Policies in the Third World,* edited by Haleh Afshar and Carolyne Dennis. Houndmills, Basingstoke, Hampshire: Macmillan Academic and Professional, 1992.

Emmerij, Louis. "Development Thinking, Globalisation and Cultural Diversity." Paper prepared for the North South Roundtable on Imperatives of Tolerance and Justice in a Globalized World, Cairo, 26–27 November 2002.

Emmerij, Louis, Richard Jolly, and Thomas G. Weiss. *Ahead of the Curve? UN Ideas and Global Challenges.* Bloomington: Indiana University Press, 2001.

Entering the 21st Century: World Development Report 1999/2000. New York: Oxford University Press for the World Bank, 2000.

Eriksen, Thomas Hylland. "Globalization and the Politics of Identity." *UN Chronicle* (Autumn 1999). Available at folk.uio.no/geirthe/UNChron.html.

Fraser, Arvonne S. "The Convention on the Elimination of All Forms of Discrimination Against Women (The Women's Convention)." In *Women, Politics, and the United Nations,* edited by Anne Winslow. Westport, Conn.: Greenwood Press, 1995.

Friedman, Elisabeth J. "The Effects of 'Transnationalism Reversed' in Venezuela: Assessing the Impact of UN Global Conferences on the Women's Movement." *International Feminist Journal of Politics* 1, no. 3 (Winter 1999): 357–381.

Fukuda-Parr, Sakiko. "The Human Development Paradigm: Operationalizing Sen's Ideas on Capabilities." *Feminist Economics* 9, nos. 2 and 3 (July/November 2003): 301–317.

Gachukia, Eddah. "Education, Women, and Politics in Kenya." In *Developing Power,* edited by Arvonne S. Fraser and Irene Tinker. New York: Feminist Press, 2004.

Galey, Margaret E. "Forerunners in Women's Quest for Partnership." In *Women, Politics, and the United Nations,* edited by Anne Winslow. Westport, Conn.: Greenwood Press, 1995.

———. "Gender Roles and UN Reform." *PS: Political Science & Politics* XXII, no. 4 (December 1989): 813–820.

———. "Promoting Non-Discrimination against Women: The UN Commission on the Status of Women." *International Development Quarterly* 23, no. 2 (June 1979): 273–302.

———. "The United Nations and Women's Issues." In *Women, Gender, and World Politics: Perspectives, Policies, and Prospects,* edited by Peter R. Beckman and Francine D'Amico. Westport, Conn.: Bergin & Garvey, 1994.

———. "Women Find a Place." In *Women, Politics, and the United Nations,* edited by Anne Winslow. Westport, Conn.: Greenwood Press, 1995.

Gaudier, Maryse. "The Development of the Women's Question at the ILO, 1919–1994: 75 Years of Progress towards Equality." Available at http://www.ilo.org/public/english/bureau/inst/papers/1996/dp87/index.htm.

Giminez, Martha. "The Feminization of Poverty: Myth or Reality?" *The Insurgent Sociologist* 14, no. 3 (Fall 1987): 5–30.

Glendon, Mary Ann. *A World Made New: Eleanor Roosevelt and the Universal Declaration of the Human Rights.* New York: Random House, 2001.

Goetz, Anne Marie. "Institutionalising Women's Interests and Gender-Sensitive Accountability in Development." *IDS Bulletin* 26, no. 3 (1995).

———. *The Politics of Integrating Gender to the State Development Processes: Trends, Opportunities and Constraints in Bangladesh, Chile, Jamaica, Mali, Morocco, and Uganda.* Geneva: UNRISD and UNDP, 1995.

Goetz, Anne Marie, and Rina Sen Gupta. "Who Takes the Credit? Gender, Power, and Control over Loan Use in Rural Credit Programs in Bangladesh." *World Development* 24, no. 1 (1996): 45–63.

Goldschmidt-Clermont, Luisella. *Unpaid Work in the Household: A Review of Economic Evaluation Methods.* Geneva: ILO, 1981.

Griffen, Vanessa. "Globalization and Re-inventing the Politics of a Women's Movement." Occasional Paper No. 6, Kuala Lumpur, Malaysia, Asian and Pacific Development Centre, June 2002. Available at http://www.awid.org/publications/OccasionalPapers/occasional6.html.

Gutierrez, Martha. *Macro-Economics: Making Gender Matter: Concepts, Policies and Institutional Change in Developing Countries.* London: Zed Books, 2003.

Hannam, June, Mitzi Auchterlonie, and Katherine Holden. *International Encyclopedia of Women's Suffrage.* Santa Barbara, Calif.: ABC–CLIO, 2000.

ul Haq, Mahbub. *Reflections on Human Development.* Oxford: Oxford University Press, 1995.

Hedervary, Claire de. "The United Nations: 'Good Grief, There Are Women Here!'" In *Sisterhood Is Global,* edited by Robin Morgan. Garden City, N.J.: Anchor Books, 1984.

Heyzer, Noeleen. "Seizing the Opportunity." In *Beijing! UN Fourth World Conference on Women,* edited by Anita Anand with Gouri Salvi. New Delhi: Women's Feature Service, 1998.

Heyzer, Noeleen, ed. *A Commitment to the World's Women: Perspectives on Development from Beijing and Beyond.* New York: UNIFEM, 1995.

Higer, Amy J. "International Women's Activism and the 1994 Cairo Population Conference." In *Gender Politics in Global Governance,* edited by Mary K. Meyer and Elisabeth Prügl. Lanham, Md.: Rowman and Littlefield, 1999.

Hochstetler, Kathryn, Elisabeth J. Friedman, and Ann Marie Clark. "Latin American NGOs and Governments: Coalition-Building at UN Conferences on the Environment, Human Rights, and Women." Paper prepared for the XXII International Congress of the Latin American Studies Association, Chicago, Illinois, September 24–26, 1998.

Hussein, Aziza. "Crossroads for Women at the UN." In *Developing Power,* edited by Arvonne S. Fraser and Irene Tinker. New York: Feminist Press, 2004.

Illo, Jeanne Frances I. "Working and Living for Family: Gender, Work, and Education in Philippines." UNESCO document SHS/POP/UNIC/CWS/90/05, 1990.

Improvement of the Status of Women in the United Nations System: Report of the Secretary-General. GA document A/58/374, 17 September 2003.

Institut el Amouri. *Le Secteur informel: quelle place pour les femmes? (Cas de la Tunisie).* Tunisia: Institut el Amouri, 1989.

INSTRAW. "The Concept of Self-Reliance and the Integration of Women into Development." In UN Department of International Economic and Social Affairs, *World Survey on the Role of Women in Development.* New York: United Nations, 1986.

———. "INSTRAW's Profile for the New Millennium." Santo Domingo: INSTRAW, 1998.

———. "Women in the Secretariat: Putting the Principle into Practice." *INSTRAW News* 18 (Autumn 1992): 18–21.

International Labour Organization (ILO). "Employment, Incomes and Equity: A Strategy for Increasing Productive Employment in Kenya." Geneva: ILO, 1972.

———. *Women in the Informal Sector: Emerging Gender Issues in the Asia Pacific Region,* Unit 2: "Gender Issues in the World of Work." Available at http://www.ilo.org/public/english/region/asro/mdtmanila/training/unit2/asiainfm.htm.

International Women's Tribune Centre (IWTC). *Developing Strategies for the Future.* New York: IWTC, 1980.

———. *It's Our Move Now; A Community Action Guide to the UN Nairobi Forward Looking Strategies for the Advancement of Women.* New York: IWTC, 1987.

Ironmonger, Duncan. "Counting Outputs, Capital Inputs and Caring Labor: Estimating Gross Household Product." *Feminist Economics* 2, no. 3 (1996): 37–64.

Jackson, Cecile. "Rescuing Gender from the Poverty Trap." *World Development* 24, no. 3 (1996): 489–504.

Jain, Devaki. "Are Women a Separate Issue?" *Populi* 5, no. 1 (November 1978): 7–15.

———. "Capitalising on Restlessness: Women's Opportunity to Transform Leadership." Inaugural address delivered at Commonwealth Universities Meet, SNDT Women's University, Mumbai, 15 November 1995.

———. "The DAWN Movement." In *Routledge International Encyclopaedia of Women*, edited by Chris Kramarae and Dale Spender. New York: Routledge, 2000.

———. "Development as if Women Mattered: Can Women Build a New Paradigm?" Lecture delivered at OECD/DAC Meeting, Paris, 26 January 1983.

———. "Development Theory and Practice: Insights Emerging from Women's Experience." *Economic and Political Weekly* (Mumbai), 7 July 1990, 1454–1455.

———. *For Women to Lead: Ideas and Experience from Asia—A Study on Legal and Political Impediments to Gender Equality in Governance.* New Delhi: National Commission for Women, 1997.

———. "Gandhian Contributions toward a Feminist Ethic." In *Speaking of Faith: Cross-Cultural Perspectives on Women, Religion and Social Change,* edited by Diana L. Eck and Devaki Jain. New Delhi: Kali for Women, 1986.

———. "The Gender Issue in Formal and Informal Labour Markets." Paper prepared for the 4th Annual Workshop on Women, Work and Public Policy, Kennedy School Forum, Harvard University, 14 April 1984.

———. "Globalism and Localism: Negotiating Feminist Space." Paper presented at the conference Rethinking Gender, Democracy and Development: Is Decentralisation a Tool for Local Ownership of an Effective Political Voice? 20–22 May 2002, University of Ferrara and Modena, Modena, Italy.

———. "House Work." Paper presented at the workshop Visibility of Women in Statistics and Indicators, jointly organized by INSTRAW and the government of India, Shreemati Nathibai Damodar Thackersey Women's University, 3–7 July 1989, Mumbai, India.

———. "The Household Trap: Report on a Field Survey of Female Activity Patterns." In *The Tyranny of the Household,* edited by Devaki Jain and Nirmala Banerjee. New Delhi: Vikas Publications, 1985.

———. "Importance of Age and Sex Specific Data Collection in Household Surveys." Paper presented at the Regional Conference on Household Survey, organized by Economic and Social Commission for Asia and Pacific (ESCAP), Bangkok, 1980.

———. "India: A Condition across Race and Class." In *Sisterhood Is Global: The International Women's Movement Anthology,* edited by Robin Morgan, 305–310. New York: Feminist Press, 1996.

———. "Indian Women: Today and Tomorrow." Padmaja Naidu Memorial Lecture, Nehru Memorial Museum and Library, New Delhi, 1982.

———. "The Leadership Gap: Challenge to Feminists." Paper presented at Indian Association of Women's Studies Conference, Mysore, 1993.

———. "Letting the Worm Turn: A Comment on Innovative Poverty Alleviation." Paper presented at IFAD panel III K of 19th World Conference of the Society for International Development (SID), New Delhi, 1988.

———. "The Many New Faces of Economic Development and Some Questions on How to

Land Justice." Paper presented at the North South Roundtable on Imperatives of Tolerance and Justice in a Globalized World, Cairo, 26–27 November 2002.

———. "Minds, Not Bodies: Expanding the Notion of Gender in Development." Bradford
Morse Memorial Lecture, Beijing, 5 September 1995. Published by Beijing and Beyond,
British Council Division, British High Commission, 1996.

———. "Need of the Hour: Political Response to Violence against Women—The Perspective
from India." Paper presented at the SADC Conference on Violence against Women, Durban,
5 March 1998.

———. "Networks, People's Movements, and Alliances: Learning from the Ground." Paper
presented at the Know-How Conference 2002, Kampala, Uganda, 23–27 July 2002.

———. "Panchayat Raj: An Institutional Platform for Women's Leadership—A Success Story
from India." Paper presented at the UNDP panel on Women in Governance, New York, 24
March 1995, as part of the prepcoms for Beijing 1995.

———. "The Politics of Measurement: HDR Values." Paper presented at the conference
"Women and Human Development Report: A Brainstorming," 20–21 February 2004, Bangalore, India. Available at http://hdrc.undp.org.in/events/Gndr_n_Gvrnce/hdr_values.pdf.

———. "Quest for Healing." In *Science and Beyond: Cosmology, Consciousness and Technology
in the Indic Traditions,* edited by Sangeetha Menon, B. V. Sreekantan, Anindya Sinha, Philip
Clayton, Roddam Narasimha. Bangalore: National Institute of Advanced Studies, 2004.

———. "Role of Women in Development: An Intergovernmental Conference of Another Kind."
Women's World (27 April 1985).

———. "Valuing Women: Signals from the Ground." Lecture delivered at University of Mary-
land, United States, June 2001.

———. "Valuing Work: Time as a Measure." *Economic and Political Weekly* XXXI, no. 43 (26
October 1996).

———. *Women's Quest for Power: Five Indian Case Studies.* New Delhi: Vikas Publication, 1980.

Jain, Devaki, and Malini Chand. "Report on a Time Allocation Study: Its Methodological
Implications." Paper presented at the seminar Women's Work and Employment, Institute
of Social Studies Trust, New Delhi, 9–11 April 1982.

Jain, Devaki, and Nirmala Banerjee, eds. *Tyranny of the Household: Investigative Essays on
Women's Work.* Sahibabad, India: Shakti Books, 1985.

Jain, Devaki, and Mukul Mukherjee. "Women and Their Households: The Relevance of Men
and Macro Policies: An Indian Perspective." Paper prepared by the Institute of Social Studies Trust for the ILO (1984) and developed for Population Council Study on Indian Female
Households (1989).

Jain, Devaki, and Pam Rajput. "Introduction." In *Narratives from the Women's Studies Family:
Recreating Knowledge,* edited by Devaki Jain and Pam Rajput. New Delhi: SAGE Publications, 2003.

Jain, Devaki, and Malini Chand Shethi. "Domestic Work: Its Implications for Enumeration of
Workers." In *Women, Work and Society,* edited by K. Saradamoni. Calcutta: Indian Statistical Institute, 1985.

Jaquette, Jane S. "Crossing the Line: From Academia to the WID Office at USAID." In *Developing Power,* edited by Arvonne S. Fraser and Irene Tinker. New York: Feminist Press, 2004.

———. "Gender and Justice in Economic Development." In *Persistent Inequalities: Women and World Development,* edited by Irene Tinker. New York: Oxford University Press, 1990.

———. "Losing the Battle/Winning the War: International Politics, Women's Issues, and the 1980 Mid-Decade Conference." In *Women, Politics, and the United Nations,* edited by Anne Winslow. Westport, Conn.: Greenwood Press, 1995.

Jhabvala, Renana. "Bringing Informal Workers Centrestage." In *Informal Economy Centrestage: New Structures of Employment,* edited by Renana Jhabvala, Ratna M. Sudarshan, and Jeemol Unni. New Delhi: Sage Publications, 2003.

———. "SEWA and Home-Based Workers in India: Their Struggle and Emerging Role." Paper presented at the Workshop on Indigenising Human Rights Education in Indian Universities, Bangalore, December 2001.

Jolly, Richard, Louis Emmerij, Dharam Ghai, and Frederic Lapeyre. *UN Contributions to Development Theory and Practice.* Bloomington: Indiana University Press, 2004.

Kabeer, Naila. *Reversed Realities: Gender Hierarchies in Development Thought.* London: Verso, 1994.

Kabeer, Naila, and Tran Thi Van Anh. "Leaving the Rice Fields, but Not the Countryside: Gender, Livelihood Diversification and Pro-Poor Growth in Rural Viet Nam." UNRISD Occasional Paper No. 13, September 2000.

Kanbur, Ravi, and Lyn Squire. "The Evolution of Thinking about Poverty: Exploring the Interactions." In *Frontiers of Development Economics: The Future in Perspective,* edited by Gerald M. Meier and Joseph E. Stiglitz. Oxford: Oxford University Press, 2001.

Kardam, Nüket. "The Tripartite System of the United Nations Development Programme." In *Bringing Women In: Women's Issues in International Development Programs.* Boulder, Colo.: Lynn Rienner, 1991.

Karl, Marilee, Anita Anand, Floris Blankenberg, Allert van den Ham, and Adrian Saldanha, eds., *Measuring the Immeasurable: Planning, Monitoring and Evaluation of Networks.* New Delhi: Women's Feature Service, 1999.

Karlekar, Malavika. "The Family and the Household in India: An Overview of Research." UNESCO document SHS/POP/UNIC/CWDS/90/06, 1990.

Kerr, Joanna. "Responding to Globalization: Can Feminists Transform Development?" In *Feminists Doing Development: A Practical Critique,* edited by Marilyn Porter and Ellen Judd. New York: St. Martin's Press, 1999.

Kristiansen, Annali. "Review of UNESCO's Past and Present Work on Gender and Women." Unpublished report, 2003.

Lamas, Marta, Alicia Martínez, María Luisa Tarrés, and Esperanza Tuñon. "Building Bridges: The Growth of Popular Feminism in Mexico." In *The Challenge of Local Feminisms,* edited by Amrita Basu with Elizabeth McGrory. Boulder, Colo.: Westview Press, 1995.

Makandiwe, Thandika. "Adjustment Political Conditionality and Democratisation in Africa." In *From Adjustment to Development in Africa: Conflict, Controversy, Consensus?* edited by Giovanni Andrea Cornea and Gerald K. Helleiner. New York: St. Martin's Press, 1994.

———. "The Political Economy of Privatisation in Africa." In *From Adjustment to Development in Africa: Conflict, Controversy, Consensus?* edited by Giovanni Andrea Cornea and Gerald K. Helleiner. New York: St. Martin's Press, 1994.

Mama, Amina. "Gains and Challenges: Linking Theory and Practice." Keynote address at the Women's World's Congress. Makerere University, 21 July 2002. Available at http://web.uct. ac.za/org/agi/events/mama.htm.

———. "Postscript: Moving from Analysis to Practice?" In *Engendering African Social Sciences,* edited by Ayesha Imam, Amina Mama, and Fatou Sow. Senegal: CODESRIA, 1999.

Marchand, Marianne H., and Jane L. Parpart. "Exploding the Canon: An Introduction/Conclusion." In *Feminism/Postmodernism/Development.* London and New York: Routledge, 1995.

Masini, Eleonora Barbieri. "The Household, Gender, and Age Project." In *Women, Households, and Change,* edited by Eleonora Masini and Susan Stratigos. Tokyo: United Nations University Press, 1991. Available at http://www.unu.edu/unupress/unupbooks/uu10we/ uu10we04.htm.

Mathiason, John. *The Long March to Beijing.* CD-ROM.

———. "UN Secretariat: Gatekeeper of Ideas." In *Beijing! UN Fourth World Conference on Women,* edited by Anita Anand with Gouri Salvi. New Delhi: Women's Feature Service, 1998.

Mazumdar, Vina. "The Non-Aligned Movement and the International Women's Decade: A Summary of Decisions." Centre for Women's Development Studies, New Delhi, 8 March 1993.

McIntosh, Tracey. "Contested Realities: Race, Gender and Public Policy in Aotearoa/New Zealand." Paper prepared for the conference Racism and Public Policy, Durban, South Africa, 3–5 September 2001.

Mehra, Rekha, and Sarah Gammage. "Trends, Countertrends, and Gaps in Women's Employment." *World Development* 27, no. 3 (1999): 533–550.

Mehrotra, Santosh, and Mario Biggeri. "Social Protection in the Informal Economy: Home Based Women Workers and Outsourced Manufacturing in Asia." Innocenti Working Paper No. 97, UNICEF, December 2002. Available at http://www.unicef-icdc.org/publications/ pdf/iwp97.pdf.

Meier, Gerald M., and Joseph E. Stiglitz, eds. *Frontiers of Development Economics: The Future in Perspective.* Oxford: Oxford University Press, 2001.

Meyer, Mary K., and Elisabeth Prügl. *Gender Politics in Global Governance.* Lanham, Md.: Rowman and Littlefield, 1999.

Miller, Carol. "'Geneva—the Key to Equality': Inter-War Feminists and the League of Nations." *Women's History Review* 3, no. 2 (1994): 219–245.

Mingst, Karen A., and Margaret P. Karns. *The United Nations in the Post-Cold War Era.* Boulder, Colo.: Westview Press, 2000.

Mkandawire, Thandika, and Virginia Rodríguez. "Globalization and Social Development after Copenhagen: Premises, Promises and Policies." Geneva 2000 Occasional Paper No. 10, United Nations Research Institute for Social Development, June 2000.

Moghadam, Valentine. "The Feminization of Poverty? Notes on a Concept and Trends." Occasional Papers No. 2, Women's Studies Program, Illinois State University, 1997.

Molyneux, Maxine, and Shahra Razavi, eds. *Gender Justice, Development, and Rights.* Oxford: Oxford University Press, 2002.

Morris, Morris David. "Light in the Tunnel: The Changing Condition of the World's Poor."

Brown University Op-Ed Service, August 1996. Available at http://www.brown.edu/Administration/News_Bureau/Op-Eds/Morris.html.

Moser, Caroline. "From Nairobi to Beijing: The Transition from Women in Development to Gender and Development." In *Seeds 2: Supporting Women's Work around the World,* edited by Ann Leonard. New York: Feminist Press, 1995.

Murray, Jill. "Social Justice for Women? The ILO'S Convention on Part-Time Work." CELRL Working Paper No. 15. Available at http://www.law.unimelb.edu.au/celrl/assets/working%20papers/celrl-wp15.pdf.

1999 World Survey on the Role of Women in Development: Globalization, Gender and Work: Report of the Secretary-General. GA document A/54/227, 18 August 1999. Available at http://www.unhchr.ch/Huridocda/Huridoca.nsf/0/053b56b6ad21d1838025683f0059083a?Opendocument.

Odejide, Abiola. "Profile of Women's Research and Documentation Centre, Institute of African Studies, University of Ibadan, Nigeria." Available at http://www.feministafrica.org/fa%201/01-2002/wordoc.html.

Okin, Susan Moller. "Poverty, Well-Being, and Gender: What Counts, Who's Heard?" *Philosophy & Public Affairs* 31, no. 3 (2003): 280–316.

Okine, Vicky T. *The Impact of the Informal Sector on the Economy: The Survival Strategies of Poor Families and the Role of Women Therein.* Geneva: UNESCO, 1987.

Otto, Diane. "Gender Comment: Why Does the UN Committee on Economic, Social and Cultural Rights Need a General Comment on Women?" *Canadian Journal of Women and the Law* 14, no. 1 (2002): 1–48.

———. "Nongovernmental Organizations in the United Nations System: The Emerging Role of International Civil Society." *Human Rights Quarterly* 18, no. 1 (1996): 107–141.

Ozbay, Ferhunde, ed. *Women, Family and Social Change in Turkey.* Bangkok: UNESCO Principal Regional Office for Asia and the Pacific, 1990.

Patton, Charlotte G. "Women and Power: The Nairobi Conference, 1985." In *Women, Politics, and the United Nations,* edited by Anne Winslow. Westport, Conn.: Greenwood Press, 1995.

Pereira, Charmaine. "Between Knowing and Imagining: What Space for Feminism in Scholarship on Africa?" *Feminist Africa: Intellectual Politics* 1 (November/December 2002): 9–33.

Petchesky, Rosalind P. "Reproductive and Sexual Rights: Charting the Course of Transnational Women's NGOs." Geneva 2000 Occasional Paper No. 8, UNRISD, June 2000.

Philipose, Elizabeth. "From Beijing to Beijing +5." *FAFIA Newsletter* (Fall 2000). Available at http://www.fafia-afai.org/Bplus5/news1_e.htm.

Pietilä, Hilkka. *Engendering the Global Agenda: The Story of Women and the United Nations.* Geneva: UN Non-Governmental Liaison Services, 2002.

Pietilä, Hilkka, and Jeanne Vickers. *Making Women Matter: The Role of the United Nations.* London: Zed Books, 1990.

Prügl, Elisabeth. "What Is a Worker? Gender, Global Restructuring, and the ILO Convention on Homework." In *Gender Politics in Global Governance,* edited by Mary K. Meyer and Elisabeth Prügl. Lanham, Md.: Rowman and Littlefield, 1999.

Prügl, Elisabeth, and Mary K. Meyer. "Gender Politics in Global Governance." In *Gender Politics in Global Governance,* edited by Mary K. Meyer and Elisabeth Prügl. Lanham, Md.: Rowman and Littlefield, 1999.

Quisumbing, A. R., Lawrence Haddad, and Christine Peña. "Gender and Poverty: New Evidence from 10 Developing Countries." Food Consumption and Nutrition Division Discussion Paper No. 9, International Food Policy Research Institute (IFPRI), Washington D.C., 1995. Available at http://www.ifpri.org/divs/fcnd/dp/dp09.htm.

Razavi, Shahra. *Shifting Burdens: Gender and Agrarian Change under Neoliberalism.* Bloomfield, Conn.: Kumarian Press, 2002.

Razavi, Shahra, and Carol Miller. "From WID to GAD: Conceptual Shifts in the Women and Development Discourse." Occasional Paper 1, United Nations Research Institute for Social Development and United Nations Development Programme, February 1995. Available at http://www.eldis.org/static/DOC1651.htm.

———. "Gender Mainstreaming: A Study of Efforts by the UNDP, the World Bank, and the ILO to Institutionalize Gender Issues." Geneva: UNRISD and UNDP, 1995.

Reanda, Laura. "The Commission on the Status of Women." In *The United Nations and Human Rights: A Critical Appraisal,* edited by Philip Alston. Oxford: Clarendon Press/Oxford University Press, 1992.

Reeves, Hazel. "Gender Evaluation within the UN System." *BRIDGE-development-gender,* Report No. 60. Brighton: Institute of Development Studies, November 2000.

Report of the Fourth World Conference on Women, Held in Beijing from 4 to 15 September 1995; Including the Agenda, the Beijing Declaration and the Platform for Action (Extract), in *The United Nations and the Advancement of Women,* 649–735.

Report of the World Conference of the International Women's Year held in Mexico City from 19 June to July 1975; including the Agenda, the World Plan of Action for the Implementation of the Objectives of the International Women's Year, the Declaration of Mexico on the Equality of Women and Their Contribution to Development and Peace, and Resolutions and Decisions Adopted by the Conference, in *The United Nations and the Advancement of Women,* 187–211.

Report of the World Conference of the United Nations Decade for Women: Equality, Development and Peace, Held in Copenhagen from 14 to 30 July; Including the Agenda, Programme of Action for the Second Half of the United Nations Decade for Women and Resolutions Adopted by the Conference, in *The United Nations and the Advancement of Women,* 258–284.

Report of the World Conference to Review and Appraise the Achievements of the United Nations Decade for Women: Equality, Development and Peace, held in Nairobi from 15 to 26 July 1985; including the Agenda and the Nairobi Forward-looking Strategies for the Advancement of Women (Extract), in *The United Nations and the Advancement of Women,* 310–362.

Rizika, Jill. "UN and Women—After the Decade." *Africa Report* (September–October 1985).

Rose, Kalima. "SEWA: Women in Movement." In *The Women, Gender and Development Reader,* edited by Nalini Visvanathan, Lynn Duggan, Laurie Nisonoff, and Nan Wiegersma. London: Zed Books, 1997.

Sadasivam, Bharati. "After Beijing." Available at http://www.socwatch.org.uy/en/informeImpreso/pdfs/afterbeijing1999_eng.pdf.

Sandler, Joanne. "UNIFEM's Experiences in Mainstreaming for Gender Equality." Presented to the UNICEF Meeting of Gender Focal Points, 5–9 May 1997. Available at www.unifem.org/index.php?f_page_pid=188.

Save-Soderbergh, Bengt. "Democracy, a Changed World and Poverty Eradication." *International IDEA News* (Autumn 2001).

Sciolino, Elaine. "Nairobi: The Event of 1985." *Ms.* (January 1986).

Scott, Gloria. "Breaking New Ground at the UN and World Bank." In *Developing Power,* edited by Arvonne S. Fraser and Irene Tinker. New York: Feminist Press, 2004.

Seltzer, Judith R. *The Origins and Evolution of Family Planning Programs in Developing Countries.* Santa Monica, Calif.: RAND, 2002.

Sen, Amartya. "Agency and Well-Being: The Development Agenda." In *A Commitment to the World's Women: Perspectives on Development for Beijing and Beyond,* edited by Noeleen Heyzer with Sushma Kapoor and Joanne Sandler. New York: UNIFEM, 1995.

———. "Democracy as a Universal Value." *Journal of Democracy* 10, no. 3 (1999): 3–17.

———. "Development: Which Way Now?" *Economic Journal* 93 (1983). Reprinted in Sen, *Resources, Values and Development.*

———. *Development as Freedom.* New York: Anchor Books, 1999.

———. "Gender and Cooperative Conflicts." In *Persistent Inequalities: Women and World Development,* edited by Irene Tinker. New York: Oxford University Press, 1990.

———. *Resources, Values and Development.* Cambridge, Mass.: Harvard University Press, 1984.

———. "What Is Development About?" In *Frontiers of Development Economics: The Future in Perspective,* edited by Gerald M. Meier and Joseph E. Stiglitz. Oxford: Oxford University Press, 2001.

Sen, Gita, and Carmen Barroso. "After Cairo: Challenges to Women's Organizations." In *A Commitment to the World's Women: Perspectives on Development for Beijing and Beyond,* edited by Noeleen Heyzer with Sushma Kapoor and Joanne Sandler. New York: UNIFEM, 1995.

Sen, Gita, and Caren Grown. *Development, Crises, and Alternative Visions: Third World Women's Perspectives.* New York: Monthly Review Press, 1987.

Sengupta, Arjun. "The Right to Development as a Human Right." Available at http:// www.hsph.harvard.edu/fxbcenter/FXBC_WP7—Sengupta.pdf.

Simons, Helen. "Repackaging Population Control." *CovertAction* 51 (Winter 1994–1995): 33–37.

Smyth, Ines. "NGOs in a Post-Feminist Era." In *Feminists Doing Development: A Practical Critique,* edited by Marilyn Porter and Ellen Judd. New York: St. Martin's Press, 1999.

Snyder, Margaret. "Bibliographic Essay: Women and African Development." *CHOICE Magazine* 37, no. 6 (February 2000).

———. "The Politics of Women and Development." In *Women, Politics and the United Nations,* edited by Anne Winslow. Westport, Conn.: Greenwood Press, 1995.

———. *Transforming Development: Women, Poverty and Politics.* London: Intermediate Technology Publications, 1995.

———. "Walking My Own Road: How a Sabbatical Year Led to a United Nations Career." In *Developing Power,* edited by Arvonne S. Fraser and Irene Tinker. New York: Feminist Press, 2004.

———. "Women Determine Development: The Unfinished Revolution." *Signs* 29, no. 2 (Winter 2004): 619–632.

Snyder, Margaret, and Mary Tadesse. "The African Context: Women in the Political Economy." In *The Women, Gender and Development Reader,* edited by Nalini Visvanathan, Lynn Duggan, Laurie Nisonoff, and Nan Wiegersma. London: Zed Books, 1997.

————. *African Women and Development: A History.* Atlantic Highlands, N.J.: Zed Books, 1995.

Soares, Vera, Ana Alice Alcantara Costa, Cristina Maria Buarque, Denise Dourado Dora, and Wania Sant' Anna. "Brazilian Feminism and Women's Movements: A Two-Way Street." In *The Challenge of Local Feminisms: Women's Movements in Global Perspective,* edited by Amrita Basu. Boulder, Colo.: Westview Press, 1995.

Somavía, Juan. "The World Summit for Social Development: Engendering Realpoltik." In *A Commitment to the World's Women: Perspectives on Development for Beijing and Beyond,* edited by Noeleen Heyzer, Sushma Kapoor, and Joanne Sandler. New York: UNIFEM 1995.

South Commission. *The Challenge to the South: The Report of the South Commission.* New York: Oxford University Press, 1990.

Standing, Guy. *Beyond the New Paternalism: Basic Security as Equality.* London: Verso, 2002.

Staudt, Kathleen. "Bureaucratic Resistance to Women's Programs: The Case of Women in Development." In *Women, Power and Policy,* edited by Ellen Bonepath. New York: Pergamon Press, 1982.

Steady, Filomina Chioma. "African Women at the End of the Decade." *Africa Report* (March–April 1985): 4–12.

Steinem, Gloria, Angela Davis, María Jiménez, and Mililani Trask. *Feminist Family Values Forum.* Austin, Tex.: Plain View Press, 1996.

Stephenson, Carolyn M. "Feminism, Pacifism, Nationalism and the United Nations Decade for Women." *Women's Studies International Forum* 5, nos. 3/4 (1982): 287–300.

————. "Women's International Nongovernmental Organizations at the United Nations." In *Women, Politics, and the United Nations,* edited by Anne Winslow. Westport, Conn.: Greenwood Press, 1995.

Stewart, Frances. "Can Adjustment Programmes Incorporate the Interests of Women?" In *Women and Adjustment Policies in the Third World,* edited by Haleh Afshar and Carolyne Dennis. Houndmills, Basingstoke, Hampshire: Macmillan Academic and Professional, 1992.

Stienstra, Deborah. "Dancing Resistance from Rio to Beijing: Transnational Women's Organizing and United Nations Conferences, 1992–6." In *Gender and Global Restructuring: Sightings, Sites and Resistances,* edited by Marianne H. Marchand and Anne Sisson Runyan. New York: Routledge, 2000.

Streeten, Paul P. "Comment" on Kaushik Basu's "On the Goals of Development." In *Frontiers of Development Economics: The Future in Perspective,* edited by Gerald M. Meier and Joseph E. Stiglitz. New York: Oxford University Press, 2001.

Suremain, Marie-Dominique de. *Women's Involvement in the Informal Urban Economy: Colombia.* Geneva: UNESCO, 1989.

Szalai, Alexander, and Margaret Croke. "Women on the Professional Staff and at Decision-Making Levels of the United Nations System: 1971–1976." In *The United Nations & Decision-Making: The Role of Women,* edited by Davidson Nicol and Margaret Croke. New York: UNITAR, 1978.

Tickner, Ann J. *Gender in International Relations: Feminist Perspectives on Achieving Global Security.* New York: Columbia University Press, 1993.

Timothy, Kristen. "Equality for Women in the United Nations Secretariat." In *Women, Politics, and the United Nations,* edited by Anne Winslow. Westport, Conn.: Greenwood Press, 1995.

———. "Walking on Eggshells at the UN." In *Developing Power,* edited by Arvonne S. Fraser and Irene Tinker. New York: Feminist Press, 2004.

Tinker, Irene. "Challenging Wisdom, Changing Policies: The Women in Development Movement." In *Developing Power: How Women Transformed International Development,* edited by Arvonne S. Fraser and Irene Tinker. New York: Feminist Press, 2004.

———. "The Making of a Field: Advocates, Practitioners and Scholars." In *The Women, Gender and Development Reader,* edited by Nalini Visvanathan, Lynn Duggan, Laurie Nisonoff, and Nan Wiegersma. London: Zed Books, 1997.

———. "Nongovernmental Organizations: An Alternative Power Base for Women?" In *Gender Politics in Global Governance,* edited by Mary K. Meyer and Elisabeth Prügl. Lanham, Md.: Rowman and Littlefield, 1999.

———. *The Percy Amendment Promoting Women in Development: Its Origin, Meaning, and Impact.* Washington, D.C.: Equity Policy Center, 1984.

———. "Preface." In *Developing Power,* edited by Arvonne S. Fraser and Irene Tinker. New York: Feminist Press, 2004.

Tinker, Irene, ed. *Persistent Inequalities: Women and World Development.* Oxford: Oxford University Press, 1990.

Tomšič, Vida. "Policy of Non-Alignment, Struggle for the NIEO and the Role of Women in Development." In *Women, Work and Society,* edited by K. Saradamoni. Calcutta: Indian Statistical Institute, 1985.

The United Nations and the Advancement of Women, 1945–1996. New York: UN Department of Public Information, 1995.

UN Department of International Economic and Social Affairs. "International Standards of Equality and Religious Freedom: Implications for the Status of Women." In *Identity Politics & Women: Cultural Reassertions and Feminisms in International Perspective,* edited by Valentine M. Moghadam. Boulder, Colo.: Westview Press, 1994.

———. "History of an Optional Protocol." Available at http://www.un.org/womenwatch/daw/cedaw/protocol/history.htm.

———. *World Survey on the Role of Women in Development.* New York: United Nations, 1986.

United Nations Development Programme (UNDP). *Human Development Report 1993: People's Participation.* New York: Oxford University Press, 1993.

———. *Human Development Report 1995: Gender and human development.* New York: Oxford University Press, 1995.

———. *Human Development Report 2001: Making new technologies work for human development.* New York: Oxford University Press, 2001.

———. *UNDP Poverty Report 2000: Overcoming Human Poverty.* Available at http://www.undp.org.np/publications/pr2000.

UNIFEM. *Progress of the World's Women 1995.* New York: UNIFEM, 1995.

———. *Progress of the World's Women 2000.* New York: UNIFEM, 2000.

van der Gaag, Nikki. "Women: Still Something to Shout About." *New Internationalist* 270 (August 1995). Available at http://www.newint.org/issue270/270keynote.html.

Van Rooy, Alison. "The Frontiers of Influence: NGO Lobbying at the 1974 World Food Conference, the 1992 Earth Summit and Beyond." *World Development* 25, no. 1 (1997): 93–114.

Vishwanath, Tara. "Informal Economy: Safety Valve or Growth Opportunity?" Swiss Agency for Development and Cooperation, 2001. Available at http://www.eldis.org/static/DOC13160.htm.

Wach, Heike, and Hazel Reeves. *Gender and Development: Facts and Figures.* Bridge Report No. 56. Brighton, UK: Institute of Development Studies, February 2000.

Ward, Michael. *Quantifying the World: UN Ideas and Statistics.* Bloomington: Indiana University Press, 2004.

Waring, Marilyn. "Counting for Something! Recognising Women's Contribution to the Global Economy through Alternative Accounting Systems." Available at http://www.awid.org/publications/gen_dev/waring.pdf.

———. *If Women Counted: A New Feminist Economics.* San Francisco: Harper and Row, 1988.

Weiss, Tom, and Tatiana Carayannis. "Whither United Nations Economic and Social Ideas? A Research Agenda." *Global Social Policy* 1, no. 1 (2001): 25–47.

West, Lois A. "The United Nations Women's Conferences and Feminist Politics." In *Gender Politics in Global Governance,* edited by Mary K. Meyer and Elisabeth Prügl. Lanham, Md.: Rowman and Littlefield, 1999.

Willitts, Peter. "The Pattern of Conferences." In *Global Issues in the United Nations' Framework,* edited by Paul Taylor and A. J. R. Groom. New York: St. Martin's Press, 1989.

Winslow, Anne. "Specialized Agencies and the World Bank." In *Women, Politics, and the United Nations,* edited by Anne Winslow. Westport, Conn.: Greenwood Press, 1995.

Winslow, Anne, ed. *Women, Politics, and the United Nations.* Westport, Conn.: Greenwood Press, 1995.

Women Go Global: The United Nations and the International Women's Movement, 1945–2000. CD-ROM, United Nations, 2003.

Women in a Changing Global Economy: 1994 World Survey on the Role of Women in Development. New York: United Nations, 1995.

Women's Feature Service. "The Legacy of the Women's Caucus." *Women's Feature Service* (7 September 1994). Available at www.iisd.ca/Cairo/wfslegac.txt.

———. *Measuring the Immeasurable: Planning, Monitoring and Evaluation of Networks.* New Delhi: Women's Feature Service, n.d.

Woodward, Alison. "Building Velvet Triangles: Gender in EU Policy Making." Paper prepared for the European Consortium for Political Research 28th Joint Sessions, Copenhagen, April 2000.

World Labour Report 1992. Geneva: ILO, 1992.

The World's Women 1970–1990: Trends and Statistics. New York: United Nations, 1991.

The World's Women 2000: Trends and Statistics. New York: United Nations, 2000.

Yusuf, Shahid, and Joseph Stiglitz. "Development Issues: Settled and Open." In *Frontiers of Development Economics: The Future in Perspective,* edited by Gerald M. Meier and Joseph E. Stiglitz. Washington: Oxford University Press and The World Bank, 2001.

Index

Note: Page numbers in italics indicate tables and charts.

About the Author

Devaki Jain is a development economist and activist. She graduated in economics from Oxford University and has taught at Delhi University. Her academic research and advocacy, influenced largely by Gandhian philosophy, have focused on issues of equity, democratic decentralization, people-centered development, and women's rights. She has been an active member of the local, national, and international women's movement and has held positions in national and international expert commissions and councils with a special focus on justice. Jain is co-editor (with Pam Rajput) of *Narratives from the Women's Studies Family: Recreating Knowledge* and (with Diana L. Eck) of *Speaking of Faith: Cross-Cultural Perspectives on Women, Religion, and Social Change.* Devaki Jain resides in Bangalore, India.

About the United Nations
Intellectual History Project

Ideas and concepts are a main driving force in human progress, and they are arguably the most important contribution of the United Nations. Yet there has been little historical study of the origins and evolution of the history of economic and social ideas cultivated within the world organization and of their impact on wider thinking and international action. The United Nations Intellectual History Project is filling this knowledge gap about the UN by tracing the origin and analyzing the evolution of key ideas and concepts about international economic and social development born or nurtured under UN auspices. The UNIHP began operations in mid-1999 when the secretariat, the hub of a worldwide network of specialists on the UN, was established at the Ralph Bunche Institute for International Studies of The CUNY Graduate Center.

The UNIHP has two main components, oral history interviews and a series of books on specific topics. The seventy-three in-depth oral history interviews with leading contributors to crucial ideas and concepts within the UN system provide the raw material for this volume. Complete and indexed transcripts will be made available to researchers and the general public in 2006.

The project has commissioned fifteen studies about the major economic and social ideas or concepts that are central to UN activity, which are being published by Indiana University Press.

- *Ahead of the Curve? UN Ideas and Global Challenges,* by Louis Emmerij, Richard Jolly, and Thomas G. Weiss (2001)
- *Unity and Diversity in Development Ideas: Perspectives from the UN Regional Commissions,* edited by Yves Berthelot with contributions from Adebayo Adedeji, Yves Berthelot, Leelananda de Silva, Paul Rayment, Gert Rosenthal, and Blandine Destremeau (2003)
- *Quantifying the World: UN Contributions to Statistics,* by Michael Ward (2004)
- *UN Contributions to Development Thinking and Practice,* by Richard Jolly, Louis Emmerij, Dharam Ghai, and Frédéric Lapeyre (2004)
- *The UN and Global Political Economy: Trade, Finance, and Development,* by John Toye and Richard Toye (2004)

- *UN Voices: The Struggle for Development and Social Justice,* by Thomas G. Weiss, Tatiana Carayannis, Louis Emmerij, and Richard Jolly (2005)
- *Women, Development, and the UN: A Sixty-Year Quest for Equality and Justice,* by Devaki Jain (2005)

Forthcoming Titles:

- *Human Security and the UN: A Critical History,* by S. Neil MacFarlane and Yuen Foong-Khong (2006)
- *The UN and Human Rights Ideas: The Unfinished Revolution,* by Sarah Zaidi and Roger Normand (2006)
- *The UN and Development Cooperation,* by Olav Stokke (2006)
- *The UN and the Global Commons: Development Without Destruction,* by Nico Schrijver (2006)
- *The UN and Transnationals, from Code to Compact,* by Tagi Sagafi-nejad, in collaboration with John Dunning (2006)
- *The UN and Global Governance: An Idea and Its Prospects,* by Ramesh Thakur and Thomas G. Weiss (2007)
- *The United Nations: A History of Ideas and Their Future,* by Richard Jolly, Louis Emmerij, and Thomas G. Weiss (2007)

The project is also collaborating on *The Oxford Handbook on the UN,* edited by Thomas G. Weiss and Sam Daws, to be published by Oxford University Press in 2007.

For further information, the interested reader should contact:

UN Intellectual History Project
The CUNY Graduate Center
365 Fifth Avenue, Suite 5203
New York, New York 10016-4309
212-817-1920 Tel
212-817-1565 Fax
UNHistory@gc.cuny.edu
www.unhistory.org